RESTORATION THEATRE

RESTORATION THEATRE

Edited by
JOHN RUSSELL BROWN
& BERNARD HARRIS

CAPRICORN BOOKS
New York

© EDWARD ARNOLD (PUBLISHERS) LTD 1965

CAPRICORN BOOKS EDITION 1967

Published by arrangement with
St. Martin's Press

PRINTED IN THE UNITED STATES OF AMERICA

Contents

LIST OF ILLUSTRATIONS

SIR JOHN BRUTE, *The Provoked Wife*
(Vanbrugh's Plays, 1734 edition)
between pages 14 & 15

LADY TOWNLEY, *The Provoked Husband*
(Vanbrugh's Plays, 1734 edition)
between pages 20 & 21

ANNE BRACEGIRDLE
(Biographical Mirrour, Vol. III)
between pages 26 & 27

ANNE OLDFIELD
(National Portrait Gallery)
between pages 32 & 33

Preface

HISTORIANS are acquainted with the wide range of Restoration theatrical enterprise, but few other people. Books published during the last fifteen or twenty years discuss the comedies, or a few authors, or conventions, or wit. Learned articles are still more specialised than usual—'Otway's tragic muse debauched: sensuality in *Venice Preserv'd*' or 'Dr. Pelling, Dr. Pell and Dryden's Lord Nonsuch' are representative—or they are restricted to the work of a single author. And there is a thin line of polemical writing, from L. C. Knights, John Wain, F. W. Bateson and others; for the period is known uncertainly as well as patchily. All this is strange in the present age of industrious scholarship and criticism: someone, somehow, might have been expected to provide a broadly based reappraisal. The situation reflects the special difficulties of Restoration theatre.

We have tried to face some of these in this latest volume of *Stratford-upon-Avon Studies*. We have commissioned nine authors and guided them towards topics familiar and unfamiliar.

Three of the acknowledged masters of comedy have been considered in individual chapters: Jocelyn Powell's account of Etherege judges the visual as well as the verbal force of the plays, seeking to assess instinctive and intellectual responses; Anne Righter's chapter on Wycherley shows his experimentation with form to satisfy an alert artistic conscience; and Kenneth Muir's view of Congreve is through his style. Other chapters investigate the important verbal element of this theatre: in the first chapter of the book, Bernard Harris traces the language of comedy from Etherege to Vanbrugh; in a study of Dryden, D. W. Jefferson reveals an acute poetry; and in his discussion of styles of Restoration acting, Hugh Hunt writes of the delivery of the lines as part of a complex theatrical enactment. Jocelyn Powell and Hugh Hunt are both especially concerned with plays in performance, and so is Moelwyn Merchant in his study of Shakespeare adaptations.

Merchant's chapter is one of those which represent an extension of usual critical discussion; for instead of condemning the misuse of Shakespeare or regaling his reader with curiosities, he has tried to judge these ambitious enterprises as individual and careful contributions to the theatre of the age. In the same spirit Norman Suckling has compared Restoration Comedy with Molière, not to prove indebtedness or limit it, but to sharpen our understanding of distinctive achievements; and Anne Righter, in her second chapter, considers heroic tragedies in the light of the better-known comedies. Roger Sharrock gives an account of non-dramatic satire to provide a necessary perspective for the usual background to the comedies.

So, in ten ways, this volume of *Stratford-upon-Avon Studies* deals with a major and neglected theme. There are a few regrettable omissions, notably full studies of Otway and music, but we wished to avoid a mere 'survey' and these are the price of that decision; neither Otway nor music is wholly neglected and we hope that the perspectives by which all elements of the Restoration theatre are viewed will be stimulating and informative. There are differences of opinion between the various chapters and these we welcome; the freedom in collaboration which has marked each volume of this series seems, on this theme in particular, the only way of representing contemporary opinion and, perhaps, the most hopeful in attempting to further and refine appreciation.

Each chapter has been provided with a prefatory note which gives factual information on which the following discourse depends, and a guide for further reading and study. The texts quoted in each chapter are specified here, and the titles of scholarly or critical works referred to later by their authors' names. The texts chosen are the most responsible that are generally available.

Further *Stratford Studies* are in preparation: *American Poetry* and *Later Shakespeare* will be the next volumes in the series; *Elizabethan Theatre*, *Victorian Poetry* and *American Theatre* will follow.

JOHN RUSSELL BROWN
BERNARD HARRIS

Note

Scholarship and Criticism: The style of the comedy of manners is discussed in
A. Nicoll's *A History of English Drama 1660–1900*, Vol. 1 (4th edition, 1961),
and in his *The Theatre and Dramatic Theory* (1962); Bonamy Dobrée's *Restoration Comedy 1660–1720* (1924) is standard; A. Beljame's *Men of Letters and the
English Public in the Eighteenth Century* (1881; trans. 1948) is invaluable for the
social documentation from 1660 to 1744. J. R. Sutherland studies the relationship of tone and audience in 'Prologues, Epilogues and Audience . . .' in *Of
Books and Humankind* (ed. J. Butt, 1964). Of older general accounts J. Palmer's
The Comedy of Manners (1913), T. W. Krutch's *Comedy and Conscience after the
Restoration* (1924), and H. T. F. Perry's *The Comic Spirit in Restoration Drama*
(1925)—the two last in paperback—remain useful. J. Wain surveys 'Restoration Comedy and its Modern Critics' in *Preliminary Essays* (1957), and
L. C. Knights' examination of 'Restoration Comedy: The Reality and the
Myth' is in *Explorations* (1946). Recent general studies includes J. H. Smith's
The Gay Couple in Restoration Comedy (1948), and T. H. Fujirama's *The
Restoration Comedy of Wit* (1952). K. M. Lynch's *The Social Mode of Restoration
Comedy* (1926) treats of a style in transition, conveniently viewed in A. S.
Knowland's *Six Caroline Plays* (1962) from Shirley's *Lady of Pleasure* to Killigrew's *The Parson's Wedding*. F. H. Moore's *The Nobler Pleasure: Dryden's
Comedy in Theory and Practice* (1963) is a comprehensive account; J. Barish's
Ben Jonson and the language of Prose Comedy (1960) makes pertinent relationships
and is a model for future enquiries. Colley Cibber's *Apology For His Life*
(Everyman, 1938 edition) is relevant, and much valuable early criticism is
presented in S. Elledge's *Eighteenth Century Critical Essays* (1961).

For biographical details of *Etherege, Wycherley, Dryden* and *Congreve* see their
respective chapters. Thomas Shadwell (1640–92), Dryden's 'Og' and Poet
Laureate, was the son of a J.P. of Santon Hall, Norfolk. The humours of his
Sullen Lovers (1668), the theatre burlesques of *A True Widow* (1679), the
rogues' language of *The Squire of Alsatia* (1688) and the rural buffooneries of
Squire Oldwit in *Bury Fair* (1689) suggest his range. *Works:* These four plays
make up the Mermaid volume (ed. G. Saintsbury). *The Dramatic Works* (4
vols., 1720) and *The Complete Works* (ed. M. Summers, 5 vols., 1927) are
essential. A. S. Borgman's *Thomas Shadwell, His Life and Comedies* (1928) is
useful.

Sir John Vanbrugh (1664–1726) trained as an architect, briefly, in France in 1683;
enlisted in 1686; was arrested in 1690 and released from the Bastille in 1692.
Cibber's *Love's Last Shift* prompted Vanbrugh to write *The Relapse* as a sequel
in 1696. *The Provok'd Wife* (1696) and *A Journey to London* (completed by
Cibber) are his best comedies. Captain, Knight, Clarenceux King at Arms,
architect of Blenheim and builder of the Opera House in Haymarket, Vanbrugh is a vigorously full figure. *Works: Collected Works* (2 vols., 1728); there
is a Mermaid edition by A. E. H. Swain: but Vanburgh is fortunate in having
the most scholarly edition of any Restoration dramatist in *The Complete Works*
(ed. B. Dobrée & Webb, 5 vols., 1927).

I

The Dialect of those Fanatic Times

BERNARD HARRIS

★

> The age demanded an image
> Of its accelerated grimace,
> Something for the modern stage,
> Not, at any rate, an Attic grace;
>
> Not, not certainly, the obscure reveries
> Of the inward gaze;
> Better mendacities
> Than the classics in paraphrase!

So Pound sang bitterly in 'Hugh Selwyn Mauberley' realising that

> The 'age demanded' chiefly a mould in plaster,
> Made with no loss of time,
> A prose kinema, not, not assuredly, alabaster
> Or the 'sculpture' of rhyme.

This bleak comment on the separation of poet and public in the twentieth century gives us some terms in which to discuss that easy and intimate collaboration of the dramatists and their audience in the later seventeenth century, when, as Dryden phrased it,

> The plays that take on our corrupted stage,
> Methinks, resemble the distracted age.

What seems worth observing in the comparison of the post-war worlds of the twentieth and seventeenth centuries is not any superficial similarity of behaviour—though some common ground might be found for the cynicism and flippancy of the 'twenties' and of 'good King Charles's golden days'—but the nature of what such 'ages' demanded of their literatures. In general the prodigious social changes in English life consequent upon the World War and the Civil War brought decisively new attitudes in religion, politics, sexual relationships, and in particular an 'accelerated' and self-conscious demand for 'modernity'. Pound instinctively chooses images from the supremely social art of the theatre to point the damaging contrast of the public fondness from self-reflection and the private incapacity for self-analysis, and sets the hard permanence of art against the brittle utility of synthetic substance offered by a literature which serves, not shapes, its time. Such images of modern frivolity and Greek poise, grimace and grace, mould and sculpture seem peculiarly appropriate to the consideration of the social drama of the post-Restoration and post-Revolution years, during which the theatre became socially articulate again after enforced silence, and in which the distinctive form of the comedy of manners found its full variety of expression.

'The comedy is a climate, and the climate *is* comedy' wrote Fry of his own work, and to understand the climate of early Restoration comedy we cannot do better than to consult Clarendon's account[1] of the temper of the nation in the years immediately following 1660, in the decade which closed, as Andrew Marvell wrote to William Popple in 1670-1, when 'The Court is at the highest Pitch of Wanton Luxury, and the People full of discontent'. Comments of that kind are so many that we cannot discount Clarendon's 'Life by Himself' as merely the special pleading of a skilled, embittered advocate and discarded chief counsellor. Certainly his broad strictures have a moralist's all-embracing warmth, finding that instead of generosity 'a vile and sordid love of money was entertained as the truest wisdom', that there was 'a total decay, or rather final expiration of all friendship', and such neglect of conscience and social obligation that 'to dissuade a man from anything he affected . . . was thought an impertinence unworthy a wise man, and received with reproach and contempt'. But what most convinces us of Clarendon's analysis is the unrealised extent of the disquieting propriety of his own prose. Believing that the many disruptive quarrels had their origins in the Civil War he ranges his main generalisations in battle order: thus, the natural opposition of parents and children is called an 'unnatural antipathy' having 'its first rise from the beginning of the rebellion, when the fathers and sons engaged themselves in the contrary parties, the one choosing to serve the king, the other the parliament'; again, finding it necessary to admit the moral discipline of Cromwell's army superior to that of the king's followers, the praise of the royalist politician contains its own neat disclaimer, 'insomuch that

[1] *Selections from Clarendon* (ed. G. Huehns), pp. 374-82.

sure there never was any such body of men so without rapine, swearing, drinking, or any other debauchery but the wickedness of their
hearts'. But the test of Clarendon's prose, as of his life, comes in his
consideration of his king, and nowhere are his words more carefully
weighed and weighted than in treating of the opposition to Charles's
personal rule and the king's response to restriction. Finding no way 'by
which he might extricate himself out of those many difficulties and
labyrinths in which he was involved' Charles, we learn,

> grew more disposed to leave all things to their natural course, and
> God's providence; and by degrees unbent his mind from the knotty
> and ungrateful part of his business, grew more remiss in his applica-
> tion to it, and indulged to his youth and appetite that licence and
> satisfaction that it desired, and for which he had opportunity enough,
> and could not be without ministers abundant for any such negotia-
> tions; the time itself, and the young people thereof of either sex
> having been educated in all the liberty of vice, without reprehension
> or restraint.

Such language proves capable of all the required movements, stooping
heavily to a delicate topic, masking contempt behind a derisive sympathy, permitting a cordial recollection of lust and a knowing minis-
terial quip, but straightening up again at the thought of the younger
generation and recovering a tone of righteous reproof. In such a paragraph the world of Charles's court is toppled, but syntactically the
blame rests comfortably on the atlas-shoulders of 'the time itself' before
being transferred to those of the younger generation.

L. C. Knights has noted[2] of Halifax's prose in his 'Character of
Charles II', that 'the even tone, the sinuous ease of movement and the
clarity of the analysis mark the passage as unmistakably post-Restoration', finds 'the achievement represented by his style was far from being
a merely individual achievement', and that to contemplate Congreve
alongside Halifax is to show 'Congreve's style as nerveless in the comparison'. In fact

> The observation to start from is that the prose in which Restoration
> comedy is written—select which dramatist you like—is poor and
> inexpressive in comparison with the staple non-dramatic prose.

This position itself, however, is reached by perceiving that 'The common mode of Restoration prose' had behind it 'serious pressure', with

[2] *Explorations* (1946), p. 141.

which the Royal Society is partly credited, to serve the needs of 'scientific inquiry and rational discussion', and that the English language was being made 'an instrument for rational dissection'. On this reckoning the comparison of dramatic and non-dramatic prose must be acknowledged to giv : the latter clear advantage. Indeed if the comparison were admitted it would be destructive. But perhaps we must start from the observation that the prose in which Restoration comedy is written is expressive of more fully theatrical preoccupations than rational dissection could satisfy.

The demands made upon the comic dramatists were of indulgence, and their response to such indulgence provides the rare strength as well as the frequent weakness of their comic language, whose 'sinuous ease of movement' has for its object not so much clarity of analysis as substantial human mimicry. From this aspect, which necessarily includes the viewpoint of their audience and the nature of acting, the comparison of dramatic and non-dramatic prose is unhelpful. It may well be true, as L. C. Knights maintains, that late seventeenth-century drama is inferior in kind 'not because it represents—by Elizabethan standards —a limited culture, but because it represents contemporary culture so inadequately; it has no significant relation with the best thought of the time'. But it is also true that social comedy, like the social beings with which it is concerned, achieves those relationships which are available to it. The relationship warmly offered by seventeenth-century audiences to those who entertained them was a promiscuous relationship, inhospitable to the 'best thought', and what significance it may have must be sought initially in those terms. G. Wilson Knight[3] is willing, indeed eager, to propose that 'The proper function of comedy is to assist the assimilation of instincts, especially sexual instincts'. On this reckoning the Elizabethans' 'attempt to assert the romance of marriage' was followed by the Jacobean 'concentration on criminal lust'. But neither extreme 'meets the near-distance human problem', and 'moralistic comedy' is 'a contradiction in terms'. In fact,

Morality and convention alone are impotent; the stuff of life is there whatever we think of it, and it is comedy's business to face it. The next step is accordingly a facing not of the instinct alone as a mere force of nature, but of instinct recognised simultaneously as sin, inevitable and as honourable. For such subtleties the middle classes had

[3] *The Golden Labyrinth* (1962), pp. 130–1.

SIR JOHN BRUTE

neither the inclination nor the language. Clarification could only come through an aristocratic daring and a sophisticated expression.

This notion of 'comedy's business', however differently phrased, as facing the stuff of life, is crucial to the understanding of social comedy. Lamb notoriously preferred to find his enjoyment of Restoration writers by believing that they presented 'altogether a speculative scene of things, which has no reference whatever to the world that is', but this was a luxury of literary appreciation. The Restoration comic writers offer a confrontation not a speculation. 'Beyond the society itself and beyond thoughts of the present moment', Allardyce Nicoll comments, 'they do not go.' This is necessity not choice. The writer of the comedy of manners, as Middleton Murry[4] perceived, is not

> engaged in creating a universe but in readjusting one; the ordering principle of this world is one which he accepts and with which he identifies; he measures men and women by the standards of an ideal, but the ideal is not his own, it is that of the society in which he moves, and if it has become second nature to him, that is because he feels himself free-est and most comfortable as a member of society.

The reconciliation of freedom and comfort is a social task and a comic art. As Northrop Frye[5] puts it 'The essential comic resolution . . . is an individual release which is also a social reconciliation'. That the terms of reconciliation may involve complicity must be granted. We are no longer capable of Goldsmith's wishful backward glance at the period of the Restoration as 'an age of wit and immorality' which 'produced some writers that at once served to improve our language and corrupt our hearts'. Swift was too near the experience and too percipient a critic to tolerate the separation of the quality of living from its mode of expression in language: in 'A Proposal for correcting, improving, and ascertaining the English tongue' (1711–12) he declared:

> From the civil war to the present time, I am apt to doubt whether the corruptions in our language have not at least equalled the refinements in it; and these corruptions very few of the best authors in our age have wholly escaped. During the usurpation, such an infusion of enthusiastic jargon prevailed in every writing, as was not shaken off in many years after. To this succeeded that licentiousness which entered with the Restoration, and, from infecting our religion

---

[4] *The Problem of Style* (1960 ed.), p. 56.
[5] 'The Argument of Comedy', quoted in Nicoll, *The Theatre and Dramatic Theory*, p. 125.

and morals, fell to corrupt our language; which last was not likely to be much improved by those who at that time made up the court of king Charles II; either such who had followed him in his banishment, or who had been altogether conversant in the dialect of those fanatic times.

Swift's charge is not to be answered by default, as those critics do who attend to the stylistic 'refinements' of Restoration comic dramatic prose and gloss the grossness. Even the most successful appreciative critic, as Bonamy Dobrée, flatters his subject by imitation; with him antitheses abound ('For if Dryden's mind was not profound, it was extraordinarily acute and well-balanced'), epigrams are effortlessly made (thus, 'Vanbrugh . . . took the writings of others and made what he could of them; he took life as he found it, and left it there'), and similes are much sought after (Wycherley at court is 'like some splen-did uncut diamond amid the polished stones', and as a writer 'scourged his sensuality with a brutal whip, and like a scorpion surrounded by a ring of fire, turned his sting upon himself'). These are tricks of an older rage; we do not write so well nowadays; and it is entirely possible that only fine writing properly displays the worth of 'fine' comedy. Yet the dull-witted and stubbornly appreciative critic is entitled to the temporary shelter of Millamant's spite, when she cried out against the phrase-maker

> Dear Mr. Witwoud, truce with your similitudes: for I am as sick of 'em—
> WITWOUD: As a physician of a good air—I cannot help it, madam, though 'tis against myself.
> MILLAMANT: Yet again! Mincing, stand between me and his wit.
> WITWOUD: Do, Mrs. Mincing, like a screen before a great fire. I confess I do blaze today, I am too bright.

Recent critics seem anxious to preserve this truce with similitudes, fearful perhaps of Raymond Williams'[6] shrewd censure, that

> The identification which some critics seem to make, in phantasy, between themselves and the insouciance of Cavalier rakes and whores, is usually ridiculous, if one goes on to ask to what moral tradition they themselves practically belong.

One solution certainly is to go against the accepted display of prefer-ence, as John Wain[7] does in answering his own question 'What, after

---

[6] *The Long Revolution* (1961), p. 260.   [7] *Preliminary Essays* (1957), p. 22.

all . . . are the most *enjoyable* passages in Wycherley and Congreve?'
To his mind

> The answer is clear; not the smart-Alec 'combats of wit', not the
> vaunted 'social criticism', but the passages which have some richness
> of language; and this means, in practice, their passages of broad
> comedy, when the buffoons take the stage. The only time when
> these dramatists write like poets, when any kind of colour and life
> radiate from the words on the page, is when they are writing speeches
> for their grotesques to utter. In these scenes they are the heirs of
> Shakespeare.

The praise is well meant and well deserved, and certainly one does not
want to promote any further the kind of criticism which can only earn
the condemnation which L. C. Knights devoted to Restoration comic
prose itself, quoting lines which 'have an air of preening themselves on
their acute discriminations'. But it is perhaps a modern naïveté to suppose that Restoration comic prose needed or would welcome our
approval. Indeed, Mirabell's portrait of Witwoud demolishes the
flattering follower before he makes his first entrance:

> MIRABELL: . . . He is a Fool with a good Memory, and some few
> Scraps of other Folks Wit. He is one whose Conversation can
> never be approv'd, yet it is now and then to be endur'd. He has
> indeed one good Quality, he is not Exceptious; for he so passion-
> ately affects the Reputation of understanding Raillery, that he will
> construe an Affront into a Jest; and call downright Rudeness and
> ill Language, Satire and Fire.
>
> (The Way of the World, I. v. 44)

This cruel thrust penetrates further than Raymond Williams's pinprick
('Yet again! Mincing, stand between me and his wit') into the skin of
those who would affect the reputation of understanding raillery. We
cannot demand of comic prose dramatists that they write like poets, all
satire and fire, as Rochester could demand in Prologue XLIII:

> Some powerful Muse, inspir'd for our defence,
> Arise, and save a little common Sense:
> In such a Cause let thy keen Satyr bite,
> Where Indignation bids thy Genius write.

> Mark a bold leading Coxcomb of the Town,
> And single out the Beast and hunt him down;
> Hang up his mangl'd Carcass on the Stage,
> To fright away the Vermin of the Age.

The speculative scene of the Restoration stage was not a metaphorical shambles supporting a gibbet, but a bedroom, a boudoir or a park. As Murry insists,

> The comedian is the most social of all artists. For his central activity, his measurement of the aberration from an ideal that is not only possible for but inherent in a society, prose, the medium of exactness, is the appropriate instrument. Poetry has no reinforcements to give.

Here Williams acknowledges that 'The true growth of the period was in the developed comedy of manners, which had a genuine correspondence with the narrow society on which it was based'. And if we are to be 'altogether conversant in the dialect of those fanatic times' we have to be equally attentive to the pressures of instinct as well as intellect, to the propriety not only of prose as a medium of exactness, but of women as appropriate instruments, namely as actresses. For Restoration comic prose is just as surely dependent for its development upon the human reality which uttered it, as the sensibility of the whole age depended for its moral improvement upon the truer apprehension of that sensibility. Nor can we easily come at that 'dialect' as it radiates 'from the words on the page', for whether they are writing combats of wit, passages of social criticism, or speeches for grotesques to utter, these social dramatists keep in mind the investment of language in human personality, social being, or idiosyncrasy. They strive after the hinted human reality in Clarendon's image of 'the slippery and uneasy posture of affairs', testing the precision of their malice, observation or sheer buffoonery against the manifest evidence afforded by 'the time itself'. Perhaps the best descriptive adjective for this characteristic activity of their prose is implied by the word 'susceptible', which appropriately enters the language in Clarendon's vocabulary. Restoration comic prose is fully 'susceptible' to the society it delineates.

The nature of this susceptibility of style and age is well treated in J. R. Sutherland's[8] inspection of the 'good reasons for claiming that after 1660 English prose made a fresh start'. Dismissing the old claim that the Royal Society might take credit for the change, in its insistence upon a 'close, natural way of speaking . . . preferring the language of artizans, countrymen, and merchants, before that of wits and scholars', Sutherland observes that 'it is one thing to have a programme, and

[8] *On English Prose* (1957), p. 67.

another to carry it out', reminds us that Restoration literature, in the main, was 'dominated by the aristocracy, who set the tone for it, and exercised an unquestioned control over the mode of expression', and sees this prevailing mode as so extensive that 'Restoration prose is, in the main, a slightly formalised variation of the conversation of gentlemen'. Such conversation, Sutherland assures us, is 'imperturbable', has 'a casual way of making devastating remarks', is 'always polite', never 'mealy-mouthed', and above all has 'no middle-class inhibitions'.

This improvement in the standard of conversation Dryden called 'the last and greatest advantage of our writing', and in a famous passage credited it to the court, after the king's example had loosened the courtiers 'from their stiff forms of conversation, and made them easy and pliant to each other in discourse'. George Williamson[9] notes of this remark that though it may be

> no more than a flattering fiction, we cannot deny its veracity as the description of something that happened in prose, something that distinguishes the *Essay of Dramatic Poesy* from earlier critical writing.

By contrast Burton's conversational norm was 'his own, not that of a social group', and the distinction is important. For although Dryden sometimes tried to widen the bounds of the group, stressing that 'perfect knowledge of a tongue was never attained by any single person. The Court, the college, and the town, must be joined in it', he more often was content to repeat the prescription with which he approved of the practice of Beaumont and Fletcher, namely, that 'Imitation of the conversation of gentlemen was the right imitation of nature in matters of style'. The conversational form of *The Essay of Dramatic Poesy* is conspicuously successful in fulfilling its author's insistence upon 'easiness' in writing: it is also one of many works which justify Sutherland's further remark that

> Restoration prose is not only conversational in tone, but actually is on many occasions a sort of conversation carried on by the writer with some individual, real or imaginary.

The most considerable exhibition of Restoration prose as a 'sort of conversation' is provided by realistic social comedy, where conversation is not just another word for stage dialogue, but the essential mode

[9] *The Senecan Amble* (1951), p. 330.

of the comedy of manners and the typical mode of most court comedies. Dryden's *Marriage à la Mode* is eminent among the latter, and
in its famous dedication to Rochester Dryden suggested that

> if there be anything in this play, wherein I have raised myself beyond
> the ordinary lowness of my comedies, I ought wholly to acknow-
> ledge it to the favour of being admitted into Your Lordship's
> conversation.

Furthermore, Dryden maintained, 'the best comic writers of our age'
would similarly acknowledge

> that they copied the gallantries of courts, the delicacy of expression,
> and the decencies of behaviour, from Your Lordship, with more
> success, than if they had taken their models from the court of
> France.

And when Dryden's politic subservience has been discounted it remains true that the special form which this comedy took, and the
nature of the development of the language with which it is related,
requires repeated emphasis upon the close connection of social and
verbal manner, and the prominence given to the social art of conversation, at court, in town, or on the stage, is inescapable. Yet the serious
attention given to polite conversation in the early eighteenth century,
by Steele, Swift or Shaftesbury, who wrote in 1709 that 'We polish
one another and rub off our corners and rough sides by a sort of
amicable collision', is scarcely to be found immediately after the Restoration, when the style of much conversation would be better described as provocative, insinuative or insulting, rather than amicable or
agreeable. 'I do believe', wrote the author[10] of *Remarques on the Humours
and Conversations of the Town* (1673), 'that never in any Age was there
such a violent and universal thirst after the Fame of being Wits.' The
consequence was an audience both excessive and egocentric in its demands, nourishing its extravagance upon the rhymed heroic plays and
its egotism upon the wit of social comedy. 'As for Comedy' as Dryden
noted

> Repartee is one of the chiefest graces; the greatest pleasure of the
> Audience is a chace of wit kept up on both sides, and swiftly man-
> aged. And this our forefathers, if not we, have had in Fletchers

[10] Cf. J. R. Sutherland's 'Prologues, Epilogues and Audience in the Restoration Theatre' (*op. cit.* p. 54).

LADY TOWNLEY

Playes, to a much higher degree of perfection than the French Poets can arrive at.

This judgement of Dryden's, made in the *Essay* some years before the main body of Restoration comedy was written, is notably informed in that he pointed to Fletcher, who had been dead for thirty-five years, and not Shirley, doyen of the Caroline playwrights, and still living. In preferring Fletcher to Shirley, *The Wild-Goose Chase* to *The Lady of Pleasure*, Dryden was establishing a series of related preferences, of prose over verse, the wild couple over the witty fair one, profligate courtiers over sophisticated citizens. Indeed, it might be claimed that the comparative neglect of Shirley's best social comedies by the Restoration audience is a sharp corrective to many easy assumptions about the essential continuity of social experience in the pre-Restoration and post-Restoration periods. *Love Tricks, or The School of Complements*, as its sub-title suggests, was a realistic linguistic comedy, capable of attracting some fashionable interest by its word-play. Even so, the new Prologue written for the revival of 1667 is diffident enough to show why Shirley's best realistic plays, like *The Example* or *The Lady of Pleasure*, were not seen at the Restoration:

> In our Old Plays, the humor Love and Passion
> Like Doublet, Hose, and Cloak, are out of fashion:
> That which the World call'd Wit in Shakespears Age,
> Is laught at, as improper for our Stage;
> Nay Fletcher stands Corrected, what hope then
> For this poor Author, Shirley, whose soft Pen
> Was fill'd with Air in Comick Scenes, alas,
> Your Guards are now so strict he'l never pass.

To itemise what Shirley failed to carry past these guards it is only necessary to display for comparison the language of Shirley and Dryden in handling an identical theme, that of the basic supposition in the whole history of the comedy of society, that urban living is vital, and rural mortifying. *The Lady of Pleasure* opens with this primary situation:

STEWARD: Be patient, madam; you may have your pleasure.
ARETINA: 'Tis that I came to town for. I would not
  Endure again the country conversation
  To be the lady of six shires—the men
  So near the primitive making they retain
  A sense of nothing but the earth, their brains

And barren heads standing as much in want
Of ploughing as their ground; to hear a fellow
Make himself merry, and his horse, with whistling
Sellinger's Round; to observe with what solemnity
They keep their wakes and throw for pewter candlesticks!
How they become the morris, with whose bells
They ring all in to Whitsun ales, and sweat
Through twenty scarfs and napkins till the hobby-horse
Tire, and Maid Marian, dissolv'd to a jelly,
Be kept for spoon meat!
STEWARD: These, with your pardon, are no argument
To make the country life appear so hateful.

In effect Aretina and her steward are still presenting arguments about the respective merits of town and country existence, for the comedy of manners has not yet acquired its ideal audience, and the viewpoints are balanced in detail. In *Marriage à la Mode* the town lady is herself scorned:

MELANTHA: I declare, I had rather of the two be *rallied*, nay, *mal traitee* at court, than be deified in the town: for, assuredly, nothing can be so *ridicule* as a mere town lady.

DORALICE: Especially at court. How I have seen 'em crowd and sweat in the drawing-room on a holiday-night! for that's their time to swarm and invade the presence.

The court circle is Melantha's sole test of her own social identity, and is placed by Doralice as the touchstone of social status:

MELANTHA: When I have been at grass in the summer, and am new come up again, methinks I'm to be turned into *ridicule* by all that see me; but when I have been once or twice at court, I begin to value myself again, and to despise my country acquaintance.

ARTEMIS: There are places where all people may be adored, and we ought to know ourselves so well as to choose them.

DORALICE: That's very true; your little courtier's wife, who speaks to the king but once a month, need but go to a town lady, and there she may vapour and cry 'The King and I', at every word. Your town lady, who is laughed at in the circle, takes her coach into the city, and there she's called 'Your honour', and has a banquet from the merchant's wife, whom she laughs at for her kindness. And, as for my finical cit, she removes but to her country house, and there insults over the country gentlewoman that never comes

up; who treats her with frumity and custard, and opens her dear
bottle of *mirabilis* beside, for a gill-glass of it at parting.

(III. i)

Such prose has the assurance of its social attitudes behind it, the
grammar of social status has been learned and is accurately recited. The
style is easy, but still formal in a courtly manner by contrast with the
flexible mode of Etherege. Here, in *The Man of Mode*, country life and
people are briefly commented upon in passing:

MRS. LOVEIT: I could chide you; where have you been these two
   days?
BELINDA: Pity me rather, my dear, where I have been so tired with
   two or three country gentlewomen, whose conversation has been
   more insufferable than a country fiddle.
MRS. LOVEIT: Are they relations?
BELINDA: No, Welsh acquaintances I made when I was last year at
   St. Winifrid's; they have asked me a thousand questions of the
   modes and intrigues of the town, and I have told 'em almost as
   many things for news that hardly were so when their gowns were
   in fashion.
MRS. LOVEIT: Provoking creatures, how could you endure 'em?

Later, these rustics stray across the line of fire and are glancingly hit:

MRS. LOVEIT: Where do these country gentlewomen lodge, I pray?
BELINDA: In the Strand, over against the Exchange.
MRS. LOVEIT: That place is never without a nest of 'em; they are
   always as one goes by fleering in balconies or staring out of
   windows.

Perhaps the precision of this prose may be better judged by contrasting
Oscar Wilde's handling of what he terms 'the agricultural depression':
this is part of a conversation in the opening scene of *The Importance of
Being Earnest*:

ALGERNON: Where have you been since last Thursday?
JACK: In the country.
ALGERNON: What on earth do you do there?
JACK: When one is in the town one amuses oneself. When one is in
   the country one amuses other people. It is excessively boring.
ALGERNON: And who are the people you amuse?
JACK: Oh, neighbours, neighbours!
ALGERNON: Got nice neighbours in your part of Shropshire?

JACK: Perfectly horrid! Never speak to one of them.

ALGERNON: How immensely you must amuse them. . . .

The climate of their times can be precisely studied only in the full dramatic context, but even these passages suggest some of the main stylistic emphases. Shirley's language is verbose, not shaping the blank verse with any precision, and cataloguing country life in a pleasantly satirical vein not altogether dissimilar from the nostalgic tone of much subsequent sentimental comedy: Dryden's language is tightly controlled, making play with appropriate foreign phrases, and condescending: Wilde's conversation is leisurely, its verbal thinness distilled to the point of languor. In Etherege we have a fuller interplay of conversation, an easier social confidence and contempt. Aretina is petulant, Melantha and Doralice affected, Algernon and Jack bored, but Belinda and Mrs. Loveit are cruel. Yet the essential point about the style of the two Restoration writers is that they share an ability to use social detail with precision: where Shirley accumulates and Wilde sheds, both Dryden and Etherege select the discriminating particular. For Doralice country people 'crowd and sweat' and 'swarm' and 'invade', unsupported by Shirley's adjectives. Melantha has 'been at grass', but once back at court begins to 'value' herself again, and the chosen phrases perfectly reflect and embody the distinct activities. Similarly Etherege's language has a capacity for assimilating the vast discrepancies of social differences and digesting them in a phrase: the country women, in town, in the Strand, by the Exchange, are pilloried in an image that has followed them from the country, and the mention of a habit incurably provincial: 'That place is never without a nest of 'em', and 'fleering in balconies or staring out of windows'. This capacity for incorporating substantial metaphor within easy social discourse is an achievement which Etherege shares with Congreve, and is a characteristic which requires further mention.

Before turning to it, however, it seems worth commenting upon another aspect of the relationship of style and substance with which Dryden's language presents us. The clarity, balance, antithesis, of his style may too easily be granted a verbal consideration merely, when its full appreciation involves a human recognition also. Dryden wrote his first comedy, *The Wild Gallant*, for enactment by Nell Gwynn and Hart, and their influence remained. His prose style cannot adequately be estimated without reference to this personal factor. Its supreme achievement, in *Marriage à la Mode*, may be inseparable from this human and theatrical complexity. Sutherland tells us[11] of an old gentleman of eighty-six who wrote to the *Gentleman's Magazine* in 1745 that this play

> made its first appearance with extraordinary lustre. Divesting myself of the old man, I solemnly declare that you have seen no such acting, no, not in *any* degree, since.

And Colley Cibber, as Sutherland reminds us, paid tribute later to the performance of Mrs. Verbruggen as Melantha. The tribute is worth repeating in detail as an indication of the degree to which Dryden's prose proved capable not merely of verbal accuracy but of human, and therefore dramatic, 'realisation'. 'Mrs. Mountfort, whose second marriage gave her the name of Verbruggen, was mistress of more variety of humour', Cibber tells us, 'than I ever knew in any one woman actress.' She had the necessary capacity of giving 'many heightening touches to characters but coldly written', but what 'found most employment for her whole various excellence at once, was the part of Melantha'. And though Cibber doubts that 'it will be a vain labour, to offer you a just likeness of Mrs. Mountfort's action, yet the fantastick impression is so strong in my memory, that I cannot help saying something, tho' fantastically, about it':

> The first ridiculous airs that break from her are upon a gallant, never seen before, who delivers her a letter from her father, recommending him to her good graces as an honourable lover. Here now, one would think she might show naturally a little of the sex's decent reserve, tho' never so slightly cover'd! No, sir; not a tittle of it; modesty is the virtue of a poor-soul'd country gentlewoman; she is too much a court lady, to be under so vulgar a confusion; she reads the letter, therefore, with a careless, dropping lip, and an erected brow, humming it hastily over, as if she were impatient to outgo her father's commands, by making a compleat conquest of him at once; and that the letter might not embarrass her attack, crack! she crumbles it at once into her palm, and pours upon him her whole artillery of airs, eyes and motion; down goes her dainty diving body, to the ground, as if she were sinking under the conscious load of her own attractions; then launches into a flood of fine language, and compliment, still playing her chest forward in fifty falls and risings, like a swan upon waving water; and to complete her impatience, she is so rapidly fond of her own wit, that she will not give her lover

[11] Edition of *Marriage à la Mode*, p. x.

leave to praise it. Silent assenting bows, and vain endeavours to speak, are all the share of the conversation he is admitted to, which, at last, he is relieved from by her engagement to half a score visits, which she *swims* from him to make, with a promise to return in a twinkling.

If we turn back from Cibber's eloquence to Dryden's prose on the page we are likely to experience some of the latter's irritation with *Bussy D'Ambois* when he brought his memory of the performance to bear upon the text; thinking to find a star he was cozened with a jelly. Melantha is no Beatrice, whose wit is poetically phrased and shaped by intelligence. Melantha is a coquette with an empty head and a mouthful of affected French. The words on the page are breathless, they have to be paced; they are 'but coldly written' and only human warmth could possibly make them seem 'fine language'. Mrs. Verbruggen played the scene like a swan; whether the actresses of Nell Gwynn's era had such an elegance is an open question, but that Melantha must play this scene with her body is evident from the fact that Palamede, when left alone on the stage, revenges himself in imagination upon her person because he has no other answer to her language:

> 'Tis true, in the daytime, 'tis tolerable, when a man has field-room to run from it; but, to be shut up in a bed with her, like two cocks in a pit, humanity cannot support it. I must kiss all night, in my own defence, and hold her down, like a boy at cuffs, nay, and give her the rising blow every time she begins to speak.   (II. i)

Such prose is typical of Dryden's manner, whose characteristic tone is of licentious indulgence: his prologues and epilogues are provocative, his scenes sensational, and his most ambitious stylistic device innuendo. If one of the purposes of comedy is to assist the assimilation of sexual instincts Dryden was more than willing to play his part. His view of comedy was low, and he prostituted his art because he was realistic enough to see that the art itself in his day depended upon prostitutes. But before we censure his comic prose style as a warning example of language in an over-susceptible relationship with its clients, we ought to remember that in putting his language in the service of basic human instincts Dryden was not only surrendering to his courtly audience; he was making more possible in the drama the fuller presentation of experience.

This problem of adequately full presentation of experience within

ANNE BRACEGIRDLE

the self-imposed conventions of the comedy of manners provides the severest test of its prose resources. The task involves bringing within the range of realistic conversation something of the possibilities of other modes of dialogue. Wycherley's reliance upon a mingled vocabulary derived from Shakespeare, Jonson or Fletcher, French influence and Roman satire makes his an impure art by comparison with that of Etherege. The full range of prose styles displayed in Wycherley's *Country Wife* and *The Plain Dealer* is formidably extensive; the stylistic devices include paradox, passages of 'character' writing, parodies of moral platitudes, frequent soliloquy and asides, irruptions of technical vocabulary, like the litigious language of the Blackacre scenes, and sustained *double entendre* like that of the notorious 'china' scene. The tone is rarely constant for long, except for the serious denunciation and satiric railing of *The Plain Dealer*, and Wycherley satisfies his restless and aggressive feelings by choosing plots of complex intrigue dependent upon surprise more than in many instances of realistic comedy. The nearest approach to balance in Wycherley's turbulent writing is typically through paradoxical assertions of perverse authority, such as Manly's 'no man can be a great enemy but under the name of a friend'. Elsewhere there are signs of difficulty in bringing the plot narrative within social exchange, as in the following sentence:

> VINCENT: I told you I had sent my man to Christina's this morning, to inquire of her maid, (who seldom denies him a secret,) if her lady had been at the Park last night; which she peremptorily answered to the contrary, and assured him she had not stirred out since your departure.   (*Love in a Wood*, IV. v)

Wycherley's characters are rarely phrase-makers of distinction, they use the language to abuse its structure, much as Horner confesses in his discussion with Harcourt and Dorilant:

> DORILANT: Did I ever think to see you keep company with women in vain?
> HORNER: In vain: no—'tis since I can't love 'em, to be revenged on 'em.
> HARCOURT: Now your sting is gone, you looked in the box amongst all those women like a drone in the hive; all upon you, shoved and ill-used by 'em, and thrust from one side to t'other.
> DORILANT: Yet he must be buzzing amongst 'em still, like other beetle-headed liquorish drones. Avoid 'em, and hate 'em, as they hate you.

HORNER: Because I do hate 'em, and would hate 'em yet more, I'll frequent 'em. You may see by marriage, nothing makes a man hate a woman more than her constant conversation. In short, I converse with 'em, as you do with rich fools, to laugh at 'em and use 'em ill.   (*The Country Wife*, III, ii)

This effective but laboured use of insect imagery may serve to introduce a comparison between the handling of such images from the natural life in the work of true prose stylists of the comedy of manners such as Etherege or Congreve, and writers in a miscellany of modes such as Wycherley or Shadwell. The comparison of human and non-human life is a powerful device for the writer concerned with behaviour. But when Wycherley makes Harcourt and Horner talk of the drones, or Horner make a conventional comparison of the nature of women and spaniels, or Alithea and Mrs. Pinchwife converse about their own existence in terms of cage birds, the intention is to make a moral judgement, or provocative comparison, or sentimental homily. Wycherley's assumption is that human life ought to be manifestly distinct. Similarly Shadwell, whose prose is richer in the detail of all forms of life than any of his contemporaries, moves his broad sympathies behind his country characters, and in *Bury Fair* even shifts his scene out of London to effect the full comparison. Wildish the spokesman for city life engages Lord Bellamy in a typical encounter:

BELLAMY: I have as pleasant a house and seat as most in England, that is thine as much as thine, Ned.
WILDISH: But 'tis in the country; a pretty habitation for birds and cattle. But man is a herded animal, and made for towns and cities.
BELLAMY: So many pens of wild beasts upon two legs, undermining, lying in wait, preying upon, informing against, and hanging one another: a crowd of fools, knaves, whores, and hypocrites.

(I. ii)

Shadwell's characters are much taken up in the discussion of natural and unnatural breeding, and he pairs opposites in a simple debating manner, like Mrs. Gertrude who counters Lady Fantast's notion of 'the art of refined conversation' with 'Art! Conversation ought to be free, easy, and natural' and offers her own account of true breeding:

A lady may look after the affairs of a family, the demeanour of her servants, take care of her nursery, take all her accounts every week, obey her husband, and discharge all the offices of a good wife with her native tongue; and this is all I desire to arrive at; and this is to be of some use in a generation; while your fantastic lady, with all those trappings and ornaments you speak of, is good for no more than a dancing mare, to be led about and shown. (II. i)

The easy reference to animal life slips out naturally again when she is humiliated by playing the false social game of courtship:

indeed it makes me smile, to think of a grave mother, or, for want of her, a wise father, putting a daughter into a room, like a hare out of a basket, and letting her loose; that is, to act the part of a lover before marriage, and never think of it afterwards.

(III. i)

Shadwell's plays contain a prodigious array of prose styles, from country dialects, rogues' canting terms, stilted dialogues of formal cits, romantic exchanges, to the sober conversation of gentlemen. The styles are distinct and faithfully represented: like Dryden, Shadwell must often have been 'put to a stand, in considering whether what I write be the Idiom of the Tongue'. But though Shadwell's plays are unfairly neglected the very scope of his achievement may be responsible. Shadwell uses his arts of language to preserve a traditional morality; his prose displays the differences of opinions and of behaviour, but he assumes that the artificial and the natural are distinct. By contrast Etherege organises his comic universe on a unified principle; his similitudes from the natural life offer a relationship to the human, not a distinction or even a parallel. In *The Man of Mode*, for instance, there is a persistent relationship effected between the forms of life. In the opening scene Dorimant talks with the Orange Woman over her fruit basket, and the syntax directs us to equate the subjects of their conversation with the activity:

ORANGE WOMAN: Here, bid your man give me an angel.

(*Sets down the fruit*)

DORIMANT: Give the bawd her fruit again.

ORANGE WOMAN: Well, on my conscience, there never was the like of you. God's my life, I had almost forgot to tell you there is a young gentlewoman lately come to town with her mother, that is so taken with you.

DORIMANT: Is she handsome?

ORANGE WOMAN: Nay, gad, there are few finer women, I tell you but so, and a hugeous fortune, they say. Here, eat this peach, it comes from the stone; 'tis better than any Newington y'have tasted.

DORIMANT: This fine woman, I'll lay my life, (*Taking the peach*) is some awkward, ill-fashioned, country toad. . . .

Medley later joins them, identifies Harriet, when the Orange Woman will not, and describes

the beautifullest creature I ever saw; a fine, easy, clean shape; light brown hair in abundance; her features regular; her complexion clear and lively; large wanton eyes; but above all, a mouth that has made me kiss it a thousand times in imagination, teeth white and even, and pretty pouting lips, with a little moisture ever hanging on them, that look like the Provence rose fresh on the bush, ere the morning sun has quite drawn up the dew.

The simile is perfectly absorbed, and absorbing: 'Rapture, mere rapture!' cries Dorimant in appetite, and where he would not pay for the peach he gives ten shillings for the introduction.

Etherege's prose itself has an easy appetite for naturalising similes as in Harriet's retort to Young Bellair 'There are some, it may be, have an eye like Bartholomew, big enough for the whole fair, but I am not of the number, and you may keep your gingerbread.' It has, too, a capacity to relate the artificial affectingly, so that its detachment disturbs us, as when Harriet and Young Bellair simulate a courtship display for the benefit of Old Bellair and Lady Woodvil. The young couple take turns at instruction, and the scene concludes:

HARRIET: 'Twill not be amiss now to seem a little pleasant.

YOUNG BELLAIR: Clap your fan then in both hands, snatch it to your mouth, smile, and with a lively motion fling your body a little forwards. So,—now spread it; fall back on the sudden, cover your face with it, and break out to a loud laughter—take up! Look grave, and fall a-fanning of yourself—admirably well acted.

HARRIET: I think I am pretty apt at these matters.

OLD BELLAIR: Adod, I like this well.

LADY WOODVIL: This promises something.

OLD BELLAIR: Come! there is love i'th'case, adod there is, or will be; what say you, young lady?

HARRIET: All in good time, sir; you expect we should fall to and love, as gamecocks fight, as soon as we are set together; adod, you're unreasonable. (III. i)

Such a scene organises our feelings to receive the implications of Dorimant's subsequent encounter with Harriet and his abuse of her airs, just as it also depends for its full context on what John Wain (*loc. cit.* p. 17) rightly calls 'the truly frightening scene of Dorimant's visit to Mrs. Loveit' when 'his extreme brutality to Mrs. Loveit is itself a form of sexual display for Belinda's benefit'. So the energy generated in one scene is drawn upon as illumination in another, and both the flow of energy and the unobtrusive allusion are controlled by the precision of wit. The fruit and flower crop up again in Dorimant's flattery of Lady Woodvil; he is speaking of old women of thirty-five:

DORIMANT: . . . show me among all our opening buds a face that promises so much beauty as the remains of theirs.

LADY WOODVIL: The depraved appetite of this vicious age tastes nothing but green fruit, and loathes it when 'tis kindly ripened.

DORIMANT: Else so many deserving women, madam, would not be so untimely neglected.   (IV. i)

In the last act of the play those mysterious strangers, the country gentle-women, insist on Belinda accompanying them to the market 'to eat fruit and buy nosegays' as she scornfully relates to Mrs. Loveit:

Do you think, my dear, I could be so loathesome to trick myself up with carnations and stock gillyflowers? I begged their pardon, and told them I never wore anything but orange flowers and tuberose. That which made willing to go was a strange desire I had to eat some fresh nectarines.   (V. i)

This inexplicable desire finds its *raison d'être* when Dorimant arrives and Belinda can pretend to be taken ill, but the inconsequence gives comic point to the artifice of all nature in this play. Harriet is so in love with the town that she can 'scarce endure the country in landscapes and in hangings'; Young Bellair plays fearfully with the thought of being 'hurried back to Hampshire'; to Dorimant 'all beyond High Park's a desert'. Such muted terrors are urgently amplified in Harriet's final picture of her country home:

a great rambling lone house that looks as it were not inhabited, the family's so small; there you'll find my mother, an old lame aunt, and myself, sir, perched up on chairs at a distance in a large parlour, sitting moping like three or four melancholy birds in a spacious volery.

So are 'scatter'd follies gathered into one', and there is even music at the close. 'Methinks I hear the hateful noise of rooks already—knaw, knaw, knaw. There's music in the worst cry in London, *My dill and cucumbers to pickle.*' The fruit harvested is vegetable: they dance and depart.

Only·Congreve shares Etherege's ability to enlarge hints, as it were, from the margin of his main concern, and impress them into active service, and to give similes something of the potency of metaphors. But by Congreve's time the accumulated experience of this late seventeenth century is ripe for full exploitation. 'It sometimes happens, in the history of an art', Raymond Williams (*loc. cit.* p. 255) notes, 'that a form reaches its highest point of development when its essential conditions are already vanishing.' And certainly it is doubtful whether any comic dramatist, Shakespeare not excepted, began his career with a work of such inherited linguistic vitality, social experience, and theatrical confidence as Congreve did with *The Old Bachelor*. The devices of social delineation are positively displayed, through nomenclature of characters, appropriate vocabulary and idiosyncratic syntax; such are the military terms employed by Captain Bluffe and Sharper, the baby talk of Fondlewife, which so thoroughly ensures our odium, the honest uncomplicated phrases of Heartwell, Bellmour's attractive nautical vocabulary, or the repellent, suave antitheses of Vainlove.

This prose is remarkably alert to the dramatic interplay between word, action and total stage situation. For instance of this one may take the successive scenes of Act IV. xix–xxii. Here the discovery of the disguised Bellmour is prompted by the book entitled *The Innocent Adultery*—as Bellmour says 'If I had gone a whoring with *The Practice of Piety* in my pocket, I had never been discover'd'—and from then on Congreve uses Bellmour's disguise as Spintext to tease out texts of Scripture in a versatile array of similes ('The Devil, no, I am afraid 'tis the Flesh', 'This is Apocryphal, I may chuse whether I may believe it or no'); some of these are merely quibbling puns, but others enforce the vehemence of the quarrel with denunciatory Old Testament names; and the sequence ends with a new treaty between cynicism and faith, an uneasy equation of pious hope and accepted cuckoldom ('Well, well, sir; as long as I believe it, 'tis well enough').

Far more ambitious, but equally confident, is the interplay of language and situation in such a scene as that between Araminta and Belinda in IV. viii, beginning with Belinda's rueful contemplation of

National Portrait Gallery

ANNE OLDFIELD

her 'furious Phyz' after a coach-ride has tousled her hair; the stage business involves a mirror and pins in the restoration of dignity; the language moves from improvised distraction to apparent inconsequence:

BELINDA: ... Good Dear, pin this, and I'll tell you—Very well—So, thank you my Dear—But as I was telling you—Pish, this is the untoward'st Lock—So, as I was telling you—How d'ye like me now? Hideous, ha? Frightful still? Or how?

ARAMINTA: No, no; you're very well as can be.

BELINDA: And so—But where did I leave off, my Dear? I was telling you——

ARAMINTA: You were about to tell me something, Child—but you left off before you began.

BELINDA: Oh; a most comical Sight: A Country Squire, with the Equipage of a Wife and two Daughters, came to Mrs. Snipwell's Shop while I was there—But, oh Gad! Two such unlick'd Cubs!

ARAMINTA: I warrant, plump, Cherry-cheek'd Country Girls.

BELINDA: Ay, O my Conscience, fat as Barn-Door Fowl: But so bedeck'd, you would have taken 'em for *Friezeland* Hens, with their Feathers growing the wrong way—O such Outlandish Creatures! Such *Tramontanae*, and Foreigners to the Fashion, or any such thing in Practice! I had not Patience to behold—I undertook the modelling of one of their Fronts, the more modern Structure——

ARAMINTA: Bless me, Cousin; why would you affront any Body so? They might be Gentlewomen of a very good Family——

BELINDA: Of a very ancient one, I dare swear, by their Dress—Affront! Pshaw, hoe you're mistaken! The poor Creature, I warrant, was as full of Curtsies, as if I had been her Godmother: the Truth on't is, I did endeavour to make her look like a Christian—and she was sensible of it; for she thank'd me, and gave me two Apples, piping hot, out of her Under-Petticoat Pocket—Ha, ha, ha: And t'other did so stare and gape—I fansied her like the Front of her Father's Hall; her Eyes were the two Jut-Windows, and her Mouth the great Door, most hospitably kept open, for the Entertainment of travelling Flies.

ARAMINTA: So then; you have been diverted. What did they buy?

BELINDA: Why, the Father bought a Powder-Horn, and an Almanack, and a Comb-Case; the Mother, a great Fruz-Towr, and a fat Amber-Necklace; the Daughters only tore two Pair of Kid-leather Gloves, with trying 'em on—Oh Gad, here comes the Fool that din'd at my Lady *Freelove*'s t'other Day.

The full meanings of this prose are difficult to restrict: the whole scene of the meeting of the two women in St. James's Park is no more than a gossiping diversion before the encounter between them and Sir Joseph Wittol and Captain Bluffe. Yet the time-taking is filled with mimetic and verbal opportunities for Mrs. Mountfort's Belinda and Mrs. Bracegirdle's Araminta. Belinda has been the victim of a comic assault upon her affected elegance, 'jolted to a Jelly' and 'horridly touz'd'. The reparation of her dignity is not complete when she has tidied her hair; the mess she was in reminded her of the 'unhewn Creatures' and she recovers her poise at the expense of the country girls; the anecdote permits her to indulge a talent for face-making and malicious description and yet convince us that the social affront to the girl was not a frivolous gesture towards fashion but generous and educative.

The authority of this language is absolute; the degree of affectation is precisely controlled, and the anecdote's seeming inconsequence is pinned firmly back from the purchased comb-case and the fruz-tower headdress to Mrs. Snipwell's shop and the business of hair-tidying in which it all originated.

Congreve's prose is not always so humanly indulgent: as Mrs. Bracegirdle said in the Prologue to his first play

> He's very civil, and entreats your Favour.
> Not but the Man has Malice, would he show it . . .

Congreve's destructive malice goes and grows along with his capacity for comic creation. His characters are as skilled in verbal malice as those of any dramatist of his time, and since so much criticism is devoted to the verbal felicities, the intellectual cruelties or the emotional subtleties of this malice it seems worth emphasising more the special weight of Congreve's prose when its malice is directed against human substance. In illustration of this we may contrast some passages of comic prose on the favourite theme of anatomy. This is a conversation about Lady Love-All in Killigrew's *The Parson's Wedding*:

WANTON: Pity her? Hang her and rid the country of her. She is a thing wears out her limbs as fast as her clothes, one that never goes to bed at all nor sleeps in a whole skin, but is taken to pieces like a motion. She should be hanged for offering to be a whore.

CAPTAIN: As I live, she is in the right. I peeped once to see what she did before she went to bed. By this light, her maids were dissect-

ing her, and when they had done, they brought some of her to
bed, and the rest they either pinned or hung up, and so she lay
dismembered till morning; in which time her chamber was
strewed all over like an anatomy school.   (IV. i)

The gruesome gaiety of the whore and the soldier has a primitive insight; but not much more than is glimpsed through the key-hole.
When Vanbrugh's Heartfree tries to dissuade Constant from romantic
notions of women's nature he sets about the subject with a fuller
rhetoric:

HEARTFREE: . . . I always consider a woman, not as the tailor, the
    shoe-maker, the tire-woman, the semptress, and (which is more
    than all that) the poet makes her; but I consider her as pure nature
    has contrived her, and that more strictly than I should have done
    our old grandmother Eve, had I seen her naked in the garden; for
    I consider her turned inside out. Her heart well examined, I find
    there pride, vanity, covetousness, indiscretion; but, above all
    things, malice: plots eternally forging to destroy one another's
    reputations, and as honestly to charge the levity of men's tongues
    with the scandal; hourly debates how to make poor gentlemen in
    love with them, with no other intent but to use them like dogs
    when they have done; a constant desire of doing more mischief,
    and an everlasting war waged against truth and good-nature.
CONSTANT: Very well, sir, an admirable composition truly!
HEARTFREE: Then for outside, I consider it merely as an outside: she
    has a thin, tiffany covering; just over such stuff as you and I are
    made of. As for her motion, her mien, her airs, and all those tricks,
    I know they affect you mightily. If you should see your mistress
    at a coronation, dragging her peacock's train, with all her state and
    insolence about her, 'twould strike you with all the awful thoughts
    that heaven itself could pretend to from you: whereas, I turn the
    whole matter into a jest, and suppose her strutting, in the self-
    same stately manner, with nothing on but her stays, and her
    scanty quilted under-petticoat.
CONSTANT: Hold thy profane tongue; for I'll hear no more. (II. i)

The malice here is speculative, leisurely, verbose, playing about the
social person as nature has 'contrived her'. But when Lady Wishfort
turns on her maid the human reality standing before us is turned into
a real contrivance, a servant:

LADY WISHFORT: . . . Fetch me the Red—the Red, do you hear,
    Sweet-heart? An errant Ash colour, as I'm a Person. Look you

how this Wench stirs! Why dost thou not fetch me a little Red?
Didst thou not hear me, Mopus?

PEG: The red *Ratafia* does your Ladiship mean, or the Cherry-
Brandy?

LADY WISHFORT: *Ratafia*, Fool. No, Fool. Not the *Ratafia*, Fool—
Grant me, Patience! I mean the *Spanish* Paper, Idiot, Complexion
Darling. Paint, Paint, Paint, dost thou understand that, Changeling, dangling thy Hands like Bobbins before thee? Why dost
thou not stir, Puppet? thou wooden Thing upon Wires.

This prose bounces off Peg, who is called Peg because she is wooden;
servants have no feelings. But when Congreve's prose explores more
inwardly it encounters equally solid resistance:

SIR SAMPSON: . . . How were you engendered, Muckworm?

JEREMY: I am by my Father, the Son of a Chairman; my Mother
sold Oisters in Winter, and Cucumbers in Summer; and I came
up Stairs into the World; for I was born in a Cellar.

FORESIGHT: By your Looks, you shou'd go up Stairs out of the
World too, Friend.

SIR SAMPSON: And if this Rogue were Anatomiz'd now, and dis-
sected, he has his Vessels of Digestion and Concoction, and so
forth, large enough for the inside of a Cardinal, this Son of a
Cucumber.—These things are unaccountable and unreasonable,
Body o'me, why was not I a Bear? that my Cubs might have liv'd
upon sucking their Paws; Nature has been provident only to Bears
and Spiders; the one has its Nutriment in his own Hands; and
t'other spins his Habitation out of his own Entrails.

(*Love For Love*, II. vii)

To all that Bonamy Dobrée[12] so well said about Congreve's rhythm,
its flexibility and point, one might only want to add that it is the
articulation not only of an 'incomparable beauty' and 'seductive gentle-
ness' but of an inexhaustible human energy. The 'refinement' is fuelled
upon gross matter and when it neglects the origin of the supply the
comic creation collapses as violently as does the verbal poise of Lady
Wishfort when she discovers Foible's deceit:

Out of my House, out of my House, thou Viper, thou Serpent, that
I have foster'd; thou bosom Traitress, that I rais'd from nothing—
Begone, begone, begone, go, go,—That I took from washing of old

---

[12] *Congreve's Comedies*, Introduction, xvi–xxviii.

Gause and weaving of dead Hair, with a bleak blue Nose, over a
Chafing-dish of starv'd Embers, and Dining behind a Traverse Rag,
in a shop no bigger than a Bird-Cage,—go, go, starve again, do, do.

(*The Way of the World*, V. i)

The balance lost here, and strenuously being restored at the close of
the play, may serve to represent that major theme of Restoration social
comedy which engages in so many ways with the refined and the raw.
Rochester phrased it briefly:

> Our selves with noise of Reason we do please
> In vain, Humanity's our worst Disease.
> (*Satire LIII, Tunbridge Wells*, 173)

The tension between reason and appetite that is achieved in the prose
of Congreve is not available to Sir John Vanbrugh, who put little store
upon words. He wrote as he spoke, and Cibber tells us that actors
found 'the style of no author whatsoever gave their memory less
trouble'. What is memorable in Vanbrugh's work is riot, relapse,
buffoonery and humiliation; it is a spectacle of appetite in action.
When Sir John Brute comes home, bleeding and dirty, he insists upon
kissing his wife:

> So, now you being as dirty and as nasty as myself, we may go pig
> together. But first I must have a Cup of your Cold-Tea, Wife.
> (*The Provoked Wife*, IV. vi)

The tea cupboard yields Constant and Heartfree, of course, to whom he
is drunkenly, menacingly, polite, until they leave:

CONSTANT: Sir, when you are cool, you'll understand reason better:
so, then, I shall take the pains to inform you; if not, I wear a sword,
sir, and so good b'ye. Come along, Heartfree. .   (*Exeunt*)

SIR JOHN BRUTE: Wear a sword, sir! And what, then, sir? He comes
to my house, eats my meat, lies with my wife, dishonours my
family, gets a bastard to inherit my estate; and when I ask a civil
account of all this—'Sir,' says he, 'I wear a sword.' Wear a sword,
sir? 'Yes, sir,' says he, 'I wear a sword.' It may a good answer at
cross purposes; but 'tis a d—d one to a man in my whimsical circumstances. 'Sir,' says he, 'I wear a sword.' (*To* Lady Brute) And
what do you wear now? Eh! tell me. (*Sitting down*) What, you are
modest, and can't! why, then, I'll tell you, you slut, you: you
wear an impudent, lewd face; a d—d designing heart; and a tail—
and a tail full of—— (*Falls fast asleep*)

LADY BRUTE: So, thanks to kind heaven, he's fast for some hours![13]

Her thoughts fly up, but ours remain below. Her husband, wrapped up like a woodlouse and dreaming of revenge (as Whitwoud advised the drunken Petulent), is carried to his bed. When he wakes Sir John Brute decides that 'a living dog is better than a dead lion'.

Perhaps the most eloquent statement of human needs and Vanbrugh's approval of their essential gratification is provided by the commotion and dismay over the loss of a goose-pie, in his last, and unfinished work, *A Journey to London*. Here the Cook comes running in to cry 'Ah my Lady! we're aw undone, the Goose Pye's gwon', and tells of how two 'thin starv'd London rogues' had robbed her and run like greyhounds with 'heavy George' and 'fat Tom' in pursuit. When this pair return, bloody and defeated, it is only to tell of how one was fetched down with 'a wherry accross the Shins' and the other with a 'swap' that came 'somewhat across my Fore-head, with such a Force, that dawn came I, like an Ox'. As the talk goes on Squire Humphry murmurs 'So, the poor Pye's quite gone then', and 'It was a rare good Pye', and later 'Feather, I had rather they had run away with heavy George than the Goose Pye, a slice of it before Supper to-night would have been pure'.

But the real thief of the great goose-pie was Colley Cibber, who took upon himself to replace the scene, in his completion of the play, with one more calculated to 'Entertain the Minds of a sensible Nation': he brought in Squire Richard with a brown-paper patch on his head earned through running after the girls and getting the door slammed in his face. But more serious even than the theft of the pie was the per-version of Vanbrugh's whole intention in the interests of moral per-suasion. 'All I could gather from him of what he intended in the *Catastrophe*, was, that the Conduct of his Imaginary Fine Lady had so provok'd him, that he design'd actually to have made her Husband turn her out of his Doors.' So Cibber relates; but he thought 'such violent Measures, however just they might be in real Life, were too severe for Comedy', so he 'preserv'd the Lady's Chastity, that the Sense of her Errors might make a Reconciliation not Impracticable'. It was cer-tainly practical; the sentiments flowed freely as Lady Townley re-pented (*ed. cit.* pp. 382–4) of her folly:

[13] 'To the Reader', *The Provok'd Husband, Vanbrugh's Plays* (1734), II, pp. 283–4.

My only Joy was Power, Command, Society, Profuseness, and to lead in Pleasures! The Husband's Right to Rule, I thought a vulgar Law, which only the Deform'd, or Meanly-spirited obey'd! I knew no Directors, but my Passions; no Master, but my Will! Even you, my Lord, some time o'ercome by Love, were pleas'd with my Delights; nor, then, foresaw this mad Misuse of your Indulgence . . . That kind Indulgence has undone me! it added Strength to my habitual Failings, and in a Heart thus warm, in wild unthinking Life, no wonder if the gentler Sense of Love was lost.

The sentences pulse onwards, punctuated only by adoring asides: 'O Manly! where has this Creature's Heart been buried?' A new art was being made.

Cibber maintained (*ibid.* pp. 285–6) of *The Provoked Husband* that in it Mills surpassed himself and that in 'the last Act, I never saw any Passion take so natural a Possession of an Actor, or any Actor take so tender a Possession of his Auditors' as in the case of Wilks. But of Mrs. Oldfield's playing of Lady Townley Cibber was moved to give testimony of exceptional interest for our knowledge of her personality and her acting. Towards the end of 1727, Cibber relates

Mrs. Oldfield was, then, in her highest Excellence of Action, happy in all the rarely-found Requisites, that meet in one Person to compleat them for the Stage—She was in Stature just rising to that Height, where the Graceful can only begin to shew it self; of a lively Aspect, and a Command in her Mien, that like the principal Figure in the finest Paintings, first seizes, and longest delights the Eye of the Spectator. Her Voice was sweet, strong, piercing, and melodious: her Pronunciation voluble, distinct, and musical; and her Emphasis always placed where the Spirit of the Sense, in her Periods, only demanded it. If she delighted more in the Higher Comick, than the Tragick Strain, 'twas because the last is too often written in a lofty Disregard of Nature. But in Characters of modern practis'd Life, she found occasions to add the particular Air and Manner which distinguished the different Humours she presented. Whereas in Tragedy, the Manner of Speaking varies, as little, as the Blank Verse it is written in—She had one peculiar Happiness from Nature, she look'd and maintain'd the *Agreeable* at a time, when other Fine Women only raise Admirers by their Understanding—The Spectator was always as much informed by her Eyes, as her Elocution; for the Look is the only Proof that an Actor rightly conceives what he utters, there being scarce an Instance, where the Eyes do their Part, that the Elocution is known to be faulty. The Qualities she had *acquired*, were the *Genteel* and the *Elegant*. The one in her Air, and the other in her Dress, never had her Equal on the Stage; and the Ornaments she herself provided, (particularly in this Play) seem'd in all Respects the *Paraphernalia* of a Woman of Quality. And of that Sort were the Characters she chiefly excell'd in; but her natural good Sense and lively Turn of Conversation made her Way so easy to Ladies of the highest Rank, that it is a less Wonder, if on the Stage she sometimes *was*, what might have become the finest Woman in real Life to have supported.

To look upon the portrait of Anne Oldfield (Plate IIB) and upon a print of Anne Bracegirdle (Plate IIA) is probably as effective a way as any of marking the difference between the Sentimental and Restoration comic styles. The Restoration comic dramatists write for the 'furious Phyz' of the contemporary human grimace, not for the 'Agreeable' mien, and their art is correspondingly vulnerable. But it is as capable as any other of curing the human affliction which Shaftesbury[14] detected when he wrote

Gravity is of the very essence of imposture. It does not only make us mistake other things but is apt perpetually almost to mistake itself. For even in common behaviour how hard is it for the grave character to keep long out of the limits of the formal one? We can never be too grave if we can be assured we are really what we suppose.

[14] *Characteristics of Men, Manners, Opinions, Times* (1711).

Note

Biography. Born in 1634-5, George Etherege was the son of a gentleman of the same name who had been resident in the Bermudas. Nothing certain is known of the dramatist until his first play, *The Comical Revenge; or, Love in a Tub*, was performed at the Duke's Theatre, Lincoln's Inn Fields, in March 1664: dedicating the first edition of the same year to Earl of Dorset, he claimed that 'the Writing of it was a means to make me known to your Lordship' and it is only at this time that Etherege began to make an impression in literary London. It was said (by Oldys in *Biog. Brit.* (1750), p. 1841) that he had spent some time in France and perhaps Flanders; there is contradictory evidence as to whether he studied at Cambridge and the Inns of Court.

She Wou'd if She Cou'd was produced at Lincoln's Inn Fields in February 1668, and *The Man of Mode; or, Sir Fopling Flutter* at the Duke's House in Dorset Garden in March, 1676; both were published at the time of their first performances.

She Wou'd if She Cou'd had an unsuccessful first night and the same year Etherege went to Constantinople as secretary to the Ambassador to Turkey. Returning to England, perhaps through ill health, he wrote some occasional verses including a prologue for the opening of the Dorset Garden theatre with Dryden's *Sir Martin Mar-all*. According to Gildon's *Roscius Anglicanus*, *The Man of Mode* was an immediate and extraordinary success: 'all agreeing it to be true Comedy, and the Characters drawn to the Life'. Etherege had a wide acquaintance among the court of Charles II, being frequently associated with Rochester. In 1680 he married and was knighted, and in 1685, with the accession of James II, he left England as Resident Minister in Ratisbon. He lived in Europe after the succession of William and Mary and was reported to have died in Paris early in 1691.

Modern Editions. The plays were edited by H. F. B. Brett-Smith, as No. 6 of the Percy Reprints: *The Works of Sir George Etherege: Plays*, 2 vols. (1927). Transcripts and summaries of letters written by Etherege and his secretary's occasional comments are preserved and have been edited by Sybil Rosenfeld as *The Letterbook of Sir George Etherege* (1928). See, also, Sybil Rosenfeld, 'The Second Letterbook of Sir George Etherege', *Review of English Studies* (1952).

Scholarship and Criticism. *Critical Essays of the Seventeenth Century* have been collected by J. E. Spingarn (1908). Recent studies of Etherege are D. Underwood, *Etherege and the Seventeenth Century Comedy of Manners* (1957), and N. N. Holland, *The First Modern Comedies: the Significance of Etherege, Wycherley and Congreve* (1959). See also Clifford Leach, 'Restoration Comedy: the First Phase', *Essays in Criticism* (1951).

The influence of pre-Restoration dramatists on Etherege is discussed in Kathleen M. Lynch's *Social Mode of Restoration Comedy* (1926).

Discussions of the style of acting practised by the Commedia dell'Arte and of its influence on the French theatre can be found in C. Mic, *La Commedia dell'Arte* (Paris, 1927); G. Attinger, *L'Esprit de la Commedia dell'Arte dans le Théâtre Français* (Paris, 1950); and W. G. Moore, *Molière: a New Criticism* (1949).

II

George Etherege and the Form of a Comedy

JOCELYN POWELL

★

GEORGE ETHEREGE was a playwright by instinct: he wrote for the pleasure of writing, not to gain a living. The easy and graceful exercise of language, the witty perception of the manners and motives of others, were necessary attributes of a gentleman; they indicated grasp of life. Writing was a leisure occupation through which a man expressed and extended his own personality. The control exercised in moulding experience into an artistic form makes that experience more entirely your own, and in a society where the art of living was the highest accomplishment, art was a way of possessing life. It is this ability to bring contemporary life and manners on the stage that is the strength of Etherege's plays. It is not original; Jonson, Middleton and their followers had all used telling observation of the details of daily existence to give their plays a quality of immediacy and reality; but Etherege's realism is more from the inside. In the Jacobeans detail is used critically; the observation holds the characters up to ridicule, because their actions are selected to expose their vices; whereas Etherege's details are primarily atmospheric. They show a subjective understanding and enjoyment of experience for its own sake, rather than a satirical awareness of the absurdity and pretentiousness of man's behaviour. This subjectivity is at once the great quality and the great problem of Etherege's writing.

Etherege was a comic writer, and objectivity is built into the neo-classical theories of comedy. The conception that comedy corrects the vices and follies of men by rendering them ridiculous and contemptible presupposes an objective idea of vice and folly; it is essentially critical, and criticism demands a structure based upon a determined morality. What is more, the conventions of such comedy assist this objectivity; for a comedy of the classical tradition does not use a plot to represent life, but to provide a series of images that bring out the

43

moral implications of experience. The comic devices of disguise, mistaken identity, trickery, and triumph in marriage, are not literal redactions of experience, but analogies; they are accepted without the need for rational explanation because they give the play a new logic of fantasy. This logic can ignore the structure of material existence, and enable the dramatist to provide heightened images of the experiences about which he is writing, rich poetic analogies for life. The weddings that close the plays are frequently more important as symbols of attainment and unity than as comments upon human relationships. It is the nature of experience, not the nature of existence that is important, and this is true whether the dramatist emphasises the lyrical content of the conventions, as did Shakespeare, or tries to give them the immediacy of life by realistic detail, as did Jonson. Whether the world of the comedy was given the poetry of a dream or the vigour of city life, it was still basically a world of analogy, and analogy that originally rose from an objective critical perception.

But Etherege does not have that objective perception, and he has a hard struggle with the forms of comic criticism. There is a clear development through his three plays, each one showing an increasing economy of dramatic means and an increasing dissatisfaction with comic conventions. The weddings of *Love in a Tub* are completely emblematic. There are six of them, and in the best Middletonian manner the fools are married to whores and the true men to the ladies of their choice. The weddings act as a resolution of the characters involved, a comment on the sort of beings they are. There is no sense of relationship; it is pure analogy. But when we come to the *Man of Mode* the resolution is studied at a more complex and highly personal level, and the conventional finale has become an impertinence. The relationship of Dorimant and Harriet is left for the audience to resolve. Etherege becomes more preoccupied with the outward forms of existence and the inner realities they conceal, and the form of his last play looks not back, but far forward, to the work of that greatest writer of comedy of manners, Anton Chekhov. The plot is curtailed to a minimum, and the action is disposed so as to give the greatest possible sense of reality. The dramatist is trying to make his audience experience what it is like to be alive in these situations, to communicate the texture of existence. To do this he builds his dramatic interest on the tensions of conversation rather than on the suspense of plot, and the atmosphere is created by a detailed knowledge of the pressures developing between the characters on the stage. The sympathies of the audience are engaged in the realities of a situation, not in a rich image presented so as to appear real. Form has become a means of expressing experience, rather than idea.

If a judgement arises out of such a play it must be intuitive rather than critical. It comes from inside the play, and lies in the individual reaction to the experiences portrayed. Its centre is sympathy, not judgement, sympathy in its proper sense of the ability to feel with someone, to understand them and their actions, whether your judgement be for or against them. The objective simplifications of criticism and ridicule are gone; hero and villain have disappeared to be replaced by characters we know so intimately that all such designations must be superfluous. The comedy of judgement gives way to the comedy of experience.

*   *   *

Love in a Tub, Etherege's first play, is a remarkable piece. It contains elements of many forms of dramatic expression, blended together into something quite new; its touches of realism, excursions into the heroic and picaresque, and elaborate sequences of song and dance, combine all the basic ingredients of Restoration play-writing into a form that is all its own.

Above all it is a play of contrasts. Contrasts so great that critics have condemned it out of hand as unwieldy and ill-constructed; but it is not altogether so. It is a highly original conception executed with tremendous vitality and a great sense of fun. Deservedly it was a huge success. If it does not seem so successful to us now, this is partly due to Etherege's failure in one essential part of the drama, and partly due to a misunderstanding of the form in which it is written. When Pepys saw it on 4 January, 1664/5, he remarked that it was 'very merry, but only so by gesture, not wit at all', and the criticism gives the key to the play;[1] for Etherege holds his plots together by translating the variety of their styles and moods into dramatic energy through the impetus of music and rhythm. A unity of mood is created by extravagance and stylisation of gesture, making a dramatic fantasy of sheer exhilaration and enjoyment.

[1] Pepys adds: 'which methinks is beneath the house'. It is extraordinary how often critics insist that the emotional experience of farce is of a lower order than the intellectual experience of high comedy. They are simply two different things.

Enjoyment is one of the essential qualities of comic writing, for it is the foundation for the best type of laughter, the laughter of sympathy. This laughter is based on a sense of relationship between the man who is laughing and the man with whom he laughs, and through the laughter there is asserted the value and goodness of the experience that causes the laughter. It is the enjoyment by one human being of the life and vitality of another. The spirit of the man who laughs is broadened and stimulated by the energy of the man who makes the laughter; together they share their joy in life. In *Love in a Tub* Etherege constructs images of life in a comedy of analogy, but turns the play into anything but a critical comedy by engaging us wholly in enjoyment of its characters through the vigour with which they are presented. It is not the intellectual interdependence of theme among the plots, grouped as they are like *divertissements* on ideas of love and honour, that catches and holds the audience; the ironies created in this way are actually rather crude; it is rather through the spectacle that the experience of the play is grasped. The contrasting plots, with their contrasting values, are presented in different conventions of movement, so that the human impulses behind the various codes of behaviour are explored in terms of action; rhythms of thought and plot are translated into equivalent rhythms of movement, and the vitality of these rhythms draws one into the play, integrating it as a spectacle. It is a flamboyant exercise in pure theatre.

There are four main divisions of plot, each with its particular variation on the central themes, and its particular convention for the expression of it. In the complicated courtly difficulties of Beaufort's love for Graciana we get a conventionally idealised view of the problems of love and personal honour; the emphasis is on a perfection of conduct and is expressed in language and gesture suitable to its ideals. The characters speak in formal couplets, and act with the broad and stylised movements associated with grand passions:

GRACIANA: Sir, you mistake; 'tis not my Love I blame,
 But my Discretion; *Here the active flame
         (*Pointing to her breast.
 Shou'd yet a longer time have been conceal'd;
 Too soon, too soon I fear it was reveal'd.
          (II. ii. 5)

It is this part of the play that fails: Etherege dallies half-heartedly with conventional problems of 'platonic' love that neither his imagination

not his technique are fitted to handle; but in spite of the lack of success
the intention of the scenes is clear. They provide a lyrical handling of
the central emotion and form part of a pattern of mood and movement.

This idealism is counteracted by a plot of Middletonian realism in
which two cheats, Wheadle and Palmer, trick a foolish Puritan knight
out of his money. The two cheats turn the concepts of honour used in
the 'ideal' plot to their own nefarious ends, and engineer Sir Nicholas
Cully into a duel in which he displays his cowardice and loses his
cash. This duel, the climax of this plot, forms an ironical parallel with
the climax of the ideal plot, also a duel. The details are the same in
both: the seconds strip, leaving the principal protagonist dawdling
and arguing the case; but where Sir Nicholas is fumbling with his
doublet out of cowardice, Colonel Bruce delays on a nice point of
honour. The flamboyant movements of the tricksters' mock duel
make a comment on the vigour of the real duels of Colonel Bruce
and Lovis. The duel of dishonour and the duel of honour complement
each other.

This element of burlesque is continued when the cheats and Sir
Nicholas disguise themselves as characters from the other plots. Palmer
and Grace appear as Lord Bevill and the Widow, and behave in
marked contrast to their garments:

> PALMER: What a rogue is that *Wheadle*, to have kept such a Trea-
> sure to himself, without communicating a little to his Friends!
> *(Offers to kiss her.*
> GRACE: Forbear; you'l be out in your Part, my Lord, when Sir
> *Nich'las* comes.
> PALMER: The truth is, my Lady, I am better prepar'd at this time
> to act a Lover then a Relation.
> GRACE: That grave dress is very amorous indeed.
>
> (IV. iii. 3)

Their whole plot comes to a fine climax when Sir Nicholas takes it
upon him to imitate one of Sir Frederick's frolics:

> *Enter Cully Drunk, with a blind Fellow led before him playing on a
> Cymbal, follow'd by a number of boys hollowing, and persecuting him.*
> (V. ii)

It is the frolics, parodied here, from which Sir Frederick Frolick,
the play's central figure, takes his name, that give the piece its energy

and consistency. The two opposed worlds, the ideal and the earthy, are drawn together in a network of song and dance which unifies the extremes through its own extravagance and fantasy. Sir Frederick and his disguised fiddlers provide a vigorous and graceful series of masquerades, which are in turn complemented by the contrastingly grotesque escapades of the French valet, Dufoy. The lewd scene of the servants dancing round the sweat-tub into which Dufoy has been locked as a punishment for pretending his peakiness was due to love when it was due to the pox, forms an anti-masque to Sir Frederick's masquerades;[2] the war of the sexes which is the basis of the play finds its expression in the opposition of crude and elegant dances.

The handling of Sir Frederick's scenes is brilliant. In them Etherege finds a way of suggesting in spectacle the ironies of experience, and involving the audience in the experience by catching them up in the excitement of movement. Sir Frederick himself is a magnificent blend of freedom and ceremony, elegance and animal spirits, and this tension between the controlled and the abandoned is particularly suited to expression in the dance. By centring the scenes of his wooing of the Widow Rich round a series of midnight masquerades and musical disguises Etherege makes full use of these possibilities. He gives his hero a band of fiddlers that accompany him upon his escapades, ready to give the impetus of music wherever it is needed. They are almost always about him, either as link-boys, bailiffs, or pall-bearers *'with their Instruments tuck'd under their Cloaks'*, moving at his pleasure, so that they become extensions of their master, and spread his vigorous personality all over the stage. But while the spectacle does create an element of fantasy Etherege also uses it to point the details of the reality involved in the situation. It is not merely the energy, but also the complexity of the relationship with the Widow that is expressed in the movement. The Widow is rich and lusty and wants a man; Sir Frederick is young and extravagant and could do with a rich widow; the tension between them arises from the inevitable insecurity in both

---

[2] The justice of this punishment derives from its reference to the method of treating venereal disease by the suffumigation of the patient with cinnabar in a tub or vat normally used for pickling meat, cf. *Measure for Measure*, III. ii.

LUCIO: How does my dear morsel thy mistress? Procures she still, ha?
POMPEY: Troth, sir, she hath eaten up all her beef, and she is herself in the tub.

of them, produced by their awareness of the other's possible motivations. Sir Frederick wishes to show he is unengaged and doing the Widow a favour in return for ready cash; the Widow wishes to prove there is more to the relationship.

The struggle is handled with splendid frankness, which builds up a genuine sympathy between the two characters. As the conflict within and between them of sex, love and money develops it becomes impossible to discern the dominant motive. But the sympathy is not without its darker side. It is a very real relationship, and in their mutual attempts to make each other ridiculous and so preserve their own independence and self-respect Etherege anticipates one of the main themes of *The Man of Mode*. Their malice is both exuberant and cruel. When Sir Frederick tries to trick the Widow into mourning over his supposed corpse he is unmasked and mocked unmercifully in his turn:

SIR FREDERICK: Laugh but one minute longer I will forswear thy company, kill thy Tabby Cat, and make thee weep for ever after.

WIDOW: Farewell, Sir . . .

SIR FREDERICK: Hark you, hark you, Widow: by all those Devils that have hitherto possess'd thy Sex——

WIDOW: No swearing, good Sir *Fred'rick*.

SIR FREDERICK: Set thy face then; let me not see the remains of one poor smile: So, now I will kiss thee, and be friends.

(Widow falls out a laughing.
Not all thy wealth shall hire me to come within smell of thy breath again. Jealousie, and, which will be worse for thee, Widow, Impotence light upon me, if I stay one moment longer with thee.

(Offers to go.

WIDOW: Do you hear, Sir; can you be so angry with one that loves you so passionately she cannot survive you?

SIR FREDERICK: Widow, May the desire of a man keep thee waking till thou art as mad as I am. *(Exit Sir Frederick.*

WIDOW: How lucky was this accident! How he wou'd have insulted over my weakness else! (IV. vii)

And indeed he does so later, when the Widow mistakes his disguised fiddlers for bailiffs come to arrest him and gives them money to release him. The insults, as before, are very near the mark, and his brutality could easily lose our sympathy. The scene brilliantly exploits this ambivalence in the audience by turning the tensions of the situation into action. The fiddlers take their instruments from under their coats and play; Dufoy, who came to rescue his master and revealed the trick, dances a jig in triumph round the stage; the Widow storms, and Sir Frederick mocks her, shaking his pockets at her to make her guineas ring. 'I shall not trouble thee much,' he says, 'till this is spent.' It is a cruel moment and its cruelty is emphasised, and at the same time made acceptable by the crude energy of the stage picture—the music, the malicious gestures of the man, the angry woman, and the absurdly triumphant figure *'with a Helmet on his head, and a great Sword in his hand'* jigging in and out between them.

Such scenes as this, in which the grotesque and farcical is brought into direct contact with the elegant and witty, provide, by this juxtaposition of effects, what is apparently a commentary by one set of actions upon another; but though there is a thematic connection, the way that the scenes are handled in movement ensures that the modification of one by another has not the objectivity of comment. The images of the play are complementary in that they provide different facets of the same subject, but because they are danced rather than enacted one finds oneself simply experiencing the same idea in different ways, rather than appreciating different attitudes to it. Dance is a very subjective medium. It draws you inside an experience through the compulsive effect of rhythm working directly upon the emotions. The intellect is occupied only with the aesthetic forms of movement and the experience is apprehended without it. By his use of dance Etherege gives what is fundamentally a critical structure a new dimension. The ironies set up by the juxtapositions of the plot are crude intellectually, but they are presented so as to create a physical response. The play is a tremendous extravaganza that builds up a sense of exhilaration sufficient to enable us to take its crudities in our stride. The diversity of moods are fused and the ugly and vulgar made to take their part in a pattern of experience. They are almost exorcised by being given qualities of even greater vitality, for the greater the vitality, the greater the sympathy and enjoyment. It is the exaggeration that creates the sympathy. *Love in a Tub* should not be read as a comedy of manners that has failed, but as a comedy-ballet.

The analogies of *Love in a Tub* take us to the heart of experiences in much the same way as that employed by Molière and the Italian comedians. Molière learned much from the Commedia troupe with whom he shared a theatre, and it is possible that Etherege may have developed his instinct for the emotional significance of movement from the same source.[3] The manner of Italian comedy was to subordinate all intrigue and dialogue to the expression of feeling through movement. Plot and speech there were; but the centre of interest was the spectacle. In this they combined a realistic observation of natural movement with a stylised execution that created aesthetic poise out of the clumsy manifestations of ordinary life. All that was extraneous was pared away, leaving clear the motive and meaning of gesture. The disarray of passion was presented with perfect control. In *Love in a Tub* Etherege discovered and explored the possibilities of this type of drama, and it became a central motif in his comedy of experience, a mechanism for drawing his audience into his play.

His awareness of the character and rhythm given to action by movement comes out very clearly in his stage directions, full as they are of strong verbs and descriptive adverbs. In *Love in a Tub* we find '*Enter . . . Sir* Nicholas, *kicking a Tavern boy before him*', Palmer '*with a bag of Money under his arm, and flings it upon the Table*'; in *She Wou'd if She Cou'd:* '*Enter* Ariana *and* Gatty *with Vizards, and pass nimbly over the stage*' and '*Enter the Musick playing,* Sir Oliver *strutting, and swaggering,* Sir Joslin *singing and dancing*'; in *The Man of Mode* Dorilant '*coming up gently, and bowing*' to Harriet, who '*Starts, and looks grave*'. All these show an eye for the significance of gesture that is extremely perceptive, for the movements do not simply suggest character or situation, they can be used to express it. His directions do not show merely the sort of things a character might be seen doing, they show what he is by the way he does it.

Etherege's art is subtle and successful. He is placing realistic actions in a pattern that visualises for the audience the tensions of the scene. Recognition of natural movement gives the scene immediacy and reality, while the selection and patterning of the movements give it form. In the first scene of *The Man of Mode* Dorimant rebukes Handy for fiddling about him; on Harriet's first entrance she is rebuking Busy for the same fault. The repetition provides an immediate and illuminating connection between the two characters. The device has made the play more natural, more formal, and given an added significance.

[3] The influence of France on the Restoration dramatists is under constant argument, but it seems likely that Etherege had spent some time there (Cibber, *Lives of the Poets* (1753), III. 33). The Italian comedians first played in London in 1673 (A. Nicoll, *Masks, Mimes and Miracles* (1931), p. 344). See prefatory note to this chapter.

Etherege has the gift of the choreographer: an understanding of the meaning and aesthetic content of natural behaviour.

Here Etherege has found a thread on which to hang his new comedy of experience. In the two later plays the mood is more intimate, the texture of the action barer, the external impetus of song and dance more rarely employed. The outward forms of experience are becoming of greater importance. In his next play, *She Wou'd if She Cou'd*, they come into sharp conflict with the exuberance of his comic analogies.

*　　*　　*

In general structure *She Wou'd if She Cou'd* is a comedy of judgement. It uses most of the well-known devices of comic analogy to create an action that will focus satirical attention on the follies of the characters. The play opens and closes with technically accomplished scenes of comic intrigue, in which various persons who would be in some embarrassment to explain their presences to new arrivals on the stage, are stowed away in closets, wood-piles, or under tables, to avoid discovery. Much play is made of this sort of comic coincidence. The wrong person is always coming along at the right time: while Lady Cockwood's maid is talking to Ned Courtall, Sir Oliver arrives; when Sir Oliver and Sir Joslin go to the Bear Tavern for a little relaxation with good wine and Madame Rampant, her ladyship turns out to be in the next room; when Courtall and Freeman accompany Sir Joslin home to meet his nieces they find them to be the girls they picked up in the park that afternoon, 'Gatty *and* Ariana *seeing* Courtall *and* Freeman *shriek and* . . . *Exeunt*'. It is all a good-humoured demonstration of the way men are trapped by their deceits.

Properly this method ought to render the characters involved completely ridiculous. The audience in the theatre is always ready to laugh out of contempt for a person whose designs miscarry; there is no surer way to alienate sympathy than to fail. One of the chief devices of critical comedy is the continual frustration of plans, the contradiction of one mind by another; the passive complement to this is embarrassment, or the potential contradiction of one mind by another; frustration and embarrassment both have the effect of allying the audience with the winning mind against the absurd loser. People in these circumstances become puppets, and so lose their independence; they are, therefore, ridiculous.

But in *She Wou'd if She Cou'd* they somehow refuse to become so, despite these attempts. Etherege is basically too sympathetic to his characters. Ostensibly he has a main theme ideal for a critical comedy; but apparently instinctively he turns it into something quite different. Sir Oliver and Lady Cockwood are both prime hypocrites. The one pretends to instincts he no longer has, the other tries to conceal instincts all too strong; Sir Oliver is only too anxious to be thought a libertine; Lady Cockwood to be a whore without anyone thinking so. As the play develops we see them alternately frustrating each other's designs by being in the same place, for the same purpose, at the same time; or else at home trying to give two contrary impressions of their married life, Lady Cockwood that she is the best of wives, Sir Oliver that he is the worst of husbands. The situation is piquant, but the laughter it provokes quite uncritical.

To start with, Etherege presents them in the form of parody. The effects are all heightened so that the comedy is of the grotesque. The boisterousness with which they handle the situations in which they find themselves turns condemnation into amusement. It is the extravagance of their behaviour, not the falsity that strikes us, and we delight in it. When Sir Oliver returns home drunk, for example, we have a situation that could be treated with satirical distaste. His mock-heroics have quite another effect.

SIR OLIVER: Dan, Dan, Da ra, Dan, &c.   *(Strutting.*
    Avoid my presence, the very sight of that face makes me more impotent than an Enuch.
LADY COCKWOOD: Dear Sir *Oliver*!   *(Offering to embrace him.*
SIR OLIVER: Forbear your conjugal clippings, I will have a Wench, thou shalt fetch me a Wench, *Sentry*.
SENTRY: Can you be so inhumane to my dear Lady?

                                    (II. ii. 141)

The whole thing is dynamic. One is swept along with it, involved in the comic contrast of movement, Lady Cockwood's advances, Sir Oliver's repulses. There is simply not time to stand back and be critical, not a moment to notice the pretence or the hypocrisy. The laughter is the laughter of sympathy.

The reason for this is that again the intellect is entirely uninvolved; the audience, the characters, and the author are all responding to the situation intuitively and emotionally. Their minds are as far in the background of the experience as can be. Now where there is no mind there is no morality, for morality is an invention of reason. Where the characters on the stage operate by instinct the audience will react by instinct also, leaving the critical faculty in abeyance.

It is certainly instinct that is at work in the Cockwoods. They get themselves both into and out of every situation by the inspiration of the moment. The spontaneity of Lady Cockwood's double-thinking is breath-taking. With plans in her head for getting Sir Oliver out of the way while she spends the day with Courtall, she says, of his drunkenness:

> These are insupportable injuries, but I will bear 'em with an invincible patience, and to morrow make him dearly sensible how unworthy he has been.
> (II. ii. 215)

There is a new contradiction in every phrase.

The next day she arrives with Courtall at a tavern where she discovers Sir Oliver and Sir Joslin have engaged a room 'to solace themselves with a fresh girl or two', as the Waiter confides. The confusion of her response is wonderful:

> LADY COCKWOOD: Oh *Sentry*! Sir *Oliver* disloyal! My misfortunes come too thick upon me.
> COURTALL (aside): Now is she afraid of being disappointed on all hands.
> LADY COCKWOOD: I know not what to do, Mr. *Courtall*, I would not be surpriz'd here my self, and yet I would prevent Sir *Oliver* from prosecuting his wicked and perfidious intentions.
> (III. iii. 39)

My own feeling towards one who can contrive such a state of mind in such a situation is not of criticism but of envy. It is so ingenuous. 'Misfortunes' as a blanket term to cover the discovery of a husband's infidelity, and fear of that husband's discovering her own, is stunning! In such scenes as these Lady Cockwood may be said to be pure instinct, and as such she is in a state of innocence. She simply does not possess the knowledge of good and evil.

This innocence is elaborated in the characterisation of Sir Joslin Jolley. He is imported directly from *Love in a Tub*, and brings all Sir Frederick's animal spirits with him, as well as Sir Frederick's apparatus of music, song, and dance. His lewd ballads provide the answer of instinct to the play's title, *She Wou'd if She Cou'd*:

> I gave my Love a Green-gown
> I'th' merry month of May,
> And down she fell as wantonly,
> As a Tumbler does at Play.
> (V. i. 632)

If we were to cast a critical eye upon him he would be the tempter of the play, the country knight showing his friend the wicked pleasures of the town; but the response to him cannot be this. The scene where he coaxes Sir Oliver to go out on the town, even in his penitential suit, displays in both of them a similar innocence to that of Lady Cockwood:

SIR OLIVER: I vow thou hast such a bewitching way with thee!

SIR JOSLIN: How lovely will the Ladies look when they have a Beer-glass in their hands!

SIR OLIVER: I now have a huge mind to venture; but if this should come to my Lady's knowledge! . . .

SIR JOSLIN: A Pox upon these Qualms.

SIR OLIVER: Well, thou hast seduc'd me; but I shall look so untowardly.

SIR JOSLIN: Again art thou at it? in, in, and make all the haste that may be, *Rake-hell* and the Ladies will be there before us else.

SIR OLIVER: Well, thou art an errant Devil—hey—for the Lady's, Brother *Jolly*.

SIR JOSLIN: Hey for the Lady's, Brother *Cockwood*.
(*Exit singing.*   (III. ii. 47)

It would be possible here to give the impression of ridiculous, elderly vicariousness; but this is not done. There is too much extravagance and enjoyment, so their absurdity becomes sympathetic, not contemptible. One would be disappointed if they were to reform. Good humour is the key-note of their sinning, and their desire is good company. Their world is of instinct, without reason, and so without morals. And so, also, it is an entirely fictional world. Men in reality possess reason, so the antics of Sir Joslin have no literal reference to reality. In spite of the close observation of life in the characters, the irrationality of response moves them to a different world. But it is only in literal reference that their world is unreal. The instinct they represent is a part of everyone watching. Its energy is released in the comic analogy. The experience of the comedy is a real experience, though the life it presents is merely an image. To deny it reality is not to deny it meaning.

But, *She Wou'd if She Cou'd* is more complicated than this, for as well as this exploitation of comic analogy it contains an attempt towards comedy of experience too, which seriously disturbs the play. The Cockwoods and Sir Joslin are characters of humour; but the lovers are characters of wit. Whereas humour does without the intellect, wit depends upon it; the alternation of the two here confuses the response, the more so since Etherege begins to give his lovers a quality of naturalness and intimacy that makes them very much a part of life. The wit in their speeches is simpler and more spontaneous than those of the later dramatists; one feels it to be an accurate representation of a certain type of conversation, rather than a heightened image of polite talk; and this reality gives a quite new dimension to the operations of the comedy. It creates a confusion between the comic pattern and life as it is lived. When Gatty says of Sir Oliver 'I dare say he counterfeited his sin, and is real in his Repentance' (III. iii. 375), or Courtall suggests to Lady Cockwood, on her promising to keep out of the great business of the town for the future, ''tis a very pious resolution, Madam, and the better to confirm you in it, pray entertain an able Chaplain' (V. i. 603), the enjoyment of the emotions is arrested by the penetration of the intellect. The analogy of experience becomes a representation of life. Through the wit of the lovers, and their characterisation as real men of the town, this confusion becomes constant.

The play opens with Courtall, just risen, discussing the coming day with his friend. There is a servant 'brushing him' to give the texture of life to the scene. It is all very much routine, the start of another day. The way they start gives an effect of normality and boredom quite out of keeping with the comic coincidences that are to follow:

COURTALL: Well, *Franck*, what is to be done to day?
FREEMAN: Faith, I think we must e'ne follow the old trade; eat well, and prepare our selves with a Bottle or two of good *Burgundy*, that our old acquaintance may look lovely in our Eyes; for, for ought as I see, there is no hopes of new.   (I. i. 3)

The men are hunting after occupation; they have nothing to do; and this places the coincidences of the comedy in a new relation to actual life. For their attitude to everything is based upon just this sense of casual aquaintanceship. They take up with people always on the same grounds: the possibility of temporary amusement. Freeman says of Courtall's ripening affair with Lady Cockwood:

'Slid, I know not how proud you are, but I have thought my self
very spruce e're now in an old Suit, that has been brush'd and laid
up a while.   (I. i. 223)

The same frivolous level of relationship with other people is continued
in Courtall's regrets when he discovers the lady he met in the park
is the same as that to whom he was to have been later introduced. She
is, at the play's end, to become his future wife:

COURTALL: . . . that which troubles me most, is, we lost the hopes
    of variety, and a single intrigue in Love is as dull as a single Plot
    in a Play, and will tire a Lover worse, than t' other does an Audience.
FREEMAN: We cannot be long without some under-plots in this
    Town; let this be our main design, and if we are any thing for-
    tunate in our contrivance, we shall make it a pleasant Comedy.
                                                              (III. i. 105)

The comic intrigues become like life because it is the way the
characters see life. And their games are made more real because they
are as possessive about them as children with their toys. The life of the
young men becomes a telling comment upon a leisured society. There
is so little to do that it is necessary to create obstacles and involvements
to give life some zest. It is one of the chief needs of life to give it the
suspense of a play, and this need involves a basic pretence in all human
relationships, since once a thing is known it loses the suspense of
mystery and becomes dull. This leads us round to a motive for hypocrisy quite different to that suggested in our response to Lady Cockwood's humorous endeavours, but which lies underneath the actions
of all the ladies. In a song Gatty sings in the last act, while the two
lovers lie concealed in the closet, the dilemma of the piece is stated:

> My passion shall kill me before I will show it,
> And yet I wou'd give all the world he did know it;
> But oh how I sigh, when I think shou'd he woo me,
> I cannot deny what I know wou'd undo me!
>
> (V. i. 320)

The temper of the time is such that the truth of almost any relationship
must be concealed. Intercourse is carried on in paraphrase. In the
relationships of the lovers in *She Wou'd if She Cou'd* this insecurity is
explored, and explored not by analogy but with an attempt to give
the real feeling of the situation. In the big ensembles, in the Exchange,

or at the Bear, Etherege creates scenes that set the situation of the lovers against the life they live. The confusion of pretence and motive is excellently suggested in the counterpoints of plot and dialogue. Courtall at Sir Oliver's house, joking with his friend, and intriguing with his friend's wife and niece, creates a life-like ambiguity in the audience's attitude towards him. They are too involved to condemn, as in the Comedy of Judgement, but at the same time too disturbed to enjoy. The play does not succeed because it suspends the audience between the humour of the Cockwoods who have no sense of what they are about but respond by instinct, and the realism of the lovers, who know about good and evil and manage their lives with the mixture of the two that characterises human morality. In *Man of Mode*, his last play, written eight years after *She Wou'd if She Cou'd*, Etherege discovers the way to exploit this ambiguity: he finds a comic form that can fully express his individual response to life. The nature of this response, which prompted the stylistic experiments of the earlier plays, can be seen from a study of the third.

*   *   *

At the very opening of *The Man of Mode* we become intimately involved with the quality of life. The first scene—it is curious how Etherege always opens with his hero's awakening to a new day—is a delicate exploration of the personalities of the chief characters entirely in terms of business and conversation. Almost nothing happens in it, but we are kept awake and interested throughout and move into the main action of the play with both an intimate acquaintance with the characters and an acute feeling for their situation and way of life. It is mood drama, but brilliantly handled so that the apparent random realism of the conversation puts us in possession of all the important elements of the ensuing action. Etherege utilises the dramatic techniques explored in the earlier plays and provides a solution to the problem of creating an aesthetically satisfactory sequence which preserves the casual appearances of life, that is similar to that of Chekhov. He, too, unifies his scene by counterpointing physical action and narrative promise. The scene is held together by stage business that embodies the mood of the passage, while the attention of the audience is held by recurring hints of impending situations. This creates a drama of inaction, or more properly a drama that explores the tensions in the moments of inaction that precede action. The conversation is given at the same time intellectual direction and emotional and physical reality.

The first entrance of Dorimant with his letter for Loveit gives promise of an impending situation, his breaking with his mistress. During the scene friends and servants accumulate with endless matter for conversation, some atmospheric, some relating to later developments of the plot, but throughout the casual discussion, which gives the exact impression of 'the talk of the town', recurs the name of Loveit, and with the name the implications of the opening speech are developed and held out to us. As a further unity, Etherege, with his eye for significant and aesthetic detail, hinges the structure of the scene on the procedure of Dorimant's Levée. His friends chat to him while he dresses, the Orange Woman brings him fruit and the latest news of ladies newly come to town; the shoemaker rounds it all off, pulling on his boots, parodying in his personality the libertinism of the young gentlemen. The dressing provides the narrative framework of action, and the detail of it gives reality and atmosphere. It also is carefully selected to enable the actor to express the impulses of his character in the combination of speech and action already discussed:

ORANGE WOMAN . . . here, bid your Man give me an Angel.
(Sets down the Fruit.

DORIMANT: Give the Bawd her Fruit again.

ORANGE WOMAN: Well, on my Conscience, there never was the like of you. God's my life, I had almost forgot to tell you, there is a young Gentlewoman lately come to Town with her Mother, that is so taken with you.

DORIMANT: Is she handsome?

ORANGE WOMAN: Nay, Gad, there are few finer Women, I tell you but so, and a hugeous fortune they say. Here, eat this Peach, it comes from the Stone, 'tis better than any *Newington* y'have tasted.

DORIMANT: This fine Woman, I'le lay my life, is some awkward
(taking the Peach.

ill fashion'd Country Toad, who not having about Four Dozen of black hairs on her head, has adorn'd her baldness with a large white Fruz, that she may look sparkishly in the Fore Front of the Kings Box, at an old Play.   (I. i. 39)

Dorimant is speaking of his future wife, and the irony is beautifully caught in the business, while the characterisation of the Orange Woman, as she stalls about giving the information for which she is really paid, and plays her game about the fruit, gives an air of routine reality while introducing the central event of the play. We learn how Dorimant gets his pleasure, his attitude to it, and of the arrival of Harriet, and the sense of all this is expressed in one sequence of action.

This naturalism in the detail of the staging creates an effect of intimacy. The characters quickly become our acquaintances and our interest and sympathy is with them; but it is with all of them, for the naturalism engages us with them all. Since we are made to understand the way each mind is working the possibilities of comic analogy are lost, for our understanding of all the characters modifies our approval of each of them, and the sympathy we have for them prevents the dissociation necessary for ridicule and contempt. We are seeing them in human, not in moral terms. In a critical comedy when a fool is gulled we allow it to be justice for his foolery, but when we know him as a person not as a fool he assumes the rights of a person, and the man gulling him the limitations of humanity. In terms of critical comedy Loveit's ill-controlled and possessive passion deserves a rebuke; but in terms of humanity where is Dorimant's right to administer that rebuke? The essential difference between the comedy of criticism and the comedy of experience is that in the former, though a good character may be given faults and a bad character virtues, there is never any serious doubt as to the category to which the character belongs; whereas in the latter there are no categories. Criticism sees characters from one angle, but experience is constantly modifying the angle from which a character is seen, so that, like a shot silk, his colour changes with the light.

This exploration of the texture of experience gives Etherege the form he needs for his analysis of the tensions of boredom, politeness, and passion towards which he was feeling in *She Wou'd if She Cou'd*. It avoids the identification of the characters with moral qualities, and explores their personal predicaments realistically; experience is presented in terms of itself. Our own sympathy and understanding for the characters helps us to perceive their own lack of sympathy for each other, our connection with them, their lack of connection with each other. The absence on the stage of the human contact that exists between it and the audience throws into strong relief the emptiness of the relationships there presented. This provides a comment on the play; but it has been apprehended through the experience in the theatre. It is implication, not judgement.

Love and friendship in *The Man of Mode* arise out of and return to the self. The friendship of Dorimant and Medley exists because they find each other entertaining as companions, but they are as willing to be amused at each other's expense as in each other's company. They look upon each other, as upon everyone else, as cogs to the wheel of pleasure; the acquaintance helps in one way or other to make life go round.

> 'Tis good to have an universal taste; we should love Wit, but for Variety be able to divert ourselves with the Extravagancies of those who want it: (III. ii. 131)

Lady Townley speaks of passing acquaintances, but one feels that the sentiment is applied by and large to all human contact. Other human beings exist, not even simply for one's entertainment—that is to put it too passively—but for one's use.

The malignant aspect of this can be seen from Dorimant's relationship with young Bellair. Bellair is presented as a frank, good-natured young man who instantly acquires our sympathy, as does Emilia, the girl he wants to marry. They are both simple, unaffected people, and our interest in them is considerable, as it should be in two persons whose plans and difficulties form a central intrigue of the play. Dorimant's first scene with Bellair bears out this impression. It is jovial, intimate, and apparently open-hearted. But no sooner has the young man gone than we are presented with a very different view of the relationship:

> He's Handsome [says Dorimant], well bred, and by much the most tolerable of all the young men that do not abound in wit.
>   (I. i. 424)

There is a complacency in the judgement which is displeasing, and the displeasure is increased by Dorimant's later remarks to the effect that he is interested in the young man's marriage largely because he thinks it will make possible attempts upon the lady that are ineffective while she is a virgin. The combination of real intention and libertine bravado gives a new perspective to what appeared to be frank and open relationship. The apparent sympathy does not exist.

The emptiness of this life of isolation is given full expression in the exploration of Dorimant's relations with women. The three main affairs, of Loveit, Bellinda, and Harriet, are cleverly contrasted and build up a ruthless picture of lovelessness and boredom. Dorimant is the typical erotic, spending most of his wit on retaining his independence and achieving his pleasure. He considers his affairs to be a mutual indulgence between himself and the lady, and considers there should be no obligation incurred upon either side. Each party is responsible for their own person and their own pleasure; nothing is shared. The resulting associations are scarcely worthy of the name relationship, they are casual, and quite meaningless.

The seduction of Bellinda is obviously a typical episode in the life of Dorimant, and the tone in which it is drawn scarcely gives the impression that it has been very satisfactory. Bellinda's attitude to the affair is complicated and ambiguous. She continually hesitates to give herself, wishing to make sure the performance is one of love. She demands Dorimant should throw off Loveit to prove his feeling, but though he does so she never altogether believes him. She comes to him out of a desire she has not the power to resist. When she has finally yielded, she makes all the conventional demands on him, but apparently with little expectation of success. Her very coyness is half-hearted:

BELLINDA: Were it to do again——
DORIMANT: We should do it, should we not?
BELLINDA: I think we should: the wickeder man you to make me love so well—will you be discreet now?
DORIMANT: I will——
BELLINDA: You cannot.
DORIMANT: Never doubt it.
BELLINDA: I will not expect it.
DORIMANT: You do me wrong.
BELLINDA: You have no more power to keep the secret, than I had not to trust you with it.   (IV. ii. 11)

There is nothing between them but a momentary sensual gratification, the casualness of which is neatly stressed by a visual detail. As they come out of the bedroom we are to see 'Handy, *tying up Linnen*'. The touch is unsavoury, and by its suggestion of the usual, the stream of such acquaintances before and after, robs the situation of any glamour. The work of the household goes on; Handy, doubtless, continues to do the laundry throughout the little passage quoted above. When the lady has gone Dorimant's friends arrive, and sum up the position on sight:

MEDLEY: You have had an irregular fit, *Dorimant*.

DORIMANT: I have.

YOUNG BELLAIR: And is it off already?

DORIMANT: Nature has done her part, Gentlemen; when she falls kindly to work, great Cures are effected in little time, you know.

(IV. ii. 69)

The whole business is sordid and without hope. The almost complete lack of resistance on Bellinda's part removes the comedy that would arise from a conflict of wills, and does, indeed, do so in the case of Loveit. Bellinda has no will: simply a cynical wavering between what she would like to think love is and what she thinks she knows it to be. The disillusionment that comes to her hurts, but it was expected, and is accepted. The negatives that litter her speeches characterise her attitude, and establish the isolated nihilism of herself and her lover. It all finds expression in her injunction to him at parting:

Take no notice of me, and I shall not hate you.   (V. ii. 303)

Bellinda accepts isolation and independence, but her lack of resistance is so depressing that it sets up a curious tension with Mrs. Loveit's comic and selfish passion. We laugh at this, we find her dramatics, her pretensions, her possessiveness quite ridiculous; but at least it is positive, and at least it has something to give. Mrs. Loveit is comic because she allows Dorimant to manipulate her. She is worked on so that the effects of her actions are the contrary of those she intended. The discrepancy between her will and its effect renders her ridiculous. But this arises out of an opposition of motive. Dorimant can manage her because he is completely indifferent; he does not care what comes of the interview, and she does. She wishes to give herself to him, and the desire to submit destroys the desire to hurt. The comedy this creates is complex. We laugh with Dorimant at Loveit, because he controls her and makes her ridiculous. When she tears her fan we laugh at the impotence of the gesture to express the feeling, and her helplessness before him. But though she is selfishly clinging, she is also genuinely passionate; there is a sense of sincerity in her actions which shows well against the frivolity of his, a warmth which reflects upon his cold destructiveness. The sympathy in the laughter is undermined as it asserts itself, for we find ourselves laughing at something to which we are emotionally sympathetic, with someone whose actions deny our sympathy. We are deriding something we feel to be ultimately of value. This creates a deep sense of insecurity that is at once comic and profound.

This insecurity, arising from a sense of the value of something we are mocking, finds its complement in the relation of Dorimant and Harriet, which, partly through its contrast with the affairs of Loveit and Bellinda, and partly from within itself, continually suggests that what we find brilliant and sympathetic is actually hollow. The selfish-ness of Dorimant's previous relationships give one the impression that he is unable and unwilling to give himself to anyone, and this leaves the prospect of his marriage on a high level of difficulty. There is no doubt of the physical attraction, and of a certain sympathy arising from their equality in wit and will. The relationship is genuinely exciting: in Harriet Dorimant has met his match; but through the play we see him struggling to keep his independence, and the end shows no definitive sign that he has resigned it. The feeling is rein-forced by Harriet's own doubts on the subject.

But there are also deeper grounds for disquiet. The libertine's own independence of person has, as a necessary corollary, the desire to possess others. In all Dorimant's relations with Loveit this is uppermost in his mind. He asserts his independence through her dependence; his power over her is the mark of his superiority. He tries to show this power by manœuvring her into making a fool of herself for his sake with Sir Fopling; but Loveit turns the tables by entertaining Sir Fopling at Dorimant's expense. Each is trying to prove their power over the other. And the same is true of Dorimant and Harriet:

> HARRIET: I was inform'd you use to laugh at Love, and not make it.
> DORIMANT: The time has been, but now I must speak——
> HARRIET: If it be on that Idle subject, I will put on my serious look, turn my head carelessly from you, drop my lip, let my Eyelids fall and hang half o're my Eyes—Thus—while you buz a speech of an hour long in my ear, and I answer never a word! why do you not begin?
> DORIMANT: That the company may take notice how passionately I make advances of Love! and how disdainfully you receive 'em.
> HARRIET: When your Love's grown strong enough to make you bear being laugh'd at, I'll give you leave to trouble me with it. 'Till when pray forbear, Sir.   (IV. i. 169)

This is the iron hand in the velvet glove, right enough. Harriet, with her conscious posing, is playing a game at her lover's expense. There

is no equality or balance; she simply wishes to subdue. The nearest
they get to sharing an experience is their joint effort to enrage Loveit
and offend Sir Fopling at the end of the play; Dorimant acting out of
a natural desire to revenge his own frustration, and Harriet out of one
equally natural, that of displaying her triumph. It is true; it is very
funny; and it is distinctly unpleasant. Their last exchange does nothing
to resolve the difficulty: they are both still struggling for the last
word. Harrient paints a picture of life in the country and asks if this
does not stagger his resolution to ask for her:

> DORIMANT: Not at all, Madam! The first time I saw you, you left
> me with the pangs of Love upon me, and this day my soul has
> quite given up her liberty.
> HARRIET: This is more dismal than the Country! *Emilia!* pitty me,
> who am going to that sad place. Methinks I hear the hateful
> noise of Rooks already—Kaw, Kaw, Kaw——   (V. ii. 427)

One cannot help asking oneself who is the fool. Dorimant's line
is one we have seen him at before; Loveit and Bellinda are not so
easily forgotten: and Harriet's retort shows a steady persistence in
demanding her pound of flesh. Their marriage is ideal in Restoration
terms, being between a young wit and a fine woman with 'a hugeous
fortune'; but the two personalities, with their determined independence
and overt possessiveness, make one question its future. The best
comment upon it is perhaps Etherege's own letter written many years
later to congratulate the Earl of Arran on just such an auspicious marriage:

> It is one of the boldest actions of a man's life to marry. Whoever
> passes that Rubicon has need of the fortune of Caesar to make him
> happy; but you have made so prudent a choice that you have
> secured to yourself all the joy I can wish you. The charms my Lady
> Anne has in her own person are sufficient for this work, were they not
> joined with that of being so nearly related to my Lord President. In
> this alliance you seem to have had an equal regard to your love and
> your ambition. The daughter is the most beautiful object that you can
> sigh for, and the father is the best appui this can desire. But to be
> less serious with your Lordship, I have had the honour of your
> confidence and you have told me of mighty deeds you have per-
> formed. I should be glad to be satisfied whether you are as great a
> hero now you fight in a good cause as when you drew your sword
> in a querelle d'allemande; the truth is that sort of courage is a little

too violent for the present purpose. The business you have now on your hands is to be spun out in length and not to be ended at once.

(*Letterbook*, p. 327)

The Earl of Arran was killed in 1712 in a duel with Lord Mohun. They fought over a matter arising out of a Chancery case concerning some property he believed should have been left to his wife.

*   *   *

The particular quality of Etherege's Comedy of Manners is achieved not through a superficial, but through an actual realism. It comes from our taking his characters as real human beings and experiencing the implications of their conduct in terms of actual life.

Dorimant is a portrait of Rochester, and the mood in which he is portrayed communicates that combination of glamour and viciousness which burns so much more fiercely in Rochester's satires. The form of the play, in which one mood or attitude continually reveals the flaws in another, while our sympathies are engaged to comprehend the nature of both, creates in Dorimant a figure in which tremendous life and energy generate a sympathy which is continually frustrated by the realisation that all the energy turns back upon itself. It is useless; it becomes atrophied. The whole is a tremendous display of brilliance which has no aim. Powers of expression are called forth, but there is nothing to express. The wit, the forms and manners, the pleasure that has no end beyond itself, are almost desperate means to express an energy that has nowhere to go. The end of it all is increasing isolation and emptiness.

When Dryden, in his Epilogue to *The Man of Mode*, wrote:

> *Yet none Sir* Fopling *him, or him can call;*
> *He's Knight o'th'Shire, and represents ye all*

he gave us a clue to the mood and method of the play. The fault of Dorimant is the personal equivalent of the fault of his whole society: form has become a substitute for feeling.

Sir Fopling is a comic embodiment of this idea. In him the elements of lyrical and musical life and energy that lifted *She Wou'd if She Cou'd* and *Love in a Tub* off the ground have been pared away to a rhythmic precision conveyed through the words. He is the successor of Sir Frederick and Sir Joslin, picking up the realism of the play and turning it into a dance; he occurs as they do to give a rhythmic finish to important scenes; but, with the exception of the Masquerade, he does so without any help. The whole effect comes from his own personality unaided by music or song. He creates his own accompaniment, and the effect is at once drier, and more real: exactly suited to the texture of the play. Like Sir Frederick, too, he is not one man but eight. His 'equipage', like Sir Frederick's masquers, spreads his personality over the stage: the exquisite with the fatal flaw. The whole tension of this personality goes with them as they follow him about, a page, five Frenchmen, and an Englishman, like the famous centipede with the wooden leg. Each exquisite ripple of movement initiated by Sir Fopling collapsing in the final and inadequate execution of the ill-fated John Trott. It is a brilliant comic device, and translates into pure spectacle the empty emotionless forms of the rest of the play. Life, for Sir Fopling, is a continual pose, as it was, or had to be, for Ariana and Gatty, and as it is with Harriet with her accurate observations of behaviour designed to deceive; and, since it is so, the whole energy of his personality goes into the pastime.

The feeling is given perfectly in a little Pamphlet entitled *News From Covent Garden or The Town Gallant's Vindication*. It appeared in 1675, but it might almost have been writttten as a portrait of Etherege's hero. The Gallant is describing the difficulties of his way of life:

> To know how to discar'd the Goloshooes in due season in their proper place: to tie the knot of one's Muff Ribbon, to the best advantage: to walk with such pleasing Gate that your Swinging Arm may keep true time with your Feet, which must dance to the Musick of the Points, Ratling on your Pantaloons, and especially to provide that the Foot-Boy be observant in his distances, that he never stand just behind, but bearing a respectful point *East* or *West* from his Master. You know full well Gentlemen! tis no such easie business to discern how much of the *Handkerchief* ought to hang out of the Right Pocket, and how to Poise it Mathematically, with the Tortoise shell comb on the left: to apprehend what a boon Grace there is in some notable words keenly pronounced, with a neat shrug and a becoming lisp, to avoid the horrible absurdity of sitting both feet flat on the Ground, when one should always stand tottering on the toe, as waiting in readiness for a *Congee*!

It is all form and no meaning; manners have become a contradiction of themselves, for manners are really the means by which men and women, wishing to know each other, can express themselves and yet not impose upon the identity of those to whom they are speaking. They are the means of communicating one's deepest feelings and preserving at the same time a respect for the feelings of others. They arise out of consideration and respect for other people. But in the society Etherege portrays manners have become not a means to an end, but an end in themselves, and an end which denies their original purpose; that which was intended to express feeling, now dictates to it, and manners prevent the intercourse they were designed to aid. Instead of ensuring you do not impose yourself upon another, they ensure that others do not impose themselves on you. They have become a means of personal isolation rather than a means of personal communication, and what was designed as a medicine has become a weapon. To shame Loveit, Dorimant determines to pluck off her 'mask' and show 'the passion that lies panting under'. Feeling has become ridiculous, the mask important; the real has given place to the trivial.

The energy of love and of living is expressed in the communication between human beings; but the Restoration reaction against the repression of the Puritan conscience produced a repression as, if not more, disastrous; for licence of action was accompanied by restriction of feeling. Throughout *The Man of Mode* one is kept constantly aware that the brilliance is suppressing and vitiating the reality of life and passion. What is serious and important is being destroyed by what is brittle and frivolous. Manners no longer express but contradict reality. The secret of the form and the drama of Etherege's last play lies in the tension he creates between the lightness and elegance of fashion on the surface and the underlying reality of passion it conceals. The energy and wit of the former creates in the audience a sympathy, which is questioned by the intimacy and humanity with which the characters are drawn. All the devices of comedy, charm, cleverness and wit, encourage one to laugh with Dorimant at his victims, but the sympathy with which those victims are themselves described make us aware that the approval we have been giving through our laughter is of what we hate. We are given a double view of the situation, a view of the pretence, and of the truth, and before it we are helpless, aware that our intellectual and emotional responses form a devastating contradiction. The laughter and the experience attack each other with the ambiguity of life.

This ambiguity explains the curious contradictions that have arisen in comments upon the play. St. Evremont said that in Dorimant

Etherege gave us Rochester with his vices 'burnished to shine like perfections'.[4] Sir Richard Steele said:

> To speak plainly of this whole work, I think nothing but being lost to a sense of innocence and virtue, can make any one see this comedy, without observing more frequent occasion to move sorrow and indignation than mirth and laughter.   (*Spectator*, No. 65)

Each has taken one aspect of the play and made it into the whole. Dorimant's charm does 'burnish' his vices, but only for a moment, the next our sympathy with one of his fellows is showing us more matter for sorrow in what we laughed at before. This ambivalence, this floating between laughter and indignation, is the essence of Etherege's comedy. He knew these emotions did not exclude but reinforce each other, and that the sense of this was one of the most common experiences of life. It is this experience his plays explore. As Congreve put it: 'The two Famous Philosophers of *Ephesus* and *Abdera* have their different Sects at this day. Some Weep and others Laugh at one and the same thing.'[5] This ambiguity of response is the essence of the comedy of experience.

[4] *A Memoir of the Life of John Wilmot, Earl of Rochester . . . in The Works of the Right Honourable Earls of Rochester & Roscannon* (1707).

[5] *Concerning Humour in Comedy:* Letter to John Dennis (1695); reprinted Spingarn, III, 249.

Note

Biography. William Wycherley (*c.* 1640–1716), born at Clive in Shropshire, became a gentleman commoner of Queen's College, Oxford, shortly before the return of Charles II, but left without matriculating. He was admitted to the Inner Temple in 1659. His first comedy, *Love in a Wood*, was performed at the Theatre Royal in Bridges Street in 1671 and made him acquainted with the circle of court wits, and with the Duchess of Cleveland. In 1672, his *Gentleman Dancing Master* followed at Dorset Garden and Wycherley received a commission in Buckingham's regiment of foot; he appears to have been present at one or more of the naval battles with the Dutch. *The Country Wife* and *The Plain-Dealer* were performed at Drury Lane in 1674/5 and 1676.

In 1679, Charles II decided to appoint Wycherley tutor to his son the Duke of Richmond, but Wycherley forfeited both this position and the favour of the king by contracting a secret marriage with the widowed Countess of Drogheda. Her death (*c.* 1681) left him encumbered with law-suits and debts, and he was imprisoned for seven years. He was rescued by James II (who appears to have been reminded of his plight by a performance of *The Plain-Dealer*), and retired to his estate at Clive. In 1704, he published a folio volume of 'Miscellany Poems' which led to friendship with the young Pope. On his death-bed he married a young girl, a marriage which—according to Pope—served the three-fold purpose of paying off his creditors, providing the girl herself with a much-needed income, and baffling the expectations of Wycherley's unsympathetic heir.

Modern Editions. The works have been edited in four volumes by Montague Summers (*The Complete Works of William Wycherley*, 1924). The comedies may be read conveniently in the Mermaid edition, by W. C. Ward (1893, etc.). All quotations in the following chapter are from Summers' edition, with references to Act and Scene divisions as in the Mermaid edition followed by volume and page of Summers'.

Scholarship and Criticism. N. N. Holland's account of Wycherley as a dramatist in *The First Modern Comedies* (1959) is both perceptive and intelligent. See also the relevant sections of T. Fujimura, *The Restoration Comedy of Wit* (1952), and W. Empson's brief discussion of the word 'honest' in *The Plain-Dealer* (*The Structure of Complex Words*, 1951).

'Some Aspects of Satire in Wycherley's Plays' are considered by T. W. Craik in *English Studies* (1960), and *The Plain-Dealer* by K. M. Rogers in *E.L.H.* (1961) and by Rose A. Zimbardo in *Studies in English Literature* (1961).

Rochester is quoted in this and following chapters from *Poems by John Wilmot, Earl of Rochester*, ed. V. de Sola Pinto (1953). Shadwell from *The Works of Thomas Shadwell*, ed. Montague Summers, 5 vols. (1927). The quotation from *Mandragola* comes from *The Literary Works of Machiavelli*, ed. and trans. J. R. Hale (1961).

III

William Wycherley

ANNE RIGHTER

★

WYCHERLEY'S first play, *Love in a Wood*, was produced in 1671, just three years after Etherege had charted the basic dimensions of Restoration comedy in *She Wou'd if She Cou'd* (1668). Later, Wycherley was to claim that he had written this initial and, as the Restoration thought, triumphantly successful play in 1659, when he was only nineteen. His second comedy, *The Gentleman Dancing Master*, seems to have been staged in the summer of 1672, although here again Wycherley tried to push the date of composition back to the beginning of Charles's reign. He was not the only well-born writer of comedy who affected to have earned his fame negligently, as the result of a precocious whim and idle hours. The pretence is no more true in his case than in that of most of his contemporaries. Unmistakable topicalities in the two comedies themselves belie their author, suggesting a date close to that of their actual production, at which time Wycherley was hardly an unfledged youth. Even more important, it is clear that both plays build upon the foundation already provided by Etherege, that they are aware both of the experiment represented by *Love in a Tub* (1664) and of the resolution achieved in *She Wou'd if She Cou'd*. It is to Etherege, with some help from Dryden, that the credit belongs of having established those formal principles which were to be the inheritance of Congreve.

That Wycherley should have served a limited apprenticeship to Etherege, in particular to that second and more important of the two comedies which preceded *The Man of Mode* (1676), is scarcely surprising. The initial reception of *She Wou'd if She Cou'd* seems to have been somewhat cool; Pepys records that he thought it very silly and insipid and so did everyone sitting around him. Yet it was afterwards claimed that even on that first, doubtful occasion, the men of wit and sense in the audience recognised the importance of Etherege's achievement.

Certainly, by 1671, Shadwell was describing it confidently as 'the best Comedy that has been written since the Restauration of the Stage'. Wycherley could hardly have failed to take notice. Yet his own nature and predilections were essentially very different from those of Etherege. When, with *The Country Wife* (?1674) and *The Plain-Dealer* (1676), he created his own best comedies, he departed markedly from that Etheregean type of play which he had begun by imitating. Norman Holland has suggested, in *The First Modern Comedies*, that it is precisely in these two plays, magnificent as they are, that the sentimental triumph of the end of the century is first adumbrated. Harcourt, Manly and Fidelia are, he asserts, a-social idealists; the dramatist has divorced cleverness from goodness, evil from folly, as Etherege never did. In these comedies, the innately good man or woman who is a deviant from society triumphs at the end in an increasingly improbable way. This implausible triumph reflects a sense of schism and contains the seeds of the movement from realism to sentimentalism.

Holland's point of view is an interesting one. He is right, surely, to insist upon the originality of Wycherley's final plays, the sense in which they strike off in new directions. However, it is a point of view which perhaps needs qualification. More fundamental, even, than the split between intellectual and moral qualities which he discerns is Wycherley's covert sympathy with excess, both emotional and otherwise. It is a sympathy which effectively destroys the balance of Etheregean comedy. Nor do the emotions suggested seem to resemble the comfortable, self-indulgent sentimentalism of Cibber or of Steele; they are far more astringent, harsh, even nihilistic. From the abandonment of the Etheregean model came not only sentimentalism but also, and more immediately, a kind of 'dark comedy' in which the genius of Wycherley was joined by the less certain but even more disturbing talents of Otway, Crowne and Lee.

*   *   *

There is not much which needs to be said about *Love in a Wood*. It is a confusing and basically centreless play, full of invention, but as tangled and obscure as any of the walks and thickets of the park in which so much of the action occurs. As Holland has seen, it resembles Etherege's *Love in a Tub* in its use of a high and a low plot, although it profits from the seven years which had elapsed since the production of that play by reducing the distance between them. The intrigues of

Ranger, Lydia, Valentine and Christina on the one hand, and of Dapperwit, Gripe, Sir Simon Addleplot, Lucy, Martha and Lady Flippant on the other belong recognisably to the same world. The play does not fall apart into two halves, one of them embodying the attitudes of comedy, the other those of tragedy, like *Love in a Tub*, or Dryden's *Secret Love* (1667). Instead, there is a clear scale of success, of relative competence at the social game (combined with certain worldly and natural assets), which establishes the characters of the high plot in a position superior to those of the low. This is an enormously acquisitive society; everybody is out to get something or somebody, preferably somebody possessed of something. In the process they tend to return helplessly, like snow-blind travellers, to the point from which they started out. As if in answer to some inexorable physical law, like matches in the end with exactly that like it had originally sought to leave behind. The foolish, fortune-hunting widow ends up with the foolish, fortune-hunting knight, the would-be wit and man of fashion with the alderman's daughter pregnant by someone else, the hypocritical Puritan with the falsely innocent cast mistress. On a higher level, the rake accepts the girl he tried to deceive; the high-minded but jealous Valentine returns to his original estimate of Christina. The whole comedy presents an ironic view of characters desperately rushing forward who nevertheless remain, despite their efforts, in exactly the place to which their own value assigns them. In their actual working-out, these plots and counter-plots are ingenious but mechanical. The various pieces of the comedy never quite fit together into a whole which is any richer or more satisfying than a diagram of positions on a ladder.

The Gentleman Dancing Master is a much better play. Here, as if in conscious reaction against the overcrowded canvas of his first comedy, Wycherley has reduced some thirteen characters of almost equal importance to five. Essentially, this is a play about a young man of wit and sense and a girl possessed of equivalent qualities who succeed in obtaining one another despite the precautions of a fanatical father, a foolish fiancé and an Argus-eyed old woman. Furthermore, it is a comedy which in its attitudes and construction echoes *She Wou'd if She Cou'd*. Like Etherege's Ariana and Gatty, Courtall and Freeman, Wycherley's young lovers stand at the centre of everything, as touchstones. It is against Hippolita and Gerrard that all the other characters, young and old, are measured and found wanting. So basic is their affinity, their likeness in a world which shades off into progressive degrees of coarseness and absurdity as it departs from their standard, that Hippolita's wild ruse (by which she lures Gerrard into her acquaintance the night before her arranged marriage to a fool) loses much of its implausibility, becoming as necessary as the operation of a magnet upon steel. On the level of plot, the lovers must outwit Don Diego, M. de Paris and Mrs. Caution if they are to win through to marriage. The requirements of intrigue force Gerrard into his clumsy impersonation of a dancing master, an impersonation which clearly derives from Calderón's comedy *El Maestro de Danzar*, although Wycherley might also have gotten hints for it closer to home in the sub-plot of *The Taming of the Shrew*. A formidable series of external obstacles threatens, through almost five acts, to separate the lovers forever. These obstacles are not, however, the only ones. Running parallel with them, and even more important, are those bars to marriage and consummation which exist only in the minds of Hippolita and Gerrard. Here, Wycherley takes up the central issues of Restoration comedy: the problems of communication and the language of love, of fruition and time. The manner in which he deals with these issues associates *The Gentleman Dancing Master* firmly with comedy of the Etheregean type.

Hippolita and Gerrard do not meet until the second act of the comedy. The situation when they do is unusual, to say the least. By chicanery, Hippolita has discovered from her impossible husband-to-be the name of the man generally considered to be the finest gallant in town; through a piece of even more outrageous trickery she has contrived to summon this gallant to her, employing her own fiancé as agent. Suspicious but curious, Gerrard obeys instructions, breaks into the house, and finds himself alone with Hippolita and her maid. It is at this point, when the first stage of Hippolita's scheme has succeeded perfectly, the truewit has been found and smuggled past the guards, that the emotional difficulties begin. Gerrard is enormously attracted by the beauty and charm of the girl he sees before him, but understandably perplexed by the whole affair. As for Hippolita, she has found the man she wants, but she can scarcely explain this fact to him in cold blood. An impasse on a psychological level results from the first enfranchisement on the level of plot. Rather helplessly, Hippolita takes refuge in a pretence of extreme innocence and naïveté quite alien to her own nature. Gerrard, for his part, addresses her in an inflated, cliché-ridden language which he clearly deems appropriate for the seduction of a beautiful but completely guileless young heiress.

> My Soul, my Life, 'tis you have Charms powerful as numberless, especially those of your innocency irresistable, and do surprise the wary'st Heart; such mine was, while I cou'd call it mine, but now 'tis yours for ever. (II. ii; vol. I, p. 177)

Divided from one another as they are by mutual misapprehension and pretence, Hippolita and Gerrard nevertheless prepare to steal away together. They are prevented by the sudden arrival of Hippolita's father, Don Diego, and her aunt Mrs. Caution. This interruption, placing a considerable impediment in the way of any actual elopement, turns Gerrard into a not very convincing dancing master. It also permits Wycherley to continue his account of the changing relationship of the lovers, of their progress towards genuine understanding.

Towards the end of this same scene, Don Diego and his sister withdraw temporarily, leaving the road to freedom open once more. Gerrard is eager to seize the opportunity; Hippolita, rather surprisingly, refuses. For this abrupt turnabout, critics of the play have tended to abuse her in terms far stronger than any of those employed by Gerrard himself. Yet her motivations are clear, and by no means either trivial or unreasonable. She has simply been overcome by doubt.

> I am afraid, to know your heart, would require a great deal of time; and my Father intends to marry me, very suddenly, to my Cousin who sent you hither. (II. ii; vol. I, p. 183)

This is Hippolita's dilemma, a dilemma upon which she meditates for the remainder of the scene. 'But what has love to do with you?' she asks Gerrard, more seriously than he suspects. Somewhat pompously, he expatiates upon the well-known power of Love to transform his servants, but receives only a doubtful, hesitating reply: 'If he were your Master.' Hippolita's next move, a move that is maddening, perverse and on the surface totally irrational, has now been prepared for. She agrees to elope with Gerrard at a specific time, sends him off to make all the arrangements, and then when the moment has come, not only refuses to go but announces that she has lied to him all the while and possesses no fortune whatsoever. To this double blow Gerrard reacts in two ways, both of them, as it turns out, right. First of all, he consents to make a fool of himself by marrying her even without a portion; secondly, when she continues to refuse, he displays such unmistakably

genuine signs of passion and jealousy that Hippolita can no longer suspect his sincerity. She rewards him both with her hand and with the
twelve hundred pounds a year which she really has.

This idea of the testing of the lover, the demand that he act in a
fashion foolish by any standards except those of love, is of course
medieval in its origins. It goes back to the courts of love, to distinctions
like that which Chrétien de Troyes makes in his account of Launcelot
as Guinevere's Knight of the Cart. From Launcelot to the Restoration
gallant may seem a far cry, yet there were special reasons why this
device of the love-trial should become so important to Etherege and
his contemporaries. Restoration comedy in general is obsessed with the
idea that passion is ephemeral, that love cannot last. Basically, the truewits and their ladies are romantics cursed with an inconveniently
powerful strain of rationalism; they wish to believe in the permanence
of something which they know to be transitory. The men possess far
more freedom than the women, and this freedom permits them (for a
time) to avoid the contradiction. Sooner or later, however, despite
their libertine principles, they are caught. They try to turn away from
their customary imagery of appetite and the chase in speaking to their
love, to make promises and swear a fidelity which the wiser self knows
time may not let them keep. At this point, however, the woman im-
poses the trial. In two of Dryden's early comedies, *Secret Love* (1667)
and *An Evening's Love* (1668), the gallant fails it. The lady accepts him
anyway, since she cannot really restrain her own inclination, but prog-
nostications for the future are admittedly dark. Etherege, in both *She
Wou'd if She Cou'd* and *The Man of Mode*, does what Shakespeare had
already done in a not dissimilar situation in *Love's Labour's Lost*. He
allows the women to formulate the terms of the trial in the closing
moments of the play: Courtall and Freeman's month of constancy,
Dorimant's journey into Hampshire, and then closes the comedy with
the outcome of the test still unresolved.

Wycherley, on the other hand, like Congreve after him, preferred
to delineate the trial within the action itself. He makes it part of that
process by which Hippolita and Gerrard come to understand both their
own emotions and each other. At the end of the play, they are address-
ing one another in terms far removed from that false naïveté matched
with an equally false language of eternal passion with which their
acquaintance began. There can be no guarantee for the future, but at
least Gerrard's actions have assured Hippolita that this marriage begins

with sincerity and love, however bitterly it may end. 'Let us have a good understanding betwixt one another at first, that we may be long Friends', as she says. Their agreements and stipulations are by no means so elaborate as those which Millamant and Mirabell will exact from each other, but they belong in the same line. With the help of the trial device, two intelligent people have succeeded in establishing an equilibrium of realism and romanticism in their relationship. It is an equilibrium that is temporary, no doubt: sweet, yet not necessarily lasting. But this is the way of the world.

There is nothing in *The Gentleman Dancing Master* that runs counter to the comedy of Etherege. *The Country Wife*, however, is another matter. Its construction seems, at first sight, similar to that of Wycherley's preceding play. Again, two young lovers (Alithea and Harcourt) stand in the centre of the play. With two other figures, Horner and the shadowy Dorilant, they represent the truewits as opposed to the fools. At the beginning of the comedy, Alithea is about to deny her own intrinsic value by marrying Mr. Sparkish, a would-be wit who imitates the ways of the truewits extremely badly. Horner describes him as 'one of those nauseous offerers at wit, who, like the worst Fidlers, run themselves into all Companies' (I. i). He follows his betters everywhere, like Dapperwit in *Love in a Wood*, and his attentions are almost impossible to discourage. As Dorilant says: 'He can no more think the Men laugh at him than Women jilt him; his opinion of himself is so good' (I. i). Alithea is painfully aware of the shortcomings of her future husband, but even after she has met and fallen in love with the truewit Harcourt, she refuses to betray Sparkish for him. Her reasons for remaining faithful are, as the play points out, wrong. She feels that it would be disloyal to jilt Sparkish on the eve of their marriage because his frankness in permitting her to know Harcourt argues a sincere love founded on trust. Actually, it means nothing of the kind. Sparkish is simply so busy thinking about himself, and about his attempts to pass for a gentleman of wit and fashion, that he has no time to think about anyone else, even the woman with whom he is supposed to be in love. Harcourt, genuinely in love with Alithea, keeps telling her this, as does her own realistic waiting-woman, Lucy. Alithea, however, remains stubborn: ''tis *Sparkish's* confidence in my truth that obliges me to be so faithful to him'. She is saved from the consequences of her romantic blindness only by accident. As the result of the complications and misunderstandings of another intrigue in the play, a love-trial of the familiar sort is imposed upon her two lovers. Sparkish, once he suspects her virtue, flies into a paroxysm of jealousy and injured self-love; he insults her and casts her off without even inquiring into the accusation made against her. When Alithea tries to clear herself, the evidence seems to point even more strongly against her. It is at this moment that Harcourt steps forward and makes that romantic, knowingly foolish gesture which always wins the lady in Restoration comedy: 'I will not only believe your innocence my self, but make all the World believe it' (V. iv). As far as Alithea is concerned, the testing of her lovers has been involuntary, but she does not hesitate to act upon its result. She and Harcourt join hands, her realistic appraisal of his worth and Sparkish's folly joining with the romanticism of Harcourt's gesture to create the equilibrium characteristic of Etheregean comedy.

Essentially, this is the story of Hippolita and Gerrard, or of Dorimant and Harriet. The surprising thing about it here, of course, is that it is not the part of *The Country Wife* that one remembers. Alithea and Harcourt stand formally at the centre of the play; it is by their standard that Wycherley intends the other characters, including Horner, to be judged. Nevertheless, the interest of the play no longer lies with them. In fact, there is something a little mechanical, a little weary, about the handling of this plot as it works towards its inevitable end. Unlike Etherege, Wycherley is not really interested in his young lovers. What he is interested in is that savage vision of society which is being revealed all the time on the outskirts of the play by the activities of a renegade from the centre: Harcourt's friend, Horner.

Horner is the most memorable figure in *The Country Wife*, even as the Vice, with his energy, his realism, his cynicism about love, had been the memorable character in late medieval drama. Like the Vice, Horner stands completely alone in the play. Harcourt and Dorilant are his good friends; when it seems that Alithea will marry Sparkish after all, Horner has enough feeling to say to himself in an aside: 'Poor *Harcourt*, I am sorry thou hast mist her' (IV. iii). Yet these friends are never allowed to share the secret behind Horner's supposed impotence. Horner accepts their diffident sympathy, watches them trying to suppress the cruel jokes of Sparkish, and says nothing. Even at the end of the comedy, the nature of his pretence is clear only to people he despises: the quack, the three hypocritical ladies and (rather dimly) to Mrs. Pinchwife. Horner is a solitary, a man who has cut himself off from everyone except those female pretenders to honour who, thanks to his ruse, can sin with him joyously and still keep their reputations immaculate. For these women, Horner has profound scorn; they are devices, impersonal instruments of pleasure. Yet his purely sensual relationship with them is the only honest one he maintains.

Curiously enough, the only other character in the comedy who is at all like Horner is the country wife herself. Margery Pinchwife is hopelessly naïve and foolish; she is quite unaware of what the moral issues are. Like Horner, however, she acts purely and straightforwardly to gratify her desires. She is so much a product of the country that she has not learned that it is necessary to conceal these appetites, or to call them by other names, as Lady Fidget and her friends have learned to do so fulsomely. Mr. Horner's love is more satisfactory than that of her jealous, old 'musty husband'; she sees no reason why she should not exchange the one for the other, permanently. In fact, her public insistence upon this preference almost wrecks Horner's pretence. Mrs. Pinchwife is an amusing simpleton; Horner is both sophisticated and almost diabolically clever. Yet they have both arrived at exactly the same place, though by different roads. Their attitudes towards love are the same, Margery's because it is all she knows in the first place, Horner's because he has deliberately excluded all other possibilities. This association of Horner with the country wife makes it doubly clear that Wycherley does not intend him as the hero of the comedy. His purely behaviourist point of view is limited and distorting; like Jonson's Volpone, he is a monomaniac who pays too great a price for his undeniable success.

The trouble with *The Country Wife* is, that although the centre of the comedy clearly lies with Alithea and Harcourt, Wycherley cannot really bring himself to believe in them. It is in their love that the conflicting claims of romanticism and the realism of a Horner are reconciled, that marriage fulfils a symbolic role. The dramatist's attention remains fixed, however, upon the negative side of the picture, upon Horner the agent of destruction, the man who flays romantic and social ideals. His behaviour scarcely accords with the truewit's standard of natural elegance and decorum; it is grotesque, one-sided and excessive, yet it dominates the comedy just the same. In its overall effect, *The Country Wife* is nihilistic. Horner is a kind of rival touchstone to that represented at the centre by Harcourt and Alithea, wholly negative as it is positive. Purely animal motives are revealed in the people Horner contacts: the unvarnished, crude desire of the women behind their virtuous facades, the stupidity of their husbands, the falsity and imperceptiveness of would-be wits like Sparkish. Before Horner, women who customarily proclaim that it is an unspeakable sin for a lady of quality to neglect her honour, begin to talk in another and more honest vein:

> Our Reputation, Lord! Why should you not think, that we women make use of our Reputation, as you men of yours, only to deceive the world with less suspicion; our Virtue is like the State-man's Religion, the Quaker's Word, the Gamester's Oath, and the Great Man's Honour, but to cheat those that trust us.
>
> (V. ii; vol. II, p. 80)

All the characters of the comedy reveal their true selves in front of Horner and, with the exception of Alithea, Harcourt and Dorilant, who actually are what they seem, he profits from them all. The state of society which Horner reveals is not only somewhat frightening, its emotional weight pulls against the meaning inherent in the structure of the comedy. By the end, the young lovers are in danger of standing in almost the same relationship to the Horner plot as the love and honour heroes of Restoration tragi-comedy do to the superior reality of the comic characters.

At one point in *The Country Wife*, Horner asserts: 'I am a Machiavel in love, Madam.' It is a remark which suggests a comparison with Machiavelli's own brilliant comedy *Mandragola*, a play written in 1518 which has had an even longer and stormier history than Wycherley's. In the Italian play, a young Florentine determined to possess the beautiful, virtuous wife of an old fool, succeeds in making his way to her bed with the strenuous help of her husband, her mother, and her confessor. The girl herself struggles to resist their blandishments and preserve her honour, but the combined greed and folly of those who should support chastity is finally too much for her. She accepts the young man, not merely for the night, but in a permanent liaison. Machiavelli is as implacable about stripping the mask away from the true face of society as Wycherley; he too attacks the clergy, snobbery —when the husband boggles slightly at pimping for his own wife, the conspirators assure him that the king of France does it—self-interest and hypocrisy. What really separates *Mandragola* from the satire of *The Country Wife*, however, is that in Machiavelli's comedy, quite characteristically, the end justifies the means. The young Florentine is really in love with the girl; she is not an anonymous object of desire, as Lady

Fidget and her friends are for Horner. At the end of the play, she is saying to her lover:

> Since your cunning, the folly of my husband, my mother's lack of scruple and the wickedness of my confessor have combined to make me do what I would never have done on my own, I can only believe that some divine influence has willed this, and, as it is not for me to resist what heaven decrees, I surrender. And so I take you for my lord, and master, and guide. You must be everything to me . . . the sole source of all my happiness.   (V. iv)

Here, at the centre of his play, Machiavelli permits a genuine value to exist. Beyond the framework of society which has been proved so frail and corruptible, the honesty of love itself still stands, and in it, realism and romanticism come together.

Whether or not Wycherley was aware of the total effect of *The Country Wife*, in his next and last play, *The Plain-Dealer*, he radically altered the structure of his comedy. Like Machiavelli, he made the lover and the man who investigates the ills of society the same person: Harcourt and Horner in one. Yet *The Plain-Dealer* remains a truly disturbing play, far more so than *The Country Wife*. When it was first published, in 1677, Wycherley provided it with a bitter, mock-dedication to a London procuress, the savage spirit of which seems to inform the play as a whole. As everyone knows, *The Plain-Dealer* is modelled upon Molière's *Misanthrope*; whether it simply misunderstands and degrades its French original, or whether it represents an inspired re-working of Molière, is, however, a point upon which critics find it hard to agree. One thing certainly seems clear. Voltaire's famous comparison of the two comedies:

> All Wycherley's strokes are stronger and bolder than those of our *Misanthrope*, but then they are less delicate, and the Rules of Decorum are not so well observed in this play

is, if anything, an understatement. Manly, the plain-dealer of the title, is an Alceste who has many of the features of Horner. His extravagance, his uncontrolled sensuality and violence set him apart not only from his French prototype, but also from the ideal of wit and judgement established in comedy by Etherege. Manly is a malcontent on a grand and emotional scale, and while there is a bitter truth in much of what he says, there is also a good deal of absurdity and false judgement. He too is a monomaniac. Certainly, he represents a curious departure from the ordinary Restoration comic treatment of the man or woman who rails against society and the age.

Generally, in Restoration comedy, such characters are highly suspect. They are either old, hypocrites, or cranks, and thus disqualified from membership among the truewits. Harriet's mother Lady Woodvil in *The Man of Mode* complains that 'Lewdness is the business now; Love was the bus'ness in my Time' (IV, i. 17), and goes on to deplore what she calls 'the deprav'd appetite of this Vicious Age'. The audience knows what to think of these remarks not only from the comments of the people standing around, but from the fact that they are addressed in all innocence to Dorimant himself, the blackest devil in Lady Woodvil's hierarchy, whom she has clumsily mistaken for a sober, quiet-spoken young man called Mr. Courtage. Lady Woodvil is old, and hates it; her prejudices spring quite clearly from this fact. Shadwell's *The Virtuoso*, a comedy produced in the same year as *The Plain-Dealer*, presents another elderly hater of the age, one Snarl. The wits of the play agree with many of his strictures against the fops and the gay young fools, but not with all. They realize that in him envy and malice, the lusts of age, have replaced a longing for wine and women. 'The last Age was the Age of Modesty', Snarl begins, but he is interrupted by the gallant:

> I believe there was the same Wenching then: only they dissembled it. They added Hypocrasie to Fornication, and so made two Sins of what we make but one. (II; vol. III, pp. 131-2)

And his companion clarifies the situation further by his whispered comment: 'After all his virtue, this old Fellow keeps a Whore.' Younger malcontents were less frequent, but no more kindly treated. Certainly, Shadwell mocks the two misanthropes of *The Sullen Lovers* (1668) without mercy, allowing more reasonable characters to score off them at will. 'Why dost thou abuse this Age so?' one character inquires. 'Methinks, it's as pretty an Honest, Drinking, Whoring Age as a Man wou'd wish to live in' (I; vol. I, p. 18).

The hypocrisy of aged railers like Snarl and Lady Woodvil is identical with that delineated by Wycherley in the figure of Mrs. Caution. Hippolita made short shrift of her aunt's invidious judgements in *The Gentleman Dancing Master*:

> By what I've heard 'tis a pleasant-well-bred-complacent-free-frolick-good-natur'd-pretty-Age; and if you do not like it, leave it to us that do. (I. i; vol. I, p. 163)

This is essentially the Etheregean attitude, an attitude adopted by Congreve in his treatment of Heartwell in *The Old Bachelor* (1693). Wycherley does not abandon it entirely in *The Plain-Dealer*; certainly, it governs his contrast between the false rigour of Olivia's views and the innocent frankness of Eliza's. Olivia has captured the plain-dealer's heart by affecting to despise the age, a pretence which everyone can see through, except Manly himself. She is Wycherley's version of Molière's Célimène, but a Célimène grown vicious and positively evil, not merely injudicious and silly. Eliza, who corresponds to Molière's Éliante, constantly shows Olivia up for what she is.

> OLIVIA: O hideous! you cannot be in earnest sure, when you say
> you like the filthy World.
> ELIZA: You cannot be in earnest sure, when you say you dislike it.
> (II. i; vol. II, p. 119)

As for the plain-dealer himself, it is clear that he does not go uncriticised by his creator. Much of the invective which Manly bestows upon his friends, upon casual fops, fools and passers-by (as well as upon the perfidious Olivia) is brilliant; all of it is passionate, and scarcely any aspect of social life or of the relationships of human beings with each other goes untouched. Yet Manly's attitudes are excessive. Wycherley may have been secretly drawn to excess, but it was still in 1676 too great a sin in Restoration comedy to escape without castigation. Manly's misanthropy is a distorted attitude; it is imperceptive and even a little affected. As such, it is criticised by Freeman, Eliza, even by the rough seamen who have accompanied Manly to London. Most revealing of all is the plain-dealer's tendency to trust precisely those people who are most hypocritical and false. Olivia says of him, shrewdly:

> he that distrusts most the World, trusts most to himself, and is but
> the more easily deceiv'd, because he thinks he can't be deceiv'd:
> his cunning is like the Coward's Sword, by which he is oftner
> worsted, than defended ... I knew he loved his own singular
> moroseness so well, as to dote upon any Copy of it; wherefore I
> feign'd an hatred to the World too, that he might love me in
> earnest. (IV. ii; vol. II, p. 171)

Self-love, one of the blackest sins in Manly's list, governs his own attitude towards society.

Unlike Snarl, Lady Woodvil, Heartwell or Shadwell's sullen lovers, however, Manly is in no sense a comic character. His behaviour, while not to be imitated, is not ridiculous either. Here, Wycherley does depart radically from the conventions of contemporary comedy. At his worst, Manly expresses himself in terms which remind one of Othello at his most frantic:

> Her Love!—a Whore's, a Witches Love!—But, what, did she not kiss well, Sir? I'm sure I thought her Lips—but must not think of 'em more—but yet they are such I cou'd still kiss—grow to—and then tear off with my teeth, grind 'em into mammocks, and spit 'em into her Cuckolds face. (IV. i; vol. II, p. 160)

Frenzy of this kind outgoes even the hell-and-furies rhetoric of Etherege's Mrs. Loveit in *The Man of Mode*. The interesting thing about Manly's outburst is that it does not ask for laughter. Mrs. Loveit, whatever certain tender-hearted modern critics may feel, was meant to be absurd. When Dorimant mocked her rage with a rhyming couplet, or suggested that her fan would be more useful to her whole than torn in pieces, he embodied both sense and a horror of emotional excess central to Etheregean comedy. It was this ideal of balance, of aristocratic restraint and self-control which gave the whole device of the love-trial such force and poignancy. Dorimant, Gerrard, Harcourt, or Congreve's Valentine all depart suddenly, under the pressure of their passion, from a standard of rational behaviour, of realism and social judgement which they have hitherto represented. It is a unique, startling reaction and one which gains its effect by sheer contrast with the worldly wisdom of previous responses. In *The Plain-Dealer*, on the other hand, the love-trial (while present) is overwhelmed and lost in the extravagance of the plot as a whole. Its distinctiveness, both structural and emotional, vanishes. It is part of this new indulgence in emotion for its own sake that Manly's violence on the subject of Olivia's infidelity should be met, not with the corrective ridicule of a Dorimant, but with the uncritical sympathy of Fidelia:

> Poor Man, how uneasy is he! I have hardly the heart to give him so much pain, tho' withall I give him a cure; and to my self new life. (IV. i; vol. II, p. 160)

Fidelia herself, the Beaumont and Fletcher heroine strayed into a world nastier than anything a pastoral Sicily could produce, accentuates the imbalance of the comedy as a whole. She, of course, is a character for which there is no analogue in the *Misanthrope*. By introducing her, Wycherley not only destroyed Molière's subtle but perfectly comprehensible equilibrium between criticism and admiration of Alceste, he created a genuine confusion in his own comedy. Fidelia is a character who must be accepted entirely uncritically, or not at all, like the heroines of Restoration tragedy. It is no good trying to regard her disguise and the situation in which it involves her as representing the education of a romantic. She is a fixed pole in the comedy, a character who remains unchanged from beginning to end. Moreover, she triumphs and, by involving Manly in her triumph, effectively negates all serious criticism of the plain-dealer and his attitudes. At the end, Fidelia's devotion restores the misanthrope's faith in human nature. Unlike Alceste, Manly marries at the end of the comedy. The trouble with this resolution, as Holland has pointed out, is that neither Manly nor Fidelia have really come to terms with the world as it is; their agreement is extra-social, romantic, artificial, and almost impossible to believe in. Even more important, it is the victory of excess.

The presence of Fidelia has an important effect upon Wycherley's treatment of two other characters besides Manly. Freeman and Eliza are clearly the equivalents of Molière's Philinte and Éliante: reasonable, intelligent, sympathetic to plain-dealing up to a point, but convinced that some measure of hypocrisy is necessary for life in society. Their destinies, however, are very different from those of Molière's characters. Éliante, in the *Misanthrope*, loves Alceste. Nevertheless, she is forced in the end to reject the extremes of conduct and emotion which he represents, turning instead to Philinte. Her decision is important, because it guides the reactions of the audience. Loneliness and despair are the rewards of Alceste; he goes his way at the end of the comedy as a splendid fool, but a fool all the same, defeated. Philinte and Éliante stand quite clearly at the centre of the *Misanthrope*. They are the characters who marry, and who embody that rational and demanding ideal of the *honnête homme* which Molière is continually advancing in one form or another. There is complexity of judgement here, but no confusion. In *The Plain-Dealer*, on the other hand, something very curious has happened to Freeman and Eliza. They do not marry, in fact they scarcely seem aware of one another. Eliza is used only as a foil to Olivia, after which she is simply dropped. Freeman is more important. Throughout the comedy, he is shown forced by poverty to try either to marry or else simply to swindle a rich, ridiculous old widow with a passion for the law courts worthy of any of the victims of Jarndyce and Jarndyce. Freeman succeeds in securing the money without the old woman, in the end, by cleverly turning the widow's foolish son against her. There is much fun in all of this; the widow is a glorious absurdity and, by the standards of comedy, fair game. But it scarcely adds dignity to Freeman, in any sense that Molière—or Etherege—would understand. What it does do is to show him dealing successfully with the world by stooping to the world's own level, using hypocrisy, deceit and the most unrelenting realism to gain his own, purely materialistic ends.

In its final effect, *The Plain-Dealer* is even more nihilistic than *The Country Wife*. Manly, like Horner, is an agent of destruction. Some criticism of his attitudes is built into the comedy, but Wycherley's insistence that he should triumph at the end effectively overrides it. By minimising the role of Eliza, and degrading Freeman, Wycherley prevents them from establishing a positive value at the centre of the play. It is Manly, negative, savage, wholly self-absorbed, who dominates the action. When one considers the total implausibility of his final agreement with Fidelia, perfunctory in a way that goes beyond even the normal resolutions of romance, there is little that is left standing. Brilliant as it is, *The Plain-Dealer* is a somewhat alarming comedy. Romanticism has lost touch with realism completely; the emotional force of the play denies the artificial solution offered by the plot. Wycherley's juggling with the standard structure of Restoration comedy has resulted in a chaos only rescued by the fertility of the invention and the strength of the language from being recognisably a disaster.

*   *   *

Wycherley is an immensely individual writer, yet at the same time it is hard not to see in *The Plain-Dealer* the reflection of a more general current beginning to appear in the age. Etherege's character Dorimant, the model gallant and man of wit, was an incarnation of Rochester at his happiest. It was a portrait filled with energy and with delight in experience, with a corruscating play of intelligence: all of it kept in balance, under control. Rochester's last years, however, and the last years of the society which he adorned, were not like this. Rochester died of syphilis in 1680, four years after the appearance of *The Plain-Dealer*. He was thirty-three. During the last four years of his life, he was troubled not only by acute physical suffering, but by a conflict in his own mind between his libertine principles and an attraction towards a kind of mystical Christianity. Throughout these last years, he struggled towards that recantation which he eventually made, trying to believe, arguing against his own rationalism. These are the years during which he wrote most of his satires, poems which display the other side of the libertine's coin: the vitality and the former sense of power turned to ashes in the mouth, a loathing of society and of man himself which comes finally to a denial that he is in any way superior to the other members of the animal kingdom.

> Be Judge your self, I'le bring it to the test,
> Which is the basest *Creature Man*, or *Beast*?
> *Birds*, feed on *Birds*, *Beasts*, on each other prey,
> But Savage *Man* alone, does *Man*, betray:
> Prest by necessity, they Kill for Food,
> *Man*, undoes *Man*, to do himself no good.
> With Teeth, and Claws by Nature arm'd they hunt,
> Natures allowances, to supply their want.
> But *Man*, with smiles, embraces, Friendships, praise,
> Unhumanely his Fellows life betrays;
> With voluntary pains, works his distress,
> Not through necessity, but wantoness.
> ('A Satyr Against Mankind', l. 127)

Even more extreme is the poem 'Upon Nothing'. Here is the frank statement of that nihilism which troubles Wycherley's final comedies: a hatred of light as opposed to merciful darkness, of substance as opposed to non-being. In a strange inversion of the passage from *Genesis*, Rochester sees the tearing of light and matter from the void as a rape, a monstrous, unspeakable act:

> Matter, the wicked'st off-spring of thy Race,
> By Form assisted, flew from thy Embrace,
> And Rebel Light obscur'd thy reverend dusky Face.

The Negative is best; 'something' only returns to it stained and corrupted. Between Rochester as Dorimant (the libertine and wit) and Rochester as Manly (the author of the satires) there is an enormous difference in attitude, but almost none of time. *The Man of Mode* and *The Plain-Dealer* were, after all, both produced in the same year. Taken together, these two comedies create the Janus-face of the Restoration's apogee.

The Plain-Dealer was Wycherley's last play. In 1682, he was imprisoned for debt; he languished in Newgate prison for almost seven years. After his release, he seems to have remained poor and dispirited, encumbered with law-suits and basically at odds with the world around him. It was a world which had changed markedly from that of the early Restoration, in ways which were by no means favourable to the theatre. Not many new comedies were written during the troubled decade of the 1680's. Dramatists tended to be otherwise occupied and, in any case, there was now only one theatre in London instead of two. Those that did appear, however, declared an affinity with Wycherley rather than with Etherege. They tended to be harsh, bitter and convinced that some profound malaise lurked at the heart of all human experience. In the hands of Otway, Crowne, Lee and Southerne —all of them, significantly, men better known for their tragedy than their comedy—the tendencies of *The Plain-Dealer* were carried still further. Disgust with society, railing against the age, becomes the inevitable mark of any man of wit and sense. As one of Otway's characters says, more or less in the tone of a man reciting the trivial news of the day,

> Iniquity in general has not lost much ground. There's Cheating and Hypocrisie still in the City; Riot and Murder in the Suburbs; Grinning, Lying, Fawning, Flattery, and False-Promising at Court; Assignations at *Covent-Garden* Church; Cuckolds, Whores, Pimps, Panders, Bawds, and their Diseases, all over the Town.
>
> (*The Atheist* (1683), I. i)

It is a world of animal warfare, in which the game is won by only the slightly less dishonourable beasts.

Not surprisingly, the few stable values which had been left standing in *The Plain-Dealer* were swept away altogether in the comedies which derived from it. It had been axiomatic in Etheregean comedy that the truewit never betrayed his friend. This loyalty, in fact, was one of the features which distinguished a member of the inner circle from the Dapperwit who tried to imitate him. Even in the later Wycherley, relations between Horner and Harcourt, Manly and Freeman, though less than ideal, were nevertheless honest. In the comedies of Otway and the later Crowne, however, and in Lee's *Princess of Cleves* (1681), those characters who must be regarded as the heroes lie, cheat and cuckold each other without compunction. In every case, the dramatist is clearly aware that he is breaking a rule, shattering a convention. A positive desire to shock pervades Otway's *Friendship in Fashion* (1678), guides the treachery of Beaugard in *The Atheist*, of Chartres and Nemours in *The Princess of Cleves*. This is the comedy of complete disillusion.

Wycherley had lost interest in the love-trial in *The Country Wife*, and submerged it in *The Plain-Dealer*. His successors tended either to do away with it completely, or else to pervert its meaning. Towards the end of *The Atheist*, Sylvia decides to test her lover. 'A true Lover', she tells her maid, 'is to be found out like a true saint, by the Trial of his patience.' This sounds familiar enough. When it comes, however, the trial is simply brutal farce. The girl persuades her lover to scale her balcony, and then contrives that he should remain entangled in the ropes all night on the outside of the building, as a figure of fun. It is an idea that reveals more about the character of Sylvia than about her unfortunate lover—and more about Otway than either. This is the same man who, at the conclusion of *Friendship in Fashion*, had insisted upon bringing in two silly but essentially harmless fops with the stage direction: '*their Hands ty'd behind 'em, Fools Caps on their Heads.* CAPER *with one Leg ty'd up, and* SAUNTER *gagg'd*'. One cannot imagine Etherege finding it necessary to punish Sir Fopling Flutter in this manner, or introducing so grotesque and excessive an image into *The Man of Mode*. Wycherley's fools had also escaped relatively lightly, but there is a quality in Manly's revenge at the end of *The Plain-Dealer*—the public exposure of Olivia's lust to a gathering of the fashionable world assembled for the purpose, the jewels offered her as the price of a prostitute's hire—which points forward to the comedies of the later Restoration.

Wycherley's emotionalism, those violent extremes of feeling condoned in *The Plain-Dealer*, proved an even more dangerous legacy to the future. Hand in hand with the general feeling of disgust which characterises comedy after 1676, the nihilism which gradually destroyed the balance of Etherege, went a new attitude towards emotion. Undisciplined passion began to find general approval, sweeping away the restraint of earlier comedy. In some plays it became recognisable as sentimentalism, although it is advisable to be careful about affixing this label at too early a date. Certainly the tears and languishing of the future can be descried, however, in the emotional excesses of Lee's *Princess of Cleves*, of Crowne's *Town Sparks* (1689), or of the later comedies of Mrs. Behn. The handsome but rather frightening rake, dowered explicitly in more than one play with an active case of the pox, is adored despite (or perhaps because of) his disadvantages by a series of women who resort to all kinds of violence, including attempted suicide, to win him. A race of Mrs. Loveits, in short, except that they are no longer despised by their creator, or by the other characters of the comedy. Violent emotion has become a sign of sincerity and depth, not merely of incompetence and lack of self-control. Only one of these women can actually marry the libertine. Yet her defeated rivals tend to stand about in the last moments of the play, their hands resting apathetically in those of more honourable husbands, their eyes fixed longingly upon the blemished, but magnetic figure of the rake.

Many of these plays also reveal how powerful an influence was constituted by Wycherley's anti-heroes, Horner and Manly. Lee's Nemours, in *The Princess of Cleves*, carries their sensuality and ruthlessness one step further. Nemours is a rake whose character has been deliberately coarsened; Lee states flatly in his dedication that he set out to create 'a ruffian', a hero who would outdo in lechery and insouciance the worst of his dramatic predecessors. Nemours is a man of indiscriminate libido; he makes no distinction whatsoever between the sexes, and not very much between individuals. Yet he is irresistibly attractive to every woman in the play, including the virtuous Mme. de Cleves, and indefatigable in his pursuit. In fact, as one of his friends remarks, with more truth than delicacy, if he goes on like this he will shortly be nicknamed 'the town-bull'. On the one hand, Lee insists that Nemours is a character to be admired. Certainly, he represents a standard of wit and accomplishment which the other men in the comedy envy and fail to achieve. Also, there is a sense in which his straightforwardness is refreshing in a world of cant. Yet his position is bewilderingly undercut throughout the play by the presence of two rival standards. One of them is the memory of Rochester, that ghost from the early Restoration which haunts the action under the name of Rosidore; the other, and more important, is that represented by the honourable, blank-verse-speaking, tearful Mme. de Cleves and her husband. From this welter of disparate material not much sense can be made. Certainly, Nemours' sudden reformation in the final moments of the play is implausible in a way which goes beyond even the extra-social agreement of Manly and Fidelia. *The Princess of Cleves* as a whole, with its wild mixture of verse and prose, of nihilism and strict morality, lasciviousness and prudery, brutality and sentiment is a far more disjointed work than *The Plain-Dealer*.

Nevertheless, it is clear that Wycherley was at least partly responsible for the new directions taken by comedy in the later Restoration. Even without him, it is hard to see how the restraint and intellectuality of

Etherege could have survived the death and dispersal of the wits, the Popish Plot, and the decline of theatre attendance. Yet there can be no doubt of the influence of *The Plain-Dealer* on subsequent comedy. Not only was it extravagantly admired from the very first, its bitter railing, its passion and its abandonment to excess all prefigured a change in the temper of the age sensed by Wycherley in the moment before it became universally apparent. These were the qualities which audiences of the 1680's and even 1690's would value. And against which Congreve, looking back deliberately to Etherege, would fight his splendid but losing battle.

Note

Biography. Molière [Jean-Baptiste Poquelin] was born in 1622, and as actor and dramatist gained the patronage of Louis XIV in 1658. His major comedies date from 1664. He died in 1673.

Scholarship and Criticism. The most enlightening English book on Molière is W. G. Moore, *Molière: a New Criticism* (1949); its first chapter is an account of twentieth-century researches. L. Jouvet in *Conférencia* (1937) usefully considers the actor-author. J. D. Hubert, *Molière and the Comedy of Intellect* (1963), considers the plays in relation to ideas of the time; an earlier study in the same field is *Morale de Molière* (1945) by J. Arnavon.

For a study of Molière's France, see Erich Auerbach, *La Cour et la Ville* (1933), revised and reprinted in his *Vier Untersuchungen zur Geschichte der französischen Bildung* (1951), and Paul Bénichou, *Morales du Grand Siècle* (1948).

For the literary scene, see Stewart and Tilley, *The Classical Movement in French Literature* (1923), H. Peyre, *Le Classicisme français* (1942) and H. C. Lancaster, *History of French Dramatic Literature in the Seventeenth Century*, Part III: The Period of Molière, 2 vols. (1936).

There have been several studies of Molière's influence on English comedy; the most comprehensive is J. Wilcox, *The Relation of Molière to Restoration Comedy* (1938).

IV

Molière and English Restoration Comedy

NORMAN SUCKLING

*

WE have not been very likely, since Saintsbury, to fall into the error of supposing that Molière was the only source of English Restoration comedy. Our contemporary criticism is well aware of the Restoration dramatists' debt to Ben Jonson, which they themselves acknowledged, and of the never really broken line of development extending to them from early- and mid-seventeenth-century English comedy in general. My object here is not so much to assess their indebtedness to Molière as to point out a few ways in which they differed from him even when he was their model, and thereby perhaps to contribute in some small degree to a revaluation of both—not as wishing to raise a point of superiority on behalf of either, but simply to indicate differences of character which have equally their value in theatrical art.

It is worth noting, first, the comparative *spareness* of Molière, both in structure and in detail, as against his English contemporaries and successors. In the matter of language he is less witty than they; W. G. Moore has pointed out that we do not find in Molière's diction 'any considerable trace of a formative or poetic use of words' (p. 55); though J. D. Hubert has directed our attention on the contrary to such lines as

> Mettez, pour me jouer, vos flûtes mieux d'accord
> (*L'Étourdi*, I. iv)

in which not only the image but the double sense of *jouer* contributes to a poetic overtone. In general, when the English writers borrowed from Molière they found it necessary to complicate him. Structurally this may be due to the English tradition of the sub-plot; in any case it is of some importance that Shadwell's *The Sullen Lovers* draws on both *Les Fâcheux* and *Le Misanthrope*, and that Wycherley's *Plain-Dealer* combines elements not only from *Le Misanthrope* but from the *Critique de l'École des Femmes* and from Shakespeare's *Twelfth Night*. (Not, most of us would agree, from Racine's *Plaideurs*; as W. C. Ward said (Mermaid ed., p. 366), there is a litigious widow in both plays and there the likeness begins and ends.) The complication is to be found in detail also. Sometimes the transferences are exact, as when Olivia carries Manly's strictures on 'the world' to their logical absurdity, much as Arsinoé did those of Alceste, or when Novel welcomes Plausible whom he had just been vilifying, as Célimène had done for Arsinoé. But the 'portrait' scene of *Le Misanthrope* takes on in *The Plain-Dealer* an additional touch of humour by Novel's desperate attempts to join in it; while in the same play there is another significant example of further additions by Wycherley to a piece of basic Molière material, which seems to me to provide a key to the specific originality of Restoration comedy.

This is the carrying one step further, in *The Plain-Dealer*, of Philinte's objections to the uncompromising sincerity of Alceste. Each time Philinte asks whether Alceste is really prepared to carry out his principle in this or that case, Alceste replies 'Sans doute', and Philinte passes on to the next example; but Freeman in *The Plain-Dealer* has each time an additional and telling comment on the probable result of Manly's intransigence:

> FREEMAN: You wou'd have me speak truth against my self, I warrant, and tell my promising Friend, the Courtier, he has a bad memory?
> MANLY: Yes.
> FREEMAN: And so make him remember to forget my business; and I shou'd tell the great Lawyer too, that he takes oftner Fees to hold his tongue, than to speak!
> MANLY: No doubt on't.
> FREEMAN: Ay, and have him hang, or ruine me, when he shou'd come to be a Judge, and I before him.
>
>   (I. i; vol. II, p. 110)

Wycherley has here done more than merely complicate Molière; he has stated more unmistakably the 'absurdity', as twentieth-century writers would call it, the disproportion between principles and the conditions of existence which rob them of their satisfactory fulfilment. Manly's attempt, at the next stage of the argument, to allege profitable consequences for his *raideur*, as Bergson would have called it—

> MANLY: Your promising Courtier wou'd keep his word out of fear of more reproaches; or at least wou'd give you no more vain

hopes: Your Lawyer wou'd serve you more faithfully; for he, having no Honour but his Interest, is truest still to him he knows suspects him:

(I. i; vol. II, p. 111)

—is not very convincing, and one doubts whether Wycherley intended us to find it so. For the situation is used by him in order to point out that even the most exacting morality is liable to founder on the circumstances of life to which we try to apply it; whereas Philinte's objection is throughout that human turpitude is not such as to call for Alceste's bludgeoning—as D'Alembert was later to formulate the case,

> que les hommes sont encore plus bornés que méchants et qu'il faut les mépriser sans le leur dire[1]

—not that the blows of the bludgeon will mostly fail of their effect. The humour in Molière consists rather in Alceste's later falling short of his own rigour; the series of 'Sans doute' in the earlier scene is replaced, when it comes to an actual confrontation with Oronte and his sonnet, by a series of 'Je ne dis pas cela, mais . . .' In the end, it is true, Alceste does give a frank opinion on the sonnet, and the result is catastrophic enough; but Molière has been directing his irony throughout the act on the man Alceste and on his relative failure to live up to his professions, rather than on the *condition humaine* which deprives those professions of a worthy object. Wycherley has gone one degree further than Molière: not only does the intransigent morality of his plain-dealer appear slightly ludicrous, but one must also ask oneself who will benefit by his holding to it, the law of existence being inimical as it is to the efforts of moral rectitude—a question legitimately arising out of Molière's situation in its turn, but there forcing itself less insistently upon our attention.

Which is as much as to say that Molière is more confident of a 'norm' against which to contrast the objects of his satire. Commentators have for a long time, admittedly, been disputing what that norm was, with results variously creditable to their subject: Jacques Arnavon, for example, denied the accepted notion of a Molière given over to good sense, 'déconseillant les audaces, même les expériences' (p. 14), only in order to enlist him in the service of the most abject irrationalism and to use him as a stick with which to beat all morality not arising

---

[1] 'Lettre à M. Rousseau', in *Mélanges de Littérature*, vol. 2, p. 422.

out of 'feeling'. At any rate his notion of an *honnête homme* is sufficiently recognisable and sufficiently reasonable to disarm in advance
the criticisms of Rousseau, which proceeded so evidently from a
moral premiss even more acceptable to the Tartuffes than to the
Alcestes of this world. The extent to which this feature of an accepted
norm is present in the Restoration dramatists is more questionable.
We should not care to maintain now, I think, that they were merely
exploiting the titillation of wickedness; but it seems to me that T. S.
Eliot conceded too much when he wrote that Restoration drama
'assumes orthodox Christian morality, and laughs (in its comedy) at
human nature for not living up to it'.[2] Our comic writers were surely
more critical than this; it is just their *doubtfulness* of an accepted norm
which renders their productions of a more central, or at any rate a
more original relevance to the criticism of life. Restoration comedy
seems to have been aware of the weakness that underlies all standards of
behaviour in so far as they, by the very fact of being publicly accepted
as standards, leave something to be desired in a reasonable light. Its
morality is perhaps justifiable on grounds other than those alleged by
Eliot; for it does not merely contrast objects of satire with a moral
norm, but shows up the insufficiencies *both* of the objects *and* of what
passes for a norm. We do not need to follow Arnavon in his gratuitous
campaign to credit Molière with an advocacy of the 'heroic' and the
'saintly' virtues in order to recognise that his standard of an *honnête
homme* is vastly superior to anything that has been held up as an
alternative to it on either religious or sociological grounds; but the
English comic writers have nothing quite corresponding to the standard. They would seem prepared in the final resort to extend a kind
of Cartesian doubt to orthodox morality itself. This may be especially
English; it is certainly characteristic of English dramatists of other ages
—W. S. Gilbert for example, who turned his fire on 'centres of old
conventions and targets for reformers' but to whom 'the reforms themselves were funnier than the old conventions'.[3]

Of course one must furthermore bear in mind that the standard of
the *honnête homme* was in fact superior to any standard, or lack of
standard, obtaining in Restoration London society, whose fault was
not so much that it had reacted against Puritanism as that it had re-
tained too much of it. It is perhaps even truer of Restoration drama

---

[2] 'A Dialogue on Dramatic Poetry', in *Selected Essays* (1932), p. 45.
[3] Reginald Nettel, *Seven Centuries of Popular Song* (1956), p. 196.

than of Shakespeare (concerning whom the remark was first made)
that there is 'no background of social order,[4]—and this, more than for
any other reason, because Restoration society had not so much revolted
from as unthinkingly accepted, in company with those very Puritans
whom it would otherwise have been right in despising, a great part
of the biblically inspired morality which has always militated against
a civilised social order; so that the comic literature of the time was
obliged in some sort to mock at the standards of its age as well as at
those who infringed them. Molière was not to the same extent under
the same obligation, trouble enough though he had with moral
obscurantists over *Tartuffe* and *Don Juan*, not to mention the curious
predisposition against the theatre which in his day was stronger in the
French church than in that of any other Catholic country. For the
society on which he depended for his patronage had in some measure
broken free from these influences without, on the other hand, feeling
any great necessity to advertise its emancipation in the blatant manner
of the Restoration court. What gave its most distinctive feature to the
society of that quarter of a century (from the 1650's to about 1680), to
which modern criticism has reduced the older idea of a *grand siècle*, was
that in its most characteristic manifestations it had both avoided the
excesses of the Counter-Reformation and expelled Jansenism from its
system; the power-hungry machinations of the *cabale dévote* were felt
by that society at its best to be a betrayal of the highest human values,
and accordingly kept in check by the king—however much *his* underlying motive may have been to assert his own authority as against the
influence of religious and aristocratic cliques (Auerbach, p. 22)—and
treated with the distrust they deserved by the best minds of the age. I
am not unaware that this description is applicable only to what was
best in the quarter-century under discussion. I know that these years
furnish plenty of examples of a less admirable turn of mind, whether it
were the crop of 'conversions' such as that of the Prince de Conti about
1666 or the constricted moral tone by which so successful a book as
La Princesse de Clèves demonstrated its alienation from courtly Epi-
cureanism. I have not forgotten that from the 1680's onwards Jansenism
(always latent and finding sympathisers in high places throughout the
century) and *dévotion* of various kinds came back in force, so that
French society, like its king, suffered a decline and the reign of Louis
XIV guttered out with a stale odour of factitious sanctity. But it

[4] T. S. Eliot, *loc. cit.*, p. 53.

remains true that the *Grand Siècle* in its noble essence stands in the line of the humanistic conquest which was to be carried further by the Enlightenment:

> Le dix-huitième siècle ne fait que continuer une œuvre entreprise avant lui, et à laquelle, en dépit d'apparences superficielles, son prédécesseur n'a pas peu contribué.   (Bénichou, p. 221)

Even the pessimistic criticism of human nature, so characteristic of seventeenth-century moralists such as La Rochefoucauld, is akin to Molière's comedy rather than to the Jansenist Nicole's sermonisings; it has a humanistic rather than a comminatory tone and is more concerned to deplore the eclipse of reason than to denounce the absence of grace:

> Il y a au dix-septième siècle une certaine façon lucide de scruter les tares de la nature . . . L'angoisse et le dégoût y ont moins de place que le désir du vrai. (La Rochefoucauld, vu sous cet angle, continue Montaigne bien plus qu'il n'accompagne Port-Royal.)
> (Bénichou, p. 223 and n.)

His pessimistic comments on the average commonplace of human nature have this in common with Molière's level-headed analysis, that they evince above all a revulsion from the prospect of being governed by the average of humanity and, worse still, by the demagogues who thrive on its insufficiencies: an affirmation of the capacity of human reasonableness to envisage the truth in proportion to its independence of mere public opinion—defending the right of the human individual to satisfy his impulses while at the same time arguing for his capacity to do so as directed by his reason. It must have been in great part out of resentment at this independent-mindedness of true aristocracy—at its tendency to discredit the demagogue—that Pascal and the Jansenists, so concerned to encourage in their audiences a disposition to be governed by them and their like, wrote so disparagingly of the excellences derived by humanity from its own resources and endeavoured to reduce them all to 'the order of concupiscence', thus leaving men no option but to grovel in a conviction of 'original sin' before the power-hunger of their 'spiritual directors'. Fortunately French society of the age of Molière knew, in its more lucid hours, how much the Pascals and the Tartuffes had in common—sometimes it would even be confirmed in its knowledge by an unexpected auxiliary from among the devout themselves, as for example Bourdaloue who as a Jesuit had his own reasons for emphasising the case against the *Provinciales*, but who understood, all the better for this, what unavowable motives might be covered by the religious pretension:

> On a trouvé moyen de consacrer la médisance, de la changer en vertu, et même dans une des plus saintes vertus, qui est le zèle de la gloire de Dieu.[5]

Here it is remembered, a score of years after Molière's time, how aptly Jansenism (and not only Jesuit casuistry) could be explained in terms of *tartufferie*, and how much more was indicated by such an explanation than a mere parade of devotional practices. Molière had understood (and this is precisely why the *cabale dévote* maintained such a campaign against his comedy of *L'Imposteur*) that Tartuffe would have been odious even had he been sincere—that his real vice was that desire of moral influence which frequently involves hypocrisy but is a much worse thing than hypocrisy even when found apart from it:

> Les 'vrais dévots', ceux à qui Molière prétend rendre hommage, sont ceux qui ne cherchent pas à s'imposer à autrui . . . Tartuffe est un censeur de mœurs, et on le tient pour hypocrite dans la mesure où il se mêle de gouverner les autres.
>
> (Bénichou, pp. 206-7)

The moral of the play is that the *honnête homme*, who makes no claim to be a spiritual director, is a better guarantee against the dangers of *libertinage* than any which might be offered by the *cabale dévote*, whether in its Jansenist or any other form; that Orgon falls a victim to Tartuffe precisely because he allows *dévotion* to blind him to other realities; that

> whenever a *dévot* attempts to meddle with worldly activities he automatically becomes suspect . . . Religion has charm as long as it does not exceed the bounds of pure spirituality.
>
> (Hubert, pp. 105-6)

And the decline of the reign proved the point abundantly.

But later seventeenth-century England had nothing quite comparable with the standard of *l'honnête homme* or the model of *la cour et la ville*. The more obvious manifestations of Puritanical philistinism no longer occupied the centre of the scene, but the 'prying commonwealth's-men' (Wycherley, *Love in a Wood*, I, i) who continued to threaten the

[5] *Sermon sur la médisance* (1691), quoted by Stewart and Tilley, p. 91.

Restoration settlement, and who triumphed as Whigs in the last years of the century, had inherited enough of it to render them of very little use as a counterbalance to courtly frivolity and of very little competence in the setting of a pattern of civilised living. The 'citizen' of Restoration comedy was never the *ally* of cultured men in the way that *la ville* complemented *la cour* (*vide* Auerbach, especially pp. 22–32); and on the other hand the 'gallants' of that comedy—Horner and Harcourt, Bellmour and Vainlove, Aimwell and Archer—were never quite so differentiated from the more extravagant type of courtier as Molière's more sympathetic heroes were from his 'marquis' types, nor is there in the English plays the same recurrence of a clear-headed, well-balanced person against whom to contrast the follies of others, such as we find in the Cléante of *Tartuffe* or the Ariste of *Les Femmes Savantes*. Molière can place the objects of his ridicule against a background of some moral and social stability—even though it may be at the price of accepting the background a little too readily—whereas the comic writers of the Restoration were confident neither of the existence of such a background nor of the frequency of characteristic persons to represent it. One of the men about town who conspire to outwit Heartwell is undisguisedly called Sharper; and on the other hand 'honest' marriage has no champion other than Sir John Brute against Constant and Heartfree. Where Molière could rely on the comparative reasonableness of a code of *honnêteté* which could all the more with dignity be accepted because it was the expression of a still more than half feudal sense of honour, not of a demagogically imposed convention—the expression of an inner harmony between the impulses and the reason, which for the best minds of the seventeenth century as for Rabelais in the sixteenth,

> se produit dans les âmes généreuses, du fait que le désir s'y portant toujours vers des objets dignes de lui, n'aliène pas la liberté du moi, qui n'est qu'un autre nom de sa dignité.   (Bénichou, p. 25)

—the English dramatists were necessarily more conscious of the insufficiency which not only belies our moral codes but even enters into them; more conscious that the public opinion which prescribes rules of moral behaviour is as likely to be mistaken as those who infringe them; and more in a position to be so conscious because the public consideration of moral behaviour was coming already in their time and place to be dissociated from the spirit of philosophic enquiry (a process whose culmination was to be reached in the Victorian age) and tied to a Protestant dogma which was not even a reflexion of the best Anglican thought of the time, as it might be that of Sir Thomas Browne or the Cambridge Platonists. The work of these is irrelevant to the official morality of Restoration England in a way that Descartes, Arnauld and Bossuet—to take only three men of widely differing tendency—never were to the French society of their day; and it is not surprising that the plays of Wycherley or Congreve should imply, much more strongly than is usual in Molière, an awareness of the ease with which 'standard' behaviour degenerates into conventionality. The moral objection to Restoration comedy has almost always proceeded from a conscience afraid of any enquiry into its own foundations; and the objectors, in the seventeenth century as later in Victorian times, were of the kind who could rest content, like the complacently paradoxical C. S. Lewis in our own day, with 'stock response' to a situation as morally adequate to the treatment of it, but who—whether it were Collier or Macaulay—had no answer that a civilised intelligence could accept to what the dramatists had observed of the life about them.

For the moral tone of Restoration comedy is a direct corollary of its observation of life, not only in the immediacy of its own time or with regard to the shortcomings of this or that man or woman, but with a more general reference. It was Wycherley and Congreve, not Collier or Macaulay, who had the truer insight into the underlying human condition in the seventeenth or any other century, as James Branch Cabell ironically reminded us:

> these Restoration dramatists were the first English writers to fall into that dangerous ... practice ... of allowing their art to be seriously influenced by the life about them. For Wycherley and his confrères were the first Englishmen to depict mankind as leading an existence with no moral outcome. It was their sorry distinction to be the first of English authors to present a world of unscrupulous persons ... and to represent such persons, not merely as going unpunished, but as thriving in all things. There was really never a more disastrous example of literature's stooping to copy life.
>
> (*Beyond Life*, ch. 5, s. 6; ed. 1925, pp. 126–7)

The truth here indicated is that Restoration comedy was a more accurate comment on the *condition humaine* than anything advanced in opposition to it. Congreve's shrugging excuse to Collier, that he was always careful to moralise in a couplet at the end of a play, was in perfect accordance with the reality of the situation; since in actual fact moral force is no more influential in determining the course of events than were these cracker-mottoes in modifying the general tone of the plays. And in any case, as Macaulay pointed out, a Congreve motto or 'tag' is likely to be more in keeping with the general tone—and therefore with the observant truth of the rest, though this would not have been Macaulay's comment—than the author himself claimed. The important conclusion to be drawn is that the illusionless outlook of the English dramatists, their unromantic closeness to life, is the reason why their satire goes so deep; for it was a satire on the human condition itself. I do not wish to maintain that it went deeper than Molière's, but simply that it was differently directed: he 'concerned himself much more with human relations than with man's fate' (Hubert, p. 178), but they were satirising *life* where he satirised *men*—or rather, since the primary aim of comedy is to amuse, they set out to amuse by pointing out the deficiencies of life, he by pointing out those of men and women.

This may be further illustrated by considering the personalities introduced into the two types of comedy. Some of course, as for example the coxcomb, they have in common; but it will be profitable to examine, in particular, the feminine characters whose relation to the men held up by both types for humorous analysis—as distinct from the plain ridicule meted out to the coxcombical person—varies from that of a snag on which they founder to that of a haven into which they steer. The parallel is in some respects very close: Manly in *The Plain-Dealer* is, I think, on the one hand as much an object of amusement (though never of contempt) as Alceste in *Le Misanthrope*, and on the other, almost as much a sympathetic character, since, though less admirable in himself, his discomfiture is due to a woman considerably more odious than Célimène. Now Molière knew very well what he was doing when he introduced coquettes such as Célimène into his plays; he was well aware that the code of *galanterie précieuse*, which stands more or less at the back of her relations with Alceste and with men in general, was in no way an improvement on the more traditional family morality, no advance in the direction of genuine sexual freedom, but merely replaced one tyranny by another—and that neither of the two has much bearing on the question of what should be done to make the relations of men and women conducive to anything really worth calling freedom. But this question was one which he hardly ever treated: again because he was concerned to satirise the way in which men reacted to their situations rather than the disposition of life underlying the situations themselves—to ridicule those who in one way or another had placed themselves in awkward positions within the framework of the love-and-marriage code, not to call in doubt the validity of the code itself. One of the few among his personages who do call it in doubt is Dorimène in *Le Mariage forcé*, and *her* proposal for 'complaisance mutuelle' between herself and her husband is so evidently the utterance of one who will later be to Sganarelle what Angélique was to George Dandin that it can hardly be of any relevance to a serious discussion of the subject; one would hardly expect any relevance from such a character. When Fielding made his adaptations from Molière he added to the characters of Harriet and Mariana in *The Miser* an element of coquetry which was quite absent from Molière's Élise and Mariane. But if Harriet could have prevailed on Mariana to resemble the best of the Restoration heroines it would have been a comparatively harmless coquetry—hardly more indeed than simple flirtatiousness—of a kind which does not endanger love, because it does not underline fidelity, and could not be ascribed to those features of the *galant* code which most evidently serve the interest of the feminine power-seeker. Restoration heroines such as Doralice and Berinthia are equally free of the taint of that baser coquetry which is Célimène's— or Armande's in *Les Femmes Savantes*: she also, it will be remembered, does her best to thwart her sister's hopes of Clitandre with the ulterior motive of keeping him for herself, though of course without conceding him anything—and free, for the most part, of the jealousy which is so frequent a weapon in its hands; and as such they were something comparatively new and refreshing in comic literature. But the coquette in Molière—whether in her own person or in the claims made out for her on a more theoretical ground by the *femmes savantes*— represents, as not only the *galant* but the *courtois* code had done before her, the power-seeking motive which accounts for the whole of the feminist movement, the *feinte connue* noted by Vogüé in a quite different connection: 'crier à la persécution pour mieux dominer'.[6]

This is the motive which runs from the Précieuses, through such characters as Suzanne in the *Mariage de Figaro*, to a thousand romantic heroines of novels and plays in the nineteenth century and to the

[6] *Les Morts qui parlent* (Paris, 1910), ch. xi; Nelson ed., p. 206.

modern American cinematic scene where the protest against hus-
bandly jealousy has been triumphantly affirmed in order to impose the
restrictions of a wifely jealousy much less justifiable; from the one end
of the series to the other we may observe manifested in it 'l'ambition
féminine de dominer l'homme, de l'attacher sans rien lui accorder'
(Bénichou, p. 198), together with a willingness, from the same motive,
to disclaim all desire of sexual satisfaction, as the English dramatists
also knew very well:

> (Coquettes) keep their chastity, only because they find more plea-
> sure in doing mischief with it, than they shou'd have in parting with
> it   (Vanbrugh, *A Journey to London*, II. i: Mermaid ed., p. 473)

and thus to get the both-ways' profit of being (as Mr. Somerset
Maugham defined the modern wife) 'a prostitute who doesn't deliver
the goods'.[7]

Molière was aware on the one hand that this was the reality behind
the disposition of his coquettes—one of them even formulates it in
terms which are the *galant* and the *courtois* code over again:

> La grande marque d'amour, c'est d'être soumis aux volontés de
> celle qu'on aime.   (*Le Malade imaginaire*, II. vi)

—and, on the other, was willing to take more or less for granted the
background of traditional morality against which, as Denis de Rouge-
mont, noted, the code stood in assumed coexistence while tacitly
stultifying its most basic assumptions. This appears also in his treatment
of the relation between parents and children. He would doubtless have
been quite impervious to Rousseau's criticism of him on this ground;
he had no need to assert that Élise and Cléante ought to behave respect-
fully towards Harpagon, because he saw no ground for supposing in
their conduct any impending danger of a failure of duty towards
parents who really deserved respect. His position would probably have
been, had he ever been called upon to express it, that it was quite unnecessary for good parents to feel themselves endangered by what
Rousseau called the *air goguenard* of Élise and Cléante—and that if they
did so feel, it would mean that there was something wrong with the
foundation of family life itself, as there undoubtedly was with a
religious life which could consider itself offended by the portrayal of
Tartuffe; but that there was no irrevocable call on French society to

[7] *The Constant Wife*, Act II.

compromise itself with that kind of family morality or that kind of *dévotion*. The Restoration dramatists, being more aware of insufficiencies in the foundation, were more ready to consider the cases in which it was threatened, and in which the threat carried some show of justification. Farquhar's discussion of divorce in the case of Squire and Mrs. Sullen is more than half serious, and could hardly have occurred in Molière; but Shadwell had anticipated it a generation earlier, and with something of the same seriousness:

> Why there's no necessity we should be such Puppies as the rest of Men and Wives are, if we fall out, to live together, and quarrel on.
> (*The Sullen Lovers*, V. 2; vol. I, p. 83)

Dryden's Doralice, who begins the play of *Marriage à la Mode* with a song to very much the same effect as this, exemplifies a similarly refreshing change from the romantic and jealous heroine: she is an excellent example, as Saintsbury wrote, of 'that interesting and by no means contemptible phase of femininity'[8] the flirt—the woman who would exercise the same right of roving as the male gallant—rather than the coquette, who finds her satisfaction in exciting the passions of men without any intention of sharing or complying in them; and when the hero of a Restoration comedy finds himself balked by a flirt of this kind, he can accept his defeat good-humouredly and with no sense of shame. But Célimène in the *Misanthrope* is a coquette in the full acceptance of the term, and thus very nearly odious; she does not love Alceste at all—not even to the limited extent that Millamant loves Mirabell—but enjoys only the exercise of power over him and other men. With the result that when Wycherley attempted to provide an equivalent to her, he proceeded in full awareness of the fact that this was a situation outside the usual framework of his comedy, and gave us not a Millamant (even supposing him to have been capable of drawing such a character with Congreve's affectionate subtlety) but one to whom the nearest, perhaps the only approach in Restoration comedy is Belinda in *The Old Bachelor*: one representing the coquettish type stripped of the graces which redeem Célimène superficially: one who is, frankly, a bitch.

It is impossible to surround Olivia in *The Plain-Dealer* with any romantic aura; and the fact serves in a curious way to remind us that it is inappropriate enough to do so with the Shakespearian personage

[8] Preface to Dryden; Mermaid ed., vol. I, p. 18.

from whom she takes her name and some of her situations. We are not, presumably, to suppose that Shakespeare's Olivia was ever idealised in the seventeenth century as she came to be in the nineteenth; but in our own day it needs Wycherley's parody, more doubtless than it did in his, to demonstrate to us what were the real-life colours even of Shakespeare's original. The Olivia of *Twelfth Night* is own sister to the lascivious ladies of Massinger and Fletcher—not that this in itself makes her less acceptable than the novelettish heroine which was the usual way of presenting her as late as my own boyhood, but it is as well to remember that she is married to Sebastian in the very chapel that she has erected to the memory of her brother,[9] and that the passage between these two is fairly accurately described in Arthur Symons' disparagingly intended account of the 'wretched farce' of a favourite Massinger situation:

> a queen or a princess violently and heedlessly enamoured of a man —apparently a common man, though he generally turns out to be a duke in disguise—whom she has never seen five minutes before.[10]

Wycherley's Olivia is the logical conclusion of some of the less creditable features implied in her Shakespearian namesake; and it is this disillusioned presentation of her that renders her, at the same time, an apt incarnation of qualities in Célimène which Molière himself had not found it necessary to emphasise. Only a sentimentalist would suggest that she gets other than her deserts at the hands of Manly; but Molière is not troubling either to mete out poetic justice to Célimène or to show her ironically as escaping it. It is perhaps a further evidence of his concern with 'human relations rather than man's fate' that the *dénouements* of his plays are usually a mere contrivance for bringing immediate difficulties to an end (as Faguet among others pointed out) and in no way a comment on the essential issues involved. The fact that the right people are married at the end of *Les Femmes Savantes* or *L'Avare* is of less concern to morality, on the whole, than the fact that Amanda and Berinthia stay as they are—again because Molière would seem to have felt no need to underline a normality which he could take for granted. It may indicate an *unusual* concern, on his part,

[9] J. Dover Wilson, *Shakespeare's Happy Comedies* (1962), p. 172. Professor Wilson made the same point some thirty years ago in a Shute Lecture at the University of Liverpool.

[10] Preface to Massinger, Mermaid ed., p. xxvii.

to show up the equivocal 'divinity that shapes our ends' for the mindless oppressiveness that it really is, that he should have let Alceste leave the stage at the end of the last act with a reward so greatly at variance with *his* deserts—however justified J. D. Hubert may be in contending (p. 143) that Alceste himself shares in the hollowness of the society he condemns.[11]

I offer in general, therefore, the provisional suggestion that English Restoration comedy leaves less room than Molière's for the assumptions of romance—which no doubt is one reason why it was so violently rejected by a romantic age in which the disillusioned outlook was regarded as vaguely reprehensible and impious. An age which could not stomach the notion, that life as such might not be fundamentally admirable, would not be likely to accept a type of comedy in which the conclusion of poetic justice simply cannot be drawn; and on the other hand the same age would find it possible to applaud Molière by drastically simplifying the moral sympathies that can be accorded to his characters—by exaggerating, for instance, the importance of those commonsensical maidservants who on a deeper scrutiny are as much figures of fun as the Jourdains and the Orgons. Both Molière and English Restoration comedy are in the last resort far removed from the blinkered and rose-tinted vision which was the mark of most European drama from the time of Sheridan to that of Ibsen; but the main difference between them was perhaps that the English writers had fewer illusions as to what *was*, Molière a stronger conviction (and maybe on a firmer ground) of what *should be*.

[11] But Hubert does not improve his case by reproaching Alceste for not leading a life of useful work—which is Marxist criticism reduced to its logical absurdity. The economic basis of living is nowhere a matter of moral significance in Molière's comedies.

Note

Texts. Some anticipations of Restoration satiric form and style are in the Cavalier verse in *Rump: or an Exact Collection of the Choicest Poems and Songs Relating to the Late Times* (1662). Collections called *Poems on Affairs of State* published between 1660 and 1714 are the main sources for the political satires and libels of the period including Marvell's (see *Poems and Letters of Andrew Marvell*, ed. H. M. Margoliouth (1952), ii. 141–205). A modern edition by G. de F. Lord is in progress: *Poems on Affairs of State*, vol. i, 1660–1678 (Yale, 1964).

The first of John Oldham's *Satires upon the Jesuits* was piratically printed in 1679; he published the whole series in 1681. His adaptations of Horace and Juvenal are in *Poems, and Translations* (1683). A mass of material in Oldham's autograph is in the Bodleian, Rawlinson Poet. 123. H. F. Brooks's edition of Oldham is still regrettably unpublished, but, by kind permission, quotations in this chapter are from his typescript. The author of this essay owes a debt to Dr. Brooks, *doyen* of students of Restoration satire, for help and advice.

Two editions of Dryden's *Absalom and Achitophel: a Poem* were published anonymously in 1681. *The Second Part of Absalom and Achitophel* (1682) is largely by Nahum Tate, but ll. 310–509 are known to be by Dryden. Dryden's *The Medal: a Satire against Sedition* and *Mac Flecknoe: or a Satire upon the True-Blue Protestant Poet, T.S., by the Author of Absalom & Achitophel* also appeared in 1682; the latter had been circulated in manuscript in 1678. Dryden's poems are quoted in this chapter from J. Kinsley's edition (1958), his *Of Dramatic Poesy and other Critical Essays* from G. Watson's Everyman Library edition (1962).

The works of some minor writers of satires are conveniently collected in *The Works of the Most Celebrated Minor Poets*, 2 vols. (1749); the authors include Sheffield, Wentworth Dillon, Sackville, and George Stepney. The *Poems on Several Occasions of John Wilmot, Earl of Rochester* were published in 1680, 1685 and 1701; a better edition by Jacob Tonson appeared in 1691 and was several times reprinted. V. de S. Pinto edited Rochester (Muses Library, 1953).

The Poems of Horace . . . Rendered in English and Paraphrased by Several Persons (1666 and 1671) is the first collection to contain free imitations of Horace.

Scholarship and Criticism. Contemporary criticism is found in Dryden's *Discourse concerning the Original and Progress of Satire* (1693; in Watson's ed. of *Essays*). Johnson's *Life of Dryden* is interesting on the formal problem of *Absalom and Achitophel*. A. F. B. Clark, *Boileau and the French Classical Critics in England* (Paris, 1925), has an appendix on the rise of formal satire that is still valuable, though Clark exaggerates the influence of Boileau. C. W. Previté-Orton's chapter in *C.H.E.L.*, VIII, 80–100, on political verse and lampoons also maintains its usefulness. C. V. Wedgwood, *Poetry and Politics under the Stuarts* (1960), sets the subject in a historical perspective. The fullest modern account is Ian Jack, *Augustan Satire: 1660–1750* (1952). There are also M. T. Osborne, *Advice-to-a-Painter Poems* (1949); H. F. Brooks, 'The Imitation in English Poetry', *Review of English Studies* (1949), pp. 124–40 (an indispensable tool for all future criticism); I. Jack, 'The True Raillery', *Cairo Studies in English* (1960), pp. 9–23; V. de S. Pinto, *Enthusiast in Wit: a Portrait of Rochester* (rev. ed., 1962); and D. M. Vieth, *Attribution in Restoration Poetry* (1963).

V

Modes of Satire

ROGER SHARROCK

★

On an occasion of this kind it becomes more than a moral duty to speak
one's mind. It becomes a pleasure.—*The Importance of Being Earnest.*

THE Restoration period of our literature has often been characterised
as an age of satire. Social and moral satire permeates the stage comedy
of the time, and abounds also in its non-dramatic poetry and in much of
its prose. Milton and Bunyan stand apart: chronologically they are of
the Restoration, but their universal human appeal marks them off from
an age which liked to be conscious of itself and its modernity; in any
case, in terms of literary history they are both backward-looking,
Milton to the resources of an earlier humanism, Bunyan to the popular
tradition of moral homily. However the time-spirit does exert its pull
on Bunyan to the extent that in his character portraits we can sometimes see him doing the same thing as Etherege and Wycherley, though
for reasons so very different; in Worldly Wiseman a pompous humbug
is drawn in order to present the theological notion of worldliness, but
he could easily be imagined treading the boards as a heavy father or
a conceited citizen. Even in slight touches, like the company at Madam
Wanton's who were 'as merry as the Maids', or the sketch of Mercy's
arrogant suitor Mr. Brisk, the resemblance to the world of stage
comedy flashes out. What there is in common is the judicious blend
of hostile criticism of a social attitude with controlled irony and wit.
This is a good enough working definition of satire from which to start
out. When we pass from Bunyan and Milton to those great writers of
the age who were conscious of the demands of their society and anxious
to express them, Butler, Rochester, Dryden, and the ageing Marvell,
now entering on his second career as a poet, we see that the satiric
attitude is dominant in the best work of all of them.

The next age saw greater satirists than any the Restoration produced,

Swift and Pope, and the Gay of *The Beggars' Opera*, but it was also the age of Thomson and Young and the youthful novel; and there was not to be another literary epoch wholly dominated by satire. In the long wake of the romantic movement English satirists have been isolated figures; they have had to create their own audience, and have not been able to appeal to any established sympathy with the satiric attitude among their contemporaries: the romantic tradition of non-ironic positive assertion ran counter to that. This has the effect of making the satirist seem crotchety and querulous, or too sensitive to adapt himself to the demands of society. *Brave New World*, the novels of Evelyn Waugh, and the two anti-utopian fantasies of George Orwell all have this effect. Even when the political and social forecasting of Huxley and Orwell seems accurate and frightening, we are oppressively aware of a soured 'outsider's' sensibility that is looking at the prospect from a personal point of view. The Restoration satirist was a partici-pator, not an outsider; he could feel that he was expressing with his own wit and literary skill what was already the concern of a large body of his intelligent contemporaries; the modern satirist's endeavour is to show that he is concerned about what few of his contemporaries have perceived at all.

It is only when a situation alters that the historian can say anything fresh about what has gone before. Today the situation has altered, and thus made possible the broad generalisations about satire thrown out in the last paragraph. Among much which is merely fashionable-silly, satire and the satiric attitude have in the last few years begun to regain the public role from which they had so long been dispossessed. Before the change one might say that to call a work like *Brave New World* or *Decline and Fall* a satire meant very little. What it did mean was that either a comment was being made on the lonely, subjective critical sensibility of the author, or that the work was being in some way related to the literary genre of satire, to Dryden, Pope and Byron; inevitably the genre appeared academic and sterile after a century and a half of neglect, during which the ablest practitioners of the form, when they were not being neglected, were being praised for every reason except being good satirists. Now that the words satire and satirist are in living use again, it may be possible for us to reach a better understanding of the English classical satirists. Admittedly, an ex-tension of usage ranging from a vague opposition to hypocrisy in high places through infidelity and obscenity to the art of the night club entertainer may not seem immediately helpful. But if so much that is now called satire is not the disinterested appraisal of contemporary foibles, but on the contrary in its turn highly prejudiced, may not that teach us something about Dryden and Pope?

From a living climate of satire we may learn that the satirist is sometimes using the form as a rhetorical mode with which to state a new attitude, not to criticise an old one; the attack on real or imaginary evils is less important than the demonstration that his attitude is shared by an intelligent and admired élite. And much of the liveliness of Restoration satire comes from its defiant assertion of the new mode of life of the Town.[1] We have tended to take too much at their face-value the statements on the function of satire made by Restoration and Augustan poets. These pay lip-service, as might be expected, to the classical theory that true satire laughs vice out of countenance. Thus Sprat writes 'The true *Raillery* should be a defence for *Good* and *Virtuous Works*, and should only intend the derision of extravagant, and the disgrace of vile and dishonourable things' (*History of the Royal Society* (1667), p. 419). Dryden likewise remarks: 'How easy is it to call rogue and villain, and that wittily! But how hard to make a man appear a fool, a blockhead, or a knave, without using any of those opprobrious terms! To spare the grossness of the names, and to do the thing yet more severely, is to draw a full face, and to make the nose and cheeks stand out, and yet not to employ any depth of shadowing.' And Butler declares:

> Never for Satyr was there better times,
> Wee now are got up to the hight of Crimes;
> All that was don before was mean and low
> To that, which evry Day produce's now.
> (Butler, *Satires and Miscellanies* (1928), p. 229)

It is always the best of times and the worst of times, though if one lives in London and listens to the gossip from Whitehall one may think it is only the worst. Butler and Sprat make statements of such vague generality as to leave the important questions unanswered. Dryden is

[1] In several programmes of *That Was the Week That Was* Millicent Martin appeared singing against a background of technicians moving camera equipment about. This seems to illustrate how fashionable, topical satire tends to lose sight of its satirical objectives and gradually to transform itself into a sort of romantic documentary of the present moment.

at least writing witty and poised criticism, and he applies critical analysis to distinguishing satire from mere abuse; he defines, while he advocates, the new 'fine raillery' which avoids 'the slovenly butchering of a man' and 'separates the head from the body, and leaves it standing in its place' (Ed. Watson, II. 137). But this definition of a new method still assumes with Sprat and Butler that what are railed at are the permanent vices of mankind ('rogues and villain'), that satire is the business of demolishing a reputation. It is the purpose of this chapter to maintain that in the Restoration period the assertion of an attitude and a style of life was often as important, if not more important, in social satire. Political satire was naturally more directed against particular targets; but here again the new style of good-humoured banter helped to define the ethos of a new élite.

*   *   *

The reiteration of classical precept by the satirists and the emphasis on this by modern scholars do not help to answer the question why Restoration satire is more interesting than the primitive and pedantic work of Hall, Marston and Guilpin in the Elizabethan period. They make similar statements on the moral function of their writing, but they work on the fringe of literature, looking at the London life of their day through a crabbed imitation of Latin satire, especially that of Persius. As Bernard Harris has suggested,[2] they only sound a deeper note when expressing the Counter-Renaissance disillusion with the anarchic, selfish will concealed behind all human ideals and activities; then they call upon the medieval tradition of the complaint or denunciation; but when they do, they often do ill what is done better in the great 'malcontent' characters of the drama, like Thersites and Bosola.

Only Donne stands apart, both for his originality and for his anticipation of one vital element in Augustan satire: the sense of an urgent, pulsing urban life with which the poet is thoroughly in touch:

> 'Tis ten a clock and past; All whom the Mues,
> Baloune, Tennis, Dyet, or the stewes,
> Had all the morning held, now the second
> Time made ready, that day, in flocks, are found

---

[2] Cf. B. A. Harris, 'Men like Satyrs', *Stratford-upon-Avon Studies 2: Elizabethan Poetry* (1960), pp. 175–201.

> In the Presence, and I, (God pardon mee.)
> As fresh, and sweet their Apparrells be, as bee
> The fields they sold to buy them; For a King
> Those hose are, cry the flatterers; And bring
> Them next weeke to the Theatre to sell;
> Wants reach all states; Me seemes they doe as well
> At stage, as court; All are players; who e'r lookes
> (For themselves dare not goe) o'r Cheapside books,
> Shall finde their wardrops Inventory.
>
> (Satire IV)

With the exception of Donne, the Elizabethan satirists failed by trying to force contemporary experience into the mould of Roman satire. And all, Donne included, believed that they had precedent in the writers for obscurity of style, roughness of verse, and the exercise of a violent, vituperative spirit. The history of English formal satire may be seen as an equation between the relative influence of Persius, Juvenal and Horace. Juvenal was always enjoyed; and his *saeva indignatio* appealed to the Elizabethans as it had done to the middle ages. But because difficulty was cultivated, Persius enjoyed a prestige in this earlier period which he was not to retain; Horace was well known, but less imitated than the other two, apart from certain famous commonplaces (like the episode of the bore in *Satires* I. ix followed by Donne in his Satire IV). In the course of the seventeenth century, as a full appreciation of the relaxed and colloquial manner grew, Horace came into his own; and after the Restoration the first successful Horation adaptations coincided with the change in fashion from violent invective to gentle raillery. In Dryden and some of his contemporaries the balance between Horace and Juvenal is equally maintained; there is an interesting blending of the two styles in *Macflecknoe*; Pope's temperamental affinity to Horace turns the equation more fully in his favour, since it is much easier to be correct in speech when keeping one's temper than losing it. Johnson readjusts the balance in favour of Juvenal.

The beginning of the seventeenth century brought advances in classical scholarship which led to a more intelligent and informed approach to the Latin sources of satire. Isaac Casaubon's *De satyrica Graecorum poesi et Romanorum satyra* (Paris, 1605) was a milestone, as was his editionof Persius in the same year. It had previously been believed that the word satire was derived from the hairy, goat-footed satyrs of Greek mythology, the followers of Pan (the spelling 'Satyr' persists throughout the seventeenth century), and that Latin verse satire was in a direct line from the Greek satyr-plays. Casaubon removed the confusion: he showed that satire was a purely Roman form and suggested that the word was derived from *lanx satura*, a full platter, describing old Roman satire as characterised not solely by moral invective, but by the mixture of several matters in alternate prose and verse. Once poets became aware of the loosely organised, informal character of the great Latin satires, they had the key; they could see that if they wished to imitate the form successfully they must, instead of trying to be obscure and allusive, aim at ease and naturalness; then, when an effect of convincing familiarity had been created for the reader, they must strike home hard at one of his familiar responses. Donne is groping towards this in the passage quoted above, when, after arguing that the spendthrift courtiers are players, he suggests that the inventory of their players' costumes may be found in the counting-houses of Cheapside (where their estates are mortgaged). But by drawing out the image of the courtier-player for several lines in the metaphysical manner he dulls the impact of the reference to the Cheapside ledgers. A post-Restoration poet would have hammered it out in one clean stroke within the limits of an end-stopped couplet. Indeed we find that over a century later when Pope paid Donne the compliment of bringing this satire up to date by revising it in accordance with Augustan regularity, he abandoned the Cheapside reference, no doubt considering it an unnecessary embroidery upon the thought, and concentrated his skill upon digesting the player-image into a single couplet and a single satiric blow:

> 'That's velvet for a King', the flatt'rer swears;
> 'Tis true, for ten days hence 'twill be King Lear's.

Heinsius, who followed Casaubon, showed that familiar diction could be polished as well as rough: '*Sicut humili ac familiari, ita acri partim ac dicaci, partim urbano ac jocoso sermone*' (*De satyra Horatiana*, 1612). Previously Horace had been thought obscure, and even Dryden, writing at the end of a period in which the real grace and art of Horace had been increasingly appreciated, could say that Horace would have appeared more charming if he had taken more care of his words and numbers (*Essays*, ed. Watson, II. 144); Dryden knew Heinsius and quotes his definition of satire as 'a kind of poetry without a series of action' (*De satyra*, i. 54). Perhaps the most outstanding feature of Restoration and Augustan satire is the formal freedom which permits the poet to range discursively from one topic to another; the most careful and polished language is displayed, but the scenes or comments are so loosely strung together for a poem of one to three hundred lines that one paragraph might often be exchanged with another without detriment to the whole. This is the legacy of Horace and Juvenal, and especially of the former; his epistles were influential here as well as his satires. The unity aimed at was that of a personal mood, of a single, wide-ranging speech to a friend, or of the general relation between the whole group of vices or foibles being pilloried. Juvenal prefers variations on a single theme, like the Third Satire on the vices of Rome, translated by Dryden and imitated by Boileau and Oldham, or a single dramatic episode, like the Fifth Satire on the dinner party at a stingy patron's. Persius adheres scrupulously to one subject only, and Dryden considered that this was the proper recipe for modern satire: there must, he says, alluding to the traditional derivation of the form from a hotch-potch, be a main dish in the farrago, one vice exposed, one virtue extolled; but not all his contemporaries put this principle into practice.

In addition to the results of improved scholarship, but stemming from them, the poets of the Restoration had the benefit of an increasingly intensive classical training in the great public schools. The chief instrument of this training was the set theme in verse or prose to be rendered in the manner of a particular Greek or Roman author. Dryden was a boy at Westminster under the formidable Busby, and he remembered translating the Third Satire of Persius 'for a *Thursday Nights Exercise*'. The rhetorical skill and agility needed to turn their thoughts into a classical mould also served the poets of Dryden's age when they came to reverse the process and to adapt the structure of a satire by Horace or Juvenal to a poem of modern life. Johnson adds this historical note to his criticism of Pope's *Imitations of Horace*:

This mode of imitation, in which the ancients are familiarised by adapting their sentiments to modern topicks, by making Horace say of Shakespeare what he originally said of Ennius, and accommodating his satires on Pantolabus and Nomentanus to the flatterers and prodigals of our own time, was first practised in the reign of Charles the Second by Oldham and Rochester, at least I remember no instances more ancient.

The change from the pedantries of Hall and Marston to the assured manner of the Restoration introduced a form of classical imitation which was a poem in its own right.

Better scholarship, the disappearance of myths about satire, and the privilege of having been beaten at Westminster and elsewhere for having closed one's lines with verbs and other such offences against decorum—these are not the whole story. Restoration satire may have profited from the school-room and the library, but the primary impulse that gave it birth was the pressure of great events: the Civil Wars and their aftermath. England was not politically settled till 1688. It is significant that the two most active periods of satirical writing coincide with the two most dangerous crises of the Restoration period: the attacks on the Court party after the disasters of the Second Dutch War in 1666-7, and the much more serious Whig offensive in the period from the Popish Plot to the eclipse of the Exclusion agitation, 1678–82. Satire needed real passion and prejudice to feed the flame of indignation which had burned low in the work of its earliest exponents. The greatest achievements of Restoration satire depend on the rancour of party, on Tory against Whig (*Absalom and Achitophel*), and Protestant against Catholic (*Satires on the Jesuits*); even Rochester's *A Satyr against Mankind* is an intellectual party piece, the libertine's case stated in opposition to the Puritan and his rule of right reason; and literary controversy is assimilated into the general party battle in the subtitle of *Macflecknoe*, 'A Satyr upon the True-Blue-Protestant Poet' (though this may have been added by the publisher). In the atmosphere of the time a non-party attitude in satire, preaching moderation and good sense and counselling a plague on both your houses, could only grow up slowly and with difficulty within the Horatian imitations; it was later in the hands of Pope that this type of satire reached full maturity.

So much for the impetus. The instrument was of course the new 'strong-lined' style that succeeded the Metaphysicals, and the metre was the end-stopped couplet. It is not easy to disentangle the origins of the new verse satire from those of the new verse in general. Rhetorical construction, epigrammatic point, and balance within the line, were felt to be generally desirable; but they gained their most striking successes in satire, panegyric or the familiar epistle. The recipe for a tauter form of English heroic verse had been sketched out by Puttenham. It was laid down in 'A short Institution to English Poesie' by J. D. in Joshua Poole's *English Parnassus* (1657) and the rules there were followed by Edward Bysshe in his *Art of English Poetry* (1702): the line should consist of disyllabic feet with the accent falling on the even syllables, the rhymes should be exact, and the caesura should come at the fourth syllable. George Williamson has described the new fashion for antithetic wit which accompanied these metrical reforms ('The Rhetorical Pattern of Neo-Classical Wit' in *Seventeenth Century Contexts* (1960), pp. 254 ff.): repetition with inversion (the classical *hendyadis*), antithesis (*antitheton*) and parallelism of balanced clauses (*parison*) were all employed. The new rhetoric was a conscious reaction against the wit of the Metaphysicals, which attempted to reconcile contraries by the exploitation of sensuous and verbal correspondences; the literary-political platform of Denham and Waller professed to despise this as verbal quibbling; in the view of the innovators the poet was to base his thought and imagery on the correspondence of sense (*figura sententiae*), not on merely verbal parallels. There are numerous anticipations of these reforms in the verse of the earlier seventeenth century. They are to be found where they might be expected, in a major figure like Ben Jonson; and also in the minor poets William Cartwright and George Sandys. Sandys' scriptural paraphrases were greatly admired by Dryden; in them for many lines together we can read the grammar of the new poetry: such lines are especially to be encountered in the *Paraphrase upon the Book of Job*, where Hebrew parallelism is naturally rendered into rhetorically balanced clauses within the couplet:

> Now try what patron can thy cause defend;
> What saint wilt thou solicit, or what friend?
> The storm of his own rage the fool confounds,
> And envy's rankling sting th' imprudent wounds.
>
> (Chapter 5)

Waller is only bestowing a higher polish on the same sort of rhetoric, as may be seen in many of his panegyric poems. Panegyric has this in common with satire that both depend on the exposition of a personal, and usually highly prejudiced case:

> Where'er thy navy spreads her canvas wings,
> Homage to thee, and peace to all she brings;
> The French and Spaniard, when thy flags appear,
> Forget their hatred, and consent to fear.

> So Jove from Ida did both hosts survey,
> And, when he pleased to thunder, part the fray.
>   (*To the King, on his Navy*)

Only the unpleasing juxtaposition of the two verbs in the last line disturbs the careful weighting and pairing of verbs and clauses. We can often say 'Dryden would not have written that line', but there are always plenty of lines in the verse of the period which any poet after the 'reform of numbers' might have written. To decide whether this brisk, efficient neutrality of thought and sentiment is a strength or a weakness is the crucial question for Restoration poetry.

From 1642 onwards, satire in the broad sense of humorous invective flowed into a host of forms other than that of the formal verse satire on classical lines; the national crisis called forth songs, broadside ballads, allegory, and the sheer denunciation or complaint derivative from medieval tradition. The anti-Puritan poems in the collection *Rump* (1662) vary in style and metre and are drawn from the whole period of the Civil Wars and Commonwealth; a few of them exhibit the response of the new rhetoric to events and to power in a manner which becomes more common in Restoration satire. One of these is *Pim's Juncto* (1642), in which the Parliamentary leader addresses the House of Commons in a speech of burlesque, Machiavellian villainy:

> So, to your businesse, yet ere you be gone
> Take my advice, then blessing light upon
> Your nimble Votes, and first be sure you shroud
> Your dark designs in a Religious Cloud,
> Gods Glory, Churches Good, Kings head Supreme,
> A preaching Minister must be your Theame;
> Next structure of your *Babel* to be built,
> Must speciously be varnisht o're and gilt
> With Liberty, Propriety of lives,
> And fortunes, 'gainst th' high stretcht Prerogatives.
> And then a Speech or two most neatly spent,
> For Rights and Privilege of Parliament;
> These two well mixt, you'le need no other lures
> To gain the People, and to make them yours.

The mood of later couplet satire is here, its steady advance and ironic control, though the needs of dramatic speech (and no doubt the influence of the theatre) cause more running on of lines than would be found in Oldham or Dryden. The peroration is gloomy and passionate: it employs the exalted rant of the hero-villain or Machiavel; such an ironic soliloquy was to grow into a powerful instrument of denunciation in the hands of Oldham and Marvell.

Many Restoration political satires, including those by Marvell, are collected in the series of volumes (1689-1716) usually referred to as *Poems on Affairs of State* ... (1697). Compared with the poems in *Rump* and in the Cavalier drolleries, this collection is less popular and has more poems in the couplet. A limited number of traditional forms continue to be employed: the Biblical narrative applied allegorically to contemporary events, the monologue by a ghost (with its many analogues in Elizabethan drama), the satiric last will and testament, the dialogue, sometimes between animals (as in Marvell's *Dialogue between Two Horses*), and the scurrilous character study of a political opponent.

The most striking new form to emerge is that of the various *Directions* and *Instructions to a Painter*. There had been a serious panegyric by Waller on the conduct of the war at sea. Unfortunately it appeared when the situation had changed: the Dutch had sailed up the Medway and burned English ships unopposed. A series of ironic imitations of Waller's poem followed; they contain in embryo the whole idea of mock-heroic poetry. Satire is mingled with serious patriotic concern at the mismanagement of affairs:

> Through our weak Chain their Fireships break their way,
> And our great Ships (unmann'd) become their prey:
> Then draw the fruit of our ill-manag'd Cost,
> At once our Honour and our Safety lost.

The other side of this disgust is the aspiration after the noble qualities that are lacking in the contemporary scene; when admirals and captains are found who can be approved, the satire turns into straight-forward heroic narrative:

> Oh too dear Exchange!
> He led our Fleet that day too short a space,
> But lost his Knee; since dy'd in glories Race:
> *Lawson!* whose Valour beyond fate did go,
> And still fights *Opdam* in the Lake below.

There are other deviations from satire. A vigorous low-comedy speech is given to the base-born Duchess of Albemarle, who has heard that her husband has been wounded in the sea-fight:

> Avaunt *Rotterdam*-Dog, *Ruyter* avaunt,
> Thou, Water-Rat, thou Shark, thou Cormorant;

I'll teach thee to shoot Scissors: I'll repair
Each Rope thou losest *George*, out of this Hair.
'Tis strong and coarse enough; I'll hem this shift,
E'er thou shalt lack a Sail, and lie a-drift:
Bring home the old ones; *I again will sew,*
And darn them up, to be as good as new.
   What, twice disabled! Never such a thing!
Now *Sovereign* help him that brought in the *King*.
Guard thy Posteriors, *George*, e'er all be gone,
Tho' Jury-Masts, thou'st Jury-Buttocks none.

The best painter poems are by Marvell. They have a vein of terse and bitter humour:

> Gen'ral at Land, at Plague, at Sea, at Fire.

In *An Historical Poem* the unknown author explores the satiric possibilities of Old Testament allegory before Dryden: Charles II is depicted:

> Of a Tall Stature, and of Sable Hue;
> Much like the Son of *Kish*, that lofty *Jew*:
> Twelve years compleat he suffer'd in Exile,
> And kept his Fathers Asses all the while.

Throughout the painter poems there are elements of heroic satire struggling with what is a basically anti-heroic form.

*　　　*　　　*

A greater degree of topicality in personal satire was the way chosen by those poets, usually anonymous, who wrote under the stimulus of some national crisis like the failure of Clarendon's policy or the Popish Plot; the literary men who were interested in the vicissitudes of everyday life and cultivated taste turned, under the influence of Juvenal, to general satire; their characters and episodes were carefully selected typical instances of a general theme. But there are exceptions. Oldham has a gift of personal spleen and brooding passion; he finds in Juvenal a congenial model: when therefore he writes political satire, the celebrated *Satires upon the Jesuits,* he produces a generalised and indeed wholly imaginative group of poems; the contemporary references are sparing, and the only persons in the poems are a ghost, a historical character, and the image of a saint: these are the speakers of the dramatic monologues which make up three of the four poems: they are the ghost of Garnet, the Jesuit conspirator in the Gunpowder Plot, St. Ignatius Loyola on his death-bed, and the latter's statue. Dryden on the other hand takes the road of personal innuendo and, in *Absalom and Achitophel* and *The Medal*, carries the methods of the libels and lampoons of the verse pamphleteers to the heights of art. It is convenient to divide our discussion here between political satire and social satire, and this means looking first at the *Satires upon the Jesuits* and postponing discussion of his other poems. This is not so unfair to Oldham as may at first appear, for his political poems are very different from his imitations of Juvenal and Horace. They are, too, the most traditional of the verse satires of the period. Not only do they employ the stock motives already noted; they make contact at many points with earlier English literature, with Reformation satire, with Hall and Donne, and above all with the dramatic tradition of burlesque denunciation in Marlowe and Jonson, that 'terribly serious, even savage' farce of villainy exposing itself, of which Eliot spoke.

The opening lines of the First Satire plunge splendidly into the melodramatic heart of the situation. Garnet's Ghost has appeared to address the Jesuits 'met in private Cabal after the Murder of Godfrey', the murder which set in motion a Whig terror that brought the country to the brink of a second civil war:

> By *hell* 'twas bravely done! what less than this?
> What *sacrifice* of meaner worth & price
> Could we have offer'd up for our success?

The rhetoric belongs to a non-realistic convention; it is like the technique of self-exposure which Chaucer practises in *The Pardoner's Tale*. Values are reversed so that wickedness is exalted, while yet by a curious literary double-take the ordinary counters of moral denunciation are used, and the speaker is thus partly identified with the audience whose feelings he is revolting: this is, in fact, high burlesque, and the melodramatic characters are fulfilling the same role as Orange demonstrators acting out the iniquities of Pope, Cardinal and Jesuit:

> Who e're is to the Sacred Mitre rear'd,
> Believe all Vertues with the place conferr'd,
> Think him establish'd there by Heaven, tho' he
> Has Altars rob'd for Bribes the choice to buy,
> Or pawn'd his Soul to Hell for Simony:

Tho' he be Atheist, Heathen, *Turk*, or *Jew*,
Blaspheamer, Sacriligious, Perjured too:
Tho' Pander, Bawd, Pimp, Pathick, Buggerer,
What e're Old Sodoms Nest of Lechers were:
Tho' Tyrant, Traitor, Pois'ner, Parricide,
Magician, Monster, all that's bad beside:
Fouler than Infamy; the very Lees,
The Sink, the Jakes, the Common-shore of Vice:
Straight count him Holy, Vertuous, Good, Devout,
Chast, Gentle, Meek, a Saint, a God, what not?

The great archetype of such ironic monologue or rant is the speech of Scylla's Ghost which serves as prologue to Jonson's *Catiline, his Conspiracy*:

> *Fate* will haue thee pursue
> Deedes, after which, no mischiefe can be new;
> The ruine of thy countrey; thou wert built
> For such a worke, and borne for no lesse guilt.
> What though defeated once th'hast beene, and knowne,
> Tempt it againe: That is thy act, or none.
> What all the seuerall ills, that visite earth,
> (Brought forth by night, with a sinister birth)
> Plagues, famine, fire could not reach vnto,
> The sword, nor surfets; let thy furie doe:
> Make all past, present, future ill thine owne;
> And conquer all example, in thy one.

But Oldham could find many models also in the ranting heroic tragedy of his own time, especially the plays of Lee. Weldon M. Williams has suggested that he failed because he employed a falsely inflated style, while Dryden succeeded on account of his adherence to the idiom and atmosphere of the lampoon, even though he was reacting against it as a form.[3] Against this, Ian Jack has justly pointed out that both the *Satires upon the Jesuits* and *Absalom and Achitophel* are attempts at heroic satire: Dryden's poem has survived because of its original blending of the heroic with the witty. Is this merely to say that Dryden amuses, and Oldham does not? There is more than this in the difference between them, between Oldham's passionate exaggeration

---

[3] Cf. 'The Genesis of Oldham's Satyre upon the Jesuits', *P.M.L.A.* (1943), and 'The Influence of Ben Jonson's Catiline upon Oldham's Satyre upon the Jesuits', *E.L.H.* (1944).

and Dryden's dignity tempered with wit. Dryden can convince us on a point of fact; once we have turned the key to his allegory there are many of these. To select at random, there is the description of the villainous features of Corah (Titus Oates) and of his technique of false witness:

> Sunk were his Eyes, his Voice was harsh and loud,
> Sure signs he neither Cholerick was, nor Proud:
> His long Chin prov'd his Wit; his Saintlike Grace
> A Church Vermilion, and a *Moses's* Face.
>   (Ed. Kinsley, I. 233)

The majority of Dryden's small London public would in 1682 know Oates's appearance and his methods. They could recall as yesterday the period of McCarthy-like terror when his victims could not try to wriggle out of the web of fantastic charges without seeming to doubt his role as self-appointed saviour of the state, thus involving themselves in direr guilt:

> Let *Israels* foes suspect his heav'nly call,
> And rashly judge his Writ Apocryphal;
> Our Laws for such affronts have forfeits made.

Admittedly Dryden has the advantage of looking back over a period of political madness and bloodshed from a point in time when the crisis has relaxed and when moderate men of both parties can recognise certain matters as true which were previously in dispute. Oldham was writing at the height of the alarm of a Catholic plot when mob hysteria was rampant; all was in doubt except the strong, irrational convictions that urged on the many and the cold exercise of will driving those who manipulated them. Oldham has no grip on the facts, however, because he has no facts; the poems on the Jesuits only achieve a piecemeal artistic success by the daring of his plunge into unreality. Whatever their religious and political convictions, all readers must agree that these grotesque, blood-bolted figures can tell us nothing about the real state of the Catholic Church in the seventeenth century; on the other hand, they may tell us a great deal about the state of mind in Protestant Englishmen, induced by real plots and by the fear of Spain in the previous century; they can illuminate the anti-Catholic hysteria of the London mob which had its final manifestation in the Gordon Riots. Perhaps the kindest estimate we can put upon Oldham's savagery in the *Satires* is to conclude that he shared to some extent the popular superstitions about Popery. He was the son of a dissenting minister, one of those ejected in 1662; he was outside the circle of the court wits to which Dryden belonged, a poor struggling writer living by schoolmastering. There was also a strain of surly independence in his nature which resented claims of authority: this is the side of him which responded to the note of Juvenal. It is not fanciful to imagine him closer in sympathy to the mood of the savage popular dumb-shows exhibited in the streets during the years of the Plot than any other polite writer of the time could be:

> ... past the Royal Exchange, through Cheapside to Temple-bar ... First came six whifflers; then a bell-man ringing a bell, and calling out dolefully, 'Remember Justice Godfrey!' Next a figure representing the dead body of the justice, mounted on a white horse, with one of his murderers behind to prevent him falling off, with spots of blood over his dress, &c.; then a priest, with deadmen's skulls, giving out pardons to all who would undertake to murder Protestants ... and lastly the Pope in effigy, in a grant scarlet chair of state, with two boys at his feet, and banners emblazoned with consecrated daggers for murdering Protestant kings and princes.
>
> (*An Account of the Burning of the Pope at Temple-bar*, 1679)

Oldham's satires have, then, like so much literature of a secondary order of merit, a strong anthropological interest. But in the best political satire, political good sense becomes a necessary constituent of poetic merit; this Dryden has, while Oldham can only parade his atavistic prejudices.

*   *   *

Of course *Absalom and Achitophel* was written even more purely as a party piece, and probably to comply with Charles II's request for a poem. It seems likely that it was published in mid-November 1681 in order to affect the issue of Shaftesbury's trial for high treason. Dryden was already acting as the chief pamphleteer of the Tories; he had defended the king's case as set out in *His Majesty's Declaration to all His Loving Subjects* in *His Majesty's Declaration Defended: in a Letter to a Friend*. Lately other pamphlets have been assigned to Dryden which were not previously considered his.

But Dryden was more than a pamphleteer. He had gone deeply into the relative claims of popular sovereignty and monarchical authority; there is evidence, summarised by Ward, that he had followed a deliberate course of study during the crisis years, including the reading of Davila's work on the French religious wars: all his works, prose and verse, of 1679–82 form an interrelated group devoted to the problems of the day.

He had developed a philosophic conservatism which takes more account of human personalities than of a theory; a supremely interesting human situation, the attempt of a wily, cynical statesman to use as his instrument a noble, but over-ambitious young man, provides the main subject of his poem. We know that he is making out as good a case as possible for Charles II; we may be irritated by Dryden's trait, shared with later conservatives, of appearing to speak for the nation, as though the absence of principle justified the claim to represent a majority of his countrymen. But he sustains our interest and belief in the drama because he allows the persons in it to have a life of their own, and treats them with some degree of dramatic seriousness, not merely as the victims of critical wit. The famous portrait of Shaftesbury-Achitophel has often been discussed as an example of the new, civilised satire, which argues rather than bludgeons, and grants some points to the other side: Achitophel *was* a just judge:

> Oh, had he been content to serve the Crown,
> With vertues only proper to the Gown;
> Or, had the rankness of the Soyl been freed
> From Cockle, that opprest the Noble seed:
> *David*, for him his tunefull Harp had strung,
> And Heaven had wanted one Immortal song.
> (Ed. Kinsley, I. 222)

But our modern interest in rhetorical technique must not blind us to the end of heroic satire, which is not to score points, but to show us human beings in the toils of a struggle for power, and to let that speak for itself. Earlier in the passage, where he examines the contradictions of Shaftesbury's temperament, the questions are not merely rhetorical: Dryden is up against the mystery of human self-assertion and passes his bewilderment on to the reader:

> A fiery Soul, which working out its way,
> Fretted the Pigmy Body to decay:
> And o'r inform'd the Tenement of Clay.
> A daring Pilot in extremity;
> Pleas'd with the Danger, when the Waves went high

He sought the Storms; but, for a Calm unfit,
Would Steer too nigh the Sands, to boast his Wit.
Great Wits are sure to Madness near ally'd;
And thin Partitions do their Bounds divide:
Else, why should he, with Wealth and Honour blest,
Refuse his Age the needful hours of Rest?
Punish a Body which he could not please;
Bankrupt of Life, yet Prodigal of Ease?
And all to leave, what with his Toyl he won,
To that unfeather'd, two leg'd thing, a Son.
(Ed. Kinsley, I. 221)

Dryden's satire branches out in lordly ease above the party libels, even the best of them like the poems by Marvell included in *Poems on Affairs of State*, but its roots are in that soil and are well fertilised by it. His personal insights rub shoulders with current judgements and are as often as possible made to appear to grow out of them. This may be seen first of all in the choice of the allegory. The analogy between David and Charles had already been noticed by contemporary pamphleteers. The Whigs had been described as 'they that set on Absalom to steal away the hearts of the people from the king' (in *A Letter to His Grace the Duke of Monmouth, this 15th of July, 1680*). Tom D'Urfey had already called Shaftesbury Achitophel, 'the chief Advocate for Hell'. The general parallel between England and Israel goes back earlier: from the days of the Commonwealth onwards Englishmen had been accustomed to hear their leaders and preachers interpret national events in terms of this symbolism. Dryden's use of the parallelism is never merely mocking; this would be out of keeping in a poem in which the binding nature of original sin is instanced as a serious argument against the theory of the social contract:

If those who gave the Scepter, coud not tye
By their own deed their own Posterity,
How then coud *Adam* bind his future Race?
How coud his forfeit on mankind take place?
(I. 236–7)

The Biblical parallel enables Dryden to smile at the amours of Charles who

Scatter'd his Maker's Image through the Land;

it also implies a solidarity with his readers, who had also heard sermons, and a belief in the national destiny of England which is worth viewing with heroic seriousness. For the parallel had originally been made by Puritan theologians arguing that God's pact with elect individuals might be repeated with whole states and societies, and that the Old Testament account of the Chosen People of Israel was a forecast of what history had in store for God's Englishmen. Hence arose the Solemn League and Covenant. It is in the light of this covenant theology that we should read the last two books of *Paradise Lost*; and it explains the serious concern that lies behind the urbanity of *Absalom and Achitophel* and justifies the heroic diction which interpreters like Ian Jack have done so much to make us appreciate.

Thus Dryden can appeal, by sympathy, not rhetorical sleight-of-hand, to the great backwash of the Puritan revolution in which English society still has its being. He often draws on less widely diffused attitudes, on the talk of the town, the gossip of those in the know. Some of the things said in the more libellous, direct attack on Shaftesbury in *The Medal* are strikingly close to the sketch of his character sent home from London by the adviser of the Grand Duke of Tuscany:

> Cambiò poi molte volte di partito secondo il vento, e fu sempre infedele a tutti, fin che resosi necessario al Re, nel suo ristabilimento . . . Huomo scaltro che fa il semplice e non lo è, fa l'amico di tutti e non l'è di niuno, ha parole melate e cattivissimi fatti . . . E Presbiteriano, ed il suo maggior talento è d'introddurre un negozzio e di venirne a fine secondo il suo intento, non già per una superiorità di spirito, ma per una prodigiosa affluenza di rigiri, di bugie, di partiti e di cabale.
>
> (Letter of Count Lorenzo Magalotti quoted in Anna Maria Crinò, *Il Popish Plot nelle Relazioni Inedite dei Residenti Granducali alla Corte di Londra (1678-1681)* (Rome, 1954), pp. 206-7)

One suspects that the Whig ideas of contract opposed in ll. 759-810 were the floating opinions of intellectual gossip at a time when Locke was secretary and companion to Shaftesbury and had not yet published any of his views on civil government. *Absalom and Achitophel* thus achieves the air of sophistication and contemporaneity which was an integral part of the new approach to satire. The new ethos of temperate good sense supports at every point the detached, objective analysis of the king's enemies.

Here as elsewhere Dryden has shown his skill in grouping authors and genres in new combinations. The man of letters comes to the aid of the poet. He has accepted the mixed character of the contemporary lampoon, which was, as we have seen, part critical, part positive statement of frustrated patriotism. His heroic satire is a happier blending of elements present in the body of manuscript poems in circulation, many of which were subsequently thrown together in a condition of stylistic and psychological confusion in the *Poems on Affairs of State*.

*   *   *

The Restoration was one of those periods when the present was running away from the past at just that rate of observable, interesting difference which made people acutely aware of fashion: it was the age of 'the man of mode'. The political satirists create an impression of sophistication, of being on the inside of public affairs, as a means of furthering their main design. In social and moral satire the sense of vivid contemporary immediacy is often the chief pleasure to be gained from the poem; the bullies, pedants, poetasters, and cullies are sitting targets.

The new urban world of the coffee-houses was now in existence, permitting a more tolerant, polished social interchange; before it could have a literary existence to enable men to become conscious of their fresh mode of life, a myth had to be found to serve as vehicle for that indefinable freshness they enjoyed. The myth of the Town was incarnated in the imitation of Roman satire: Juvenal and Horace now came into their own; where they had led the Elizabethan satirists down a blind alley they provided their Restoration successors with the ideal vehicle. The world they see is partly built from observation of the real world, partly an imaginative construction. It has two faces: it presents an ideal civilised elegance, or an image of urban depravity, according to whether the satirist is talking about himself and his friends, or about other people.

Oldham was again a pioneer, and a more effective one than he had been in the sphere of heroic satire. The innovation was the practice of consistent adaptation of a single original to a modern setting. Cowley and Sprat seem to have been the first in the field in satiric imitation in their version of the fable of the Town and the Country Mouse (Horace, *Satires*, II. vi) which is to be found in *The Poems of Horace . . . Rend'red in English and Paraphrased by Several Persons* (1662; 1671). This has an admirable sprightliness and freedom: the Town Mouse hums with courtly jargon:

> I pray Sir get his Graces hand to this,
> He knows me, and it reasonable is.

> When did the *Portuguez* resign *Tangier*?
> Is all in *Ireland* quiet still or no?

and when he is with his cousin in the country

> still his thought
> Upon the *cakes* and *pies* of *London* wrought.

Oldham's *An Imitation of Horace* (a version of *Satires*, I. ix—the Impertinent) reveals a colloquial accomplishment and a talent for successfully transposing the atmosphere from Rome to London that are unexpected from the author of the *Satires upon the Jesuits*. The bore boasts of his attainments:

> I'm grown the envy of the men of Wit,
> I kill'd ev'n *Rochester* with grief, and spight:
> Next for the Dancing part I all surpass,
> St. *André* never mov'd with such a grace:
> And 'tis well known, when e're I sing, or set,
> *Humphreys*, nor *Blow* could never match me yet.

The ideal view of the Town saw it as the arbiter of a standard of good sense and good speech. In Oldham's version of Horace's *Art of Poetry* we hear of those who

> Speak the fine Language of the *Park* and *Mall*,
> As if they had their training at *Whitehall*.

The bore in *An Imitation of Horace* is a foil for the quiet good sense of his victim; and this is a situation often repeated in satire of the 'seventies and 'eighties. The influences of Boileau was exerted in the direction of making satire a school of manners. Boileau's influence has probably been exaggerated in the past, and is more truly seen as supplying material for an English tradition that was already in existence. Oldham followed Boileau in his *Satire in Imitation of the Third of Juvenal*; Johnson certainly took the main idea for his sketch of the 'monsieur' (for *Graeculus esuriens*) from this poem. Oldham's *A Satire Touching Nobility* is also modelled on Boileau; and Pope follows it closely for the fourth epistle of the *Essay on Man*.

Imitation could range from adaptation image by image to the bold expansion and transformation of a short passage into a longer one. George Stepney, in a version of Juvenal, *Satire* VIII, essays a touch of Newmarket in

> . . . Who wins most plates with greatest ease, and first
> Prints with his hoofs his conquest on the dust.

and justifies this rather shyly by stating in a note: 'I have taken the liberty to give this simile a modern air, because it happens to agree exactly with the humour of our author.' Another minor poet, Thomas Wood, reaches out much more boldly on the slender pretext of Juvenal. I. 1–4:

> proelia quanta illic dispensatore videbis
> armigero? simplexne furor sestertia centum
> perdere et horrenti tunicam non reddere servo?

> Sir *Fopling* must to day at *Lockets* dine,
> Where Cards and Dice commend the Nasty wine;
> Grannums and Gold from *Satin* Purse is brought,
> And Lordships are by Jilting Fortune caught.
> Undone he stakes his Soul, tempts on his Fate,
> While's Lowsy Footmen for their wages wait.
> At length the *Gentile* Cully leaves our Isle,
> Whilst *Noise* and Bully *Thunder* share the Spoil.
> (*Juvenalis Redivivus. Or The First Satyr of Juvenal
> taught to speak plain English*, 1683)

Rochester develops the satire of the Town into high art: his sense of social immediacy is assisted by such a recording eye and ear that moments are isolated from the stream of time and fashion and given a pathetic human permanency. Such is the account of the stale clichés at the old-fashioned dinner party, where he is loosely imitating Boileau:

> And now the *Wine* began to work, mine *Host*
> Had been a *Collonel*, we must hear him boast
> Not of *Towns* won, but an *Estate* he lost
> For the *Kings* Service, which indeed he spent
> Whoring, and Drinking, but with good intent.
> He talkt much of a Plot, and *Money* lent
> In *Cromwell's* time. My *Lady* she
> Complain'd our Love was course, our *Poetry*,

Unfit for modest Eares, small *Whores*, and *Play'rs*
Were of our Hair-brain'd *Youth*, the only cares;
Who were too wild for any virtuous *League*,
Too rotten to consummate the Intrigue.
Falkland, she prais'd, and *Sucklings*, easie Pen,
And seem'd to taste their former parts again.
Mine *Host*, drinks to the best in *Christendome*,
And decently my *Lady*, quits the Room.

*   *   *

This chapter has tried to outline something of the variety of approaches to satire to be found even within the couplet tradition. Butler and the burlesque tradition lie outside my scope, and I have only glanced at Rochester because it seems to me that his genius most clearly emerges in ways that are not 'of the age' and not usually satirical. I have concentrated on Oldham and Dryden; the former owed much to the older drama, and the latter had of course a career as a dramatist parallel to his career as a poet: the prologues and epilogues he wrote for his own and other men's plays provide in themselves a kind of satirical calendar of the age. Most of the satiric attitudes found in verse are also present in the comedies of Etherege, Wycherley and Congreve. Wycherley even has a satirist for a hero: Manly, in *The Plain-Dealer*, who is an interesting mixture of Elizabethan malcontent and Juvenalian honest man; the confusion of modes is reflected in the style, where direct invective, coarse and colourful, alternates with courtly irony. The satire of the play has, too, its heroic overtones: Manly is a veteran of the Dutch war, and is at a loss among the subterfuges of the Town: he goes everywhere accompanied by two faithful tars. But there was no future for the heroic after the settlement of 1688: the way lay with mock-heroic, the acceptance of contemporary smallness and insufficiency: Dryden had initiated it in *Macflecknoe*, just as he had made the noblest attempt at heroic satire at a time when public issues were still open, and individual heroism therefore still possible. *Macflecknoe* certainly performs an effective job of demolition on its subject; in so doing it supplies the usual advertisement for the standards of the Town, the world of 'gentle George' and Dryden himself, to which Shadwell does not belong. Throughout the period those standards become more and more decorous, as invective gives way to banter and swashbuckling to well-bred mediocrity. In

Congreve's *The Double Dealer*, Lady Froth complains that Mellefont lacks 'a manner', and Cynthia asks her what she means by it:

> LADY FROTH: Some distinguishing Quality, as for Example, the *bel air* or *Brilliant* of Mr. *Brisk*; the Solemnity, yet Complaisance of my Lord, or something of his own that should look a little *Je-ne-scay-quoysh*; he is too much a Mediocrity, in my Mind.
>
> CYNTHIA: He does not indeed affect either Pertness or Formality; for which I like him. (II. i)

Oldham, Rochester, and their fellow-satirists may not have reformed the abuses of the age, but they helped to form Mellefont.

Note

Scholarship and Criticism. Dryden's critical writings remain the most useful guide to heroic tragedy; his essays and prefaces have been gathered together in the two-volume Everyman Library edition by G. Watson, *Of Dramatic Poesy and Other Critical Essays.* Bonamy Dobrée's *Restoration Tragedy, 1660–1720* (1929) and Allardyce Nicoll's *Restoration Drama, 1660–1700* (Vol. I of *A History of English Drama*, rep. 1955) provide standard surveys of the subject.

Cecil V. Deane's *Dramatic Theory and the Rhymed Heroic Play* (1931) is extremely useful, as is Clifford Leech's article 'Restoration Tragedy: a Reconsideration', in *Durham University Journal* (1950). T. S. Eliot's essay *John Dryden* (1924) contains interesting reflections, while G. W. Knight's *Golden Labyrinth* (1962) offers a reappraisal of Restoration Tragedy.

A. Mackenzie has an essay 'Venice Preserved Reconsidered' in *Tulane Studies in English* (1949), while her *Next to Shakespeare: Otway's 'Venice Preserved' and 'The Orphan' and their History on the London Stage* (1950) offers a detailed account of performances.

Modern Editions. Characteristic tragedies of Roger Boyle [Earl of Orrery], Crowne, Dryden, Lee and Settle are reprinted in *Five Heroic Plays*, edited by Bonamy Dobrée (The World's Classics, 1960).

All the plays of Orrery have been edited and provided with an introduction by W. S. Clark (2 vols., 1937). Crowne's generally underrated comedies and tragedies have been edited by J. Maidment and W. H. Logan in *Dramatic Works of John Crowne*, 4 vols., London and Edinburgh, 1873–4). There is a six-volume edition of Dryden's plays by Montague Summers (1931–2); quotations in this chapter are from Summers, the volume and page number being preceded in references with the Act and Scene as in the Mermaid edition of Saintsbury (2 vols., 1923). Otway's *Works* were edited by Summers (3 vols., 1926) and by J. C. Ghosh (2 vols., 1932); there is a one-volume Mermaid edition by R. Noel of four plays and some letters (1888). Quotation here is from Summers with reference to the Mermaid as well.

Lee's plays have been edited by T. B. Stroup and and A. L. Cooke (2 vols., 1954): Settle still awaits a modern editor; Dryden's plays are being re-edited by F. Bowers, who is also preparing a *Bibliography of Restoration Drama*.

For Dryden's biography, see the prefatory note to Chapter VII.

VI

Heroic Tragedy

ANNE RIGHTER

*

IT was characteristic of the Restoration, with its love of paradox, of contradiction and false faces, that it should have created a tragedy that was less serious than its comedy. Neo-classical precepts, French example, the lofty critical pronouncements of Dryden: even for contemporaries, all of this theorising could not quite hide the fact that the tragedies produced between 1660 and the formal end of the Restoration in 1685 were essentially frivolous. Plays in rhyme dominate the first part of this period; after 1676 they were gradually replaced by the blank-verse tragedy of pathos. In both, the furious gestures of the heroes, the rant and the declarations of passion are literary and hollow. Behind them, as behind the painted gardens and palaces of the scenery, there was nothing at all. The traditional accoutrements of Tragedy—like those coronation robes which King Charles himself sometimes lent to the playhouse—bestowed the illusion of form upon a great emptiness. From its very beginning in D'Avenant's *The Siege of Rhodes* (1656), a play with music performed shortly before the return of the king, Restoration tragedy had taken refuge in fantasy, traditionally a comic domain. Faced with the real issues of the age, with the new science and the doctrines of Hobbes, with the split between faith and reason, appearance and reality, it retreated in confusion to a land of rhetorical make-believe. Comedy, as a result of this abdication, was left to fill the gap: to accept the warring impulses of the time, as Jacobean tragedy had before it, and try to reconcile them in the momentary peace of a play.

It was not just because he was the Merry Monarch that Charles II personally preferred comedy to tragedy. 'The humour of the people' was, as Dryden remarked sourly on more than one occasion, adjusted to comedy. A natural reaction against Puritan solemnities doubtless had something to do with this. 'In a word there is nothing here but mirth', wrote a French visitor shortly after the coronation of Charles II:

> And there is a talk that there shall be a proclamacon made that any melancoly man or woman coming into this towne shall be tourned out and put to the pillory, and there to be whep [*sic*] till he hath learned the way to be mary *à la mode*.[1]

In their conversation and their letters, in lampoons and plays, the members of Charles's court customarily laughed at things which the eighteenth century would regard with awe, or else a gasp of horror, and which even the Elizabethans had treated seriously. For the Restoration wits, adultery, old age, the clergy, death, and the amatory exploits or failures of their king were all potentially funny. Their attitude towards the wages of sin in the form of the pox would make Ibsen's *Ghosts* totally incomprehensible.

This tendency to treat serious things with apparent lightness was a gift to writers of comedy. It freed them, first of all, from certain restraints in a way that later critics were to find immoral and blasphemous, but which at the time permitted comedy to enlarge its scope, to reflect the actual way of the Restoration world with astonishing fidelity. Furthermore, it endowed dramatists like Etherege and Wycherley with a ready-made complexity of attitude, a contrast between laughter and its underlying emotions which gave another kind of depth to comedies which, from the point of view of character, were usually frankly shallow. Tragedy, however, as one might expect, found this general climate of risibility anything but beneficial. Wonder and admiration, as Dryden liked to point out, were the emotions meant to be aroused by an heroic play. Yet there is a good deal of evidence to suggest that in practice audiences frequently dissolved in mirth, listening to the pomposities they were expected to find elevating. Wonder and admiration, if they existed at all, tended to spring from the spectacle itself: those machines and extravagances of costume and scenery which Aristotle had dismissed contemptuously as the province of the property-man, not the poet. More, really, than a breach of neo-classical rules underlies the sad comment of Dryden's Lisideius: 'I have observed that, in all our tragedies, the audience cannot forbear

---

[1] Denis de Repas: Hist. Manuscripts Commission, *Portland MSS.*, III (1894), 293.

laughing when the actors are to die; tis' the most comic part of the whole play' (ed. Watson, I. 51).

In the prologue to *The Rehearsal* (1671), Buckingham hints at the paradox of the Restoration theatre:

> For (changing Rules, of late, as if men writ
> In spite of Reason, Nature, Art, and Wit)
> Our Poets make us laugh at Tragoedy,
> And with their Comedies they make us cry.

The Rehearsal itself is, of course, an uninhibited demonstration of just how absurd the heroic plays could be. As such, it represented the point of view not merely of Buckingham himself, but of the court wits as a group, many of whom had helped him to write it. Realistic, intelligent, unabashed, their presence in the playhouse must have constituted a considerable hazard for tragic dramatists. Sedley, Mulgrave, Dorset, Rochester and the rest were likely to speak up suddenly, to finish a laboured couplet in their own irreverent fashion, dissent from the morality of the hero, or carry an unfortunate poetic conceit to some wild and hilarious conclusion. On 4 October, 1664, Pepys attended a peformance of Orrery's heroic play *The General*, where he heard the antagonistic voice of comedy raise itself among the spectators, in the person of Sir Charles Sedley. Sedley was exasperated with what he saw,

> and he did at every line take notice of the dullness of the poet and badness of the action, that most pertinently; which I was mightily taken with; and among others where by Altemire's command Clarimont, the Generall, is commanded to rescue his Rivall, whom she loved, Lucidor, he, after a great deal of demurre, broke out, 'Well, I'le save my Rivall and make her confess, that I deserve, while he do but possesse'. 'Why, what, pox', says Sir Charles Sydly, 'would he have him have more, or what is there more to be had of a woman than the possessing her?'

Both the reaction and the story itself are characteristic. They help to explain the uncertain fortunes of tragedy on the Restoration stage.

Certainly, it was not merely out of deference to classical principles that comedy became an unwelcome visitor in the Restoration tragic world. It was all very well for Hamlet to confront Osric, or Lear to abide the railing of his bitter Fool; the dignity of Shakespeare's Cleopatra survived the ribald assaults of the countryman who brought

her death. But Restoration comedy is the implacable enemy of Dryden's Almanzor, of his Cleopatra in *All for Love,* or of Otway's fragile
Monimia. It is, in this particular tragic context, too serious. Its realism
is inimical to the tragic pretence. When the two forms were forced
together, as they were in Dryden's tragi-comedy *Marriage à la Mode*
(1672), or Etherege's early comedy *Love in a Tub* (1664), one of two
things tended to happen. Either the play split down the centre, re-
solving into two separate and mutually exclusive halves, as Dryden's
does, or else (as Norman Holland has pointed out) the comic low
plot simply attacked and destroyed the values of the high. The nobility
of the love-and-honour heroes faded away into silliness when confronted with the honesty of the rake.

As implacably opposed forms, Restoration comedy and tragedy
appealed, as one might expect, to slightly different sections of the
contemporary audience. Realistic, essentially masculine in outlook,
always a trifle bitter, comedy cut a little too close to the bone to please
many of the women and their attendant fops. The foolish gallant Sir
Courtly Nice, in Crowne's comedy of the same name (1685), only
attends performances of tragedy because, as he says, 'comedies . . . are
so ill-bred—and sawcy with Quality, and always cramm'd with our
odious Sex—that have not always the most inviting smell' (V; vol.
III, p. 339). The defence of comedy undertaken by the truewits in
countless Restoration plays, against the cavils of fools, reflects a real
state of affairs. As does the endlessly reiterated appeal of comedy
epilogues not to permit the play to be damned by outraged fops, the
laughing-stock of both the author and of all men of wit and sense in the
playhouse. The women, for their part, seem to have tried long before
the general moral reaction at the end of the century to band together
and suppress comedies which were particularly outspoken. *The Country
Wife* (1674/5), for instance, came under attack at once, an attack
which Wycherley countered amusingly enough in *The Plain-Dealer*
the following year.

Tragedy, on the other hand, flattered exactly those romantic notions and grandiose dreams of the self which comedy set out to deflate.
It loosed no arrows of mockery at the inhabitants of Fop's Corner;
it consistently assured women that they were beings enskied and
sainted, that virtue reaped a sure reward, and that love was the con-
queror of time. Despite all the puffs it received from the theorists,
Dryden included, Restoration tragedy continued to embody a feminine

as opposed to a masculine point of view. The conflict between love
and honour, the exaltation of platonic love, stemmed by way of
D'Avenant (and French romances of the type of Astrée) from the
court of Charles I, from Queen Henrietta Maria and her friends. Its
Restoration equivalent, the platonist societies gathered around the
Duchess of Newcastle and Mrs. Philips, were again feminine in their
inspiration. The constancy, the exaggerated loyalty and pride of heroes
like Almanzor and Aurengzebe echo these slightly ludicrous real-life
attempts to attain the heroic ideal. As Addison later observed, because
the titanic figures of tragedy

> are generally Lovers, their Swelling and Blustring upon the Stage
> very much recommends them to the Fair Part of their Audience.
> The Ladies are wonderfully pleased to see a Man insulting Kings,
> or affronting the Gods, in one Scene, and throwing himself at the
> Feet of his Mistress in another. Let him behave insolently towards
> the Men, and abjectly towards the Fair One, and it is ten to one but
> he proves a Favourite of the Boxes. *Dryden* and *Lee*, in several of
> their Tragedies, have practised this Secret with good Success.
> (*Spectator*, No. 40)

Nor, apparently, did the ladies like to see their heroes deviate in any
very marked way towards the speculative issues of comedy. Crowne,
in his preface to the two parts of *The Destruction of Jerusalem* (1677),
complained that the tragedy failed in performance because its hero,
returning victorious from a great battle, disappointed the ladies in the
audience by discussing the question of religious truth, rather than love.
Somewhat wearily, he offered his defence:

> Having employ'd this and two heroes more, for almost ten acts,
> in nothing else but love, I thought I had given 'em enough for rea-
> sonable women, and might borrow this Hero to entertain the men
> for a minute with a little reason, if it were but to give him some
> respite to breath.   (vol. V, p. 236)

Even this acknowledged preference of women for tragedy, men for
comedy, is however insufficient to explain the positively schizophrenic
nature of Restoration drama. Certainly, the disjunction between the
two forms was one for which no precedent existed in any earlier
theatre. It was not merely a matter of language, subject matter, presentation and acting styles, disparate though the two were in these

respects. After all, it would be difficult to imagine extremes more widely separated than rhyme which prided itself on its very artificiality, its distance from ordinary life, and the easy, flexible prose of Etherege and his followers. The exotic countries of tragedy—Granada, Alexandria, Morocco, Peru—were divided by more than geographical distance from the contemporary London of comedy, that recognisable world of chocolate-houses and ordinaries, great houses and pleasure-gardens, which actually surrounded the theatre. Spectacle was the life and soul of much Restoration tragedy; unlike comedy, it was expected to be at least as much a feast for the eye as for the ear. Spirits descended from the clouds on golden wires; whole fleets of ships sailed across the stage on imitation oceans; curtains drew back to reveal long, perspective vistas of temples, prisons, palaces and forests. The deaths of kings had customarily been preceded, in the Elizabethan theatre, by an account of various portents and meteorological oddities; the Restoration theatre went one step farther: it provided the account in the old way, and then thoughtfully halted the tragedy while the spectators enjoyed the display. A quite characteristic stage-direction in Lee's *Sophonisba* (1675) calls for the discovery of '*a Heaven of Blood, two Suns, Spirits in Battel, Arrows shot to and fro in the Air*' etc. (II. i). An almost incredible versatility was required of those actors and actresses who played successfully in both comedy and tragedy. They were forced to master two entirely different styles, to switch back and forth between naturalism and an almost operatic manner. Cibber later remembered that he had once seen Nokes, one of the great comic actors of the Restoration, 'giving an Account of some Table-Talk, to another Actor behind the Scenes, which a Man of Quality accidentally listening to, was so deceiv'd by his manner that he asked him if that was a new Play he was rehearsing'.[2] Comedy and ordinary conversation, the acting style and the reality it imitated, could hardly be told apart. When he came to speak of the tragic acting of Betterton, on the other hand, Cibber expressed his admiration in different, and far more formal, terms:

> The Voice of a Singer is not more strictly ty'd to Time and Tune than that of an Actor in Theatrical Elocution: the least Syllable too long or too slightly dwelt upon in a Period depreciates it to nothing.[3]

[2] *Apology* (ed. 1925), i. 79.
[3] *Op. cit.*, i. 62. On acting styles, *vide infra*, Chapter IX, pp. 195–220.

Beyond these obvious differences of language, setting, acting style and manner of presentation, however, lie more fundamental contradictions. In their attitudes and values, in all of their basic presuppositions, a comedy like Etherege's *She Wou'd if She Cou'd* (1668) and a tragedy like Dryden's *Tyrannic Love* (1669) exist quite simply at opposite poles. They are, in fact, so antithetical that a curious relationship establishes itself between them as a result. Maximin, Berenice, Porphyrius and their like stand to Etherege's Ariana and Gatty, Lady Cockwood and foolish Sir Oliver much as a photographic negative stands to its developed print. Black becomes white, and white, black. Directions are exactly reversed. To look at them side by side is to feel that the same is locked together bewilderingly with the other.

*   *   *

All of the ancient Greek satyr plays, with one late and isolated exception, are lost. We shall never really understand the connection of those ritual comedies with the tragedies of Aeschylus and Sophocles which they partnered in dramatic festivals of the fifth century. That the same Athenian audience could admire both the comedies of Aristophanes and the tragedies of Euripides seems, however, in no way strange. The two dramatists may have detested one another; certainly their plays invoke wholly different dramatic conventions, suggest different styles of acting. Yet a comedy like *Lysistrata* is in no basic way incompatible with a tragedy like *The Trojan Women*. Their attitudes towards war and peace, towards human feelings and motivations, even towards the relationship of men and women—the most obvious point of comic-tragic divergence—are essentially the same. Elizabethan writers of what Philip Sidney called 'mungrell tragycomedie' had of course insisted from the very beginning upon an alliance of comedy and tragedy so close that it was the scandal of the orthodox. Orthodoxy triumphed elsewhere, in the French neoclassical theatre of the seventeenth century, separating the two *genres* with a strictness alien to the medieval-Elizabethan tradition. Yet even here, the fundamental rapport between comedy and tragedy remained unbroken. Molière's *Bourgeois Gentilhomme* and Racine's tragedy *Bérénice*, both of which appeared in 1670, are wildly dissimilar, but not contradictory plays. They share the same attitudes and values. The aristocratic ideal which in Racine glorifies Titus and Bérénice at the same time that it destroys their happiness forever is also the one which fascinates Molière's would-be gentleman. In his case, this complex code of behaviour is wholly inappropriate; he is absurd in his efforts to imitate something which he cannot, in fact, comprehend. Nevertheless, it is always at M. Jourdain that Molière directs our laughter, never at the ideal itself.

Restoration drama betrays more than a slight hint of French influence. Yet it presents a split between comedy and tragedy for which no sanction existed in the French theatre, or in any other theatre. On two fundamental issues, 'poetic justice' and the treatment of excess, comedy and tragedy adopt completely contrary positions, positions which have a profound and very different effect upon the structure of each. As for those subsidiary themes of love and pleasure, constancy, virtue and honour, marriage, and the relations of parents and children which are common to both forms, their treatment is again opposite. Mockery of heroic ideas and sentiments was, of course, standard in comedy. 'What foolish Fustian's this? you talk like an Heroic Poet', exclaims one of Shadwell's heroines to a rhapsodising lover. Her point of view represents almost a comic cliché. Less obvious, perhaps, is the way in which comedy attitudes find their way into Restoration tragedy. Over and over again the sentiments, sometimes the exact phrases of Dorimant, Harriet, Freeman and other members of the inner circle of comedy, appear in tragedy on the lips of villains. While the same appeals to virtue and honour which are the exclusive property of fools or canting deceivers in comedy fill the speech of those very heroes and heroines whom tragedy holds up to the admiration of the audience.

When, towards the end of the seventeenth century, Restoration comedy came under serious attack from the moralists, the feature which aroused more wrath than any other was the wilful neglect of 'poetic justice'. Collier begins his *Short View of the Immorality and Profaneness of the English Stage* (1698) with these words:

> The business of *Plays* is to recomend Virtue, and discountenance Vice; To shew the Uncertainty of Humane Greatness, the suddain Turns of Fate, and the Unhappy Conclusions of Violence and Injustice: 'Tis to expose the Singularities of Pride and Fancy, to make Folly and Falsehood contemptible, and to bring every Thing that is Ill Under Infamy, and Neglect.

Needless to say, such an uncompromising view of the moral obligations of drama could not regard with equanimity that multitude of adulteries which flourish, unpunished and often undiscovered, at the end of so many comedies: Horner and his bevy of lecherous ladies, or the intrigues of Brisk and Careless in Congreve's *Double-Dealer* (1694). It was not pleased either to see the rake rewarded at last with the fine lady. Nor could it approve of the way in which the lady, admiring the spirit and the unsanctified wit of the rake, set out to win him in flat disobedience to the wishes of her careful parents. Addison returns to this point constantly in his attacks upon *The Man of Mode* (1676). 'There is nothing in it', he says, 'but what is built upon the Ruin of Virtue and Innocence' (*Spectator*, No. 65). Addison was writing in 1711, after the triumph of sentimentalism, but there had been murmurs throughout the Restoration period about the haphazard nature of the justice meted out in the fifth act of comedy. Dryden, in the preface to *An Evening's Love* (1671), asserts categorically that since 'the first end of comedy is delight, and instruction only the second, it may reasonably be inferred that comedy is not so much obliged to the punishment of faults which it represents, as tragedy' (ed. Watson, I. 152). Yet he is a little uneasy. Perhaps it is because he is aware that although the living example of Etherege and Sedley will support him, the ghosts of Shakespeare and Ben Jonson may not. There is, in any case, both defensiveness and some equivocation in the sentences which follow, with their self-conscious appeal to the authority of the ancient world and far from substantiated claim that marriage, in Restoration comedy, necessarily implies the gallant's reformation.

With respect to this issue of 'poetic justice', Restoration tragedy bears a relation to comedy which is a little like that of the Looking-Glass world to the real world from which Alice enters it. It is an exact reversal. Elizabethan and Jacobean tragedy had insisted upon the destruction of evil at the end of the play, but at least a few of the innocent and good were usually sacrificed in the process. The Restoration, on the other hand, preferred not only to show evil finally defeated, but virtue triumphant and unscathed. In the end, despite some scarifying experiences, the hero and heroine marry and live happily. This is, of course, by no means an unbroken rule. There are tragedies which destroy the good as well as the wicked, particularly after 1676, when blank verse and a new appraisal of the Elizabethans began to replace rhyme and the neo-classical theorising of the early period. For the most part, however, the spirit which produced Nahum Tate's happy-ending version of *King Lear* predominated. The model tragedies of the early Restoration—Dryden's *Indian Queen* and *Indian Emperor*, his

Tyrannic Love, Conquest of Granada and *Aurengzebe*, along with the Corneillan imitations of Orrery and the first work of Settle and Crowne —all end happily for the virtuous characters. Only Nat Lee, whose obsession with death rivalled Webster's, regularly insisted upon involving all his characters, good and bad alike, in the final holocaust.

The trouble with this even-handed justice is that it is manifestly untrue. When at the end of Congreve's tragedy, *The Mourning Bride* (1697), the hero regards the lifeless forms of his enemies and reflects comfortably that

> Blessings ever wait on virtuous Deeds;
> And tho' a late, a sure Reward succeeds,
> (V. xii. 45)

by which he means here and now, not in any after-life, dramatist and spectators alike remain sadly aware that this is not the way of the world in reality, and that no amount of wishful thinking will make it so. Tragedy becomes a fairy-tale: charming perhaps, but scarcely what Aristotle meant. Nothing in fact is more ludicrous than the way in which Restoration tragic heroes, faced with the spectacle of virtue in distress, tend to take the heavens to task for temporary mismanagement of the administration. After all, as the hero of Settle's *Empress of Morocco* (1673) points out:

> What have the higher Powers to do but to take care
> Of so much Vertue and a Face so fair? (V. i)

Usually, the immortals oblige by the end of the fifth Act, at least before 1676. After that point, the repeated question, 'Why, you Gods, was virtue made to suffer?' receives answers which are both more doubtful and more honest.

> The Gods are just.—
> But how can Finite measure Infinite?
> Reason! alas, it does not know it self!
> Yet Man, vain Man, wou'd with this short-lin'd Plummet,
> Fathom the vast Abysse of Heav'nly justice.
> What ever is, is in its Causes just;
> Since all things are by Fate. But pur-blind Man
> Sees but a part o'the Chain; the nearest links;
> His eyes not carrying to that equal Beam
> That poizes all above.   (III; vol. IV, p. 388)

This is Dryden, in the blank-verse tragedy *Oedipus* (1679), a story for which no one, not even Nahum Tate or Hollywood, could have devised a happy ending.

The question of excess divides Restoration comedy and tragedy as sharply as that of 'poetic justice'. It is the great sin in the world of Etherege, condemning the emotionalism, the passionate rage of Mrs. Loveit as well as the fussiness, the overly-refined dress and manners of Sir Fopling Flutter. In Wycherley, again, the jealousy and uxoriousness of Pinchwife, the window-breaking gaiety of young Novel, the monomania of Horner and the single-minded savagery of Manly are all excessive attitudes. As such, they can neither be condoned nor taken altogether seriously. Congreve will judge the protestations of Lord and Lady Froth, the virtue of Lady Plyant, the surliness of Heartwell, and Witwoud's straining after style by the same standard. Only those characters who can temper their attitudes and reactions, who link fancy with judgement, passion with reason, find admission among the truewits. Success in that company depends upon the achievement of balance, upon the ability to deal with a world of adjustment and subtle compromise.

Restoration tragedy, by contrast, presents a world of absolutes, of black and white without any mitigating shades of grey. The whole form is built upon the idea of excess. At the beginning, these extremes were basically those of situation. *The General*, written by the Earl of Orrery, may fairly claim (despite some earlier experiments by D'Avenant) to be the first English heroic play. It was written in 1661 at the request of Charles II, who was interested to see whether tragedy in the French manner could be composed in English. Static, formal, respectful of the unities, *The General* is in effect a long, rhyming debate on the rival claims of love and honour, at the end of which a truce is worked out between the two. A Sir Charles Sedley in the audience might mock the self-sacrificing idealism of the hero, but on the whole the play is quite restrained. Orrery's second play however, *The History of Henry V*, written in 1662, deliberately repeated the situation of the first in more extreme terms. By the time of *Mustapha* (1665), Orrery was manœuvring pairs of rival lovers and rival queens into positions of positively geometric complexity. A play like *Mustapha* is really conservative by comparison with most other English heroic plays, far closer to French example. Yet in its characteristically English doubling of the plot, its complication and repetition of a central idea, it stands in something of the same relation to Corneille's *Le Cid* as does the wilful ingenuity of the vaulting in the Lady Chapel at Gloucester to the typically clear, four-part vaults of French Gothic. The maze of lierne and tiercon ribs at Gloucester serves no essential structural purpose; it is there for its own sake, simply because its intricacy pleases the English, if not the French, eye. The main-plot, sub-plot structure, the fondness for pairs of lovers or of servants, for a skein of intrigues cunningly woven together was, after all, part of the Elizabethan inheritance. It was not surprising that Restoration tragic writers should cling to it, for all the fashionable talk about unity of action. What is surprising, and often ludicrous, is what happens to this tradition once it is used in a drama committed to the juggling of absolutes, the creation of extreme situations for their own sake. The glorious impasse arrived at by the four lovers in the prison scene of Dryden's *Indian Queen* (1664) is so close to Sheridan's famous stage-direction in *The Critic* that it is hard to decide which scene is more absurd:

> *The two Nieces draw their two daggers to strike Whiskerandos; the two Uncles at the instant, with their two swords drawn, catch their two Nieces' arms and turn the points of their swords to Whiskerandos, who immediately draws two daggers and holds them to the two Nieces' bosoms.*

It was perhaps inevitable that a tragedy consciously given over to the aim of astonishing the spectators, of rousing them to wonder and surprise, should run into excess. Determined to magnify human personality and actions, to show love and hate, virtue and sin all larger than life, Restoration dramatists abandoned the ideal of balance and vied with one another in folly. Shakespeare had made men over life size too, but not by the simple expedient of taking a series of absolute qualities, blowing them up to maximum size, and then setting them down in the arena for a lumbering battle of giants. Elizabethans had often compared the great man to an eagle or a lion; Cassius and Cleopatra go so far as to imagine a Colossus. The Restoration, with its straining after sheer size, its joyous abandonment to the grotesque, went one step further and arrived at the whale. Heroic tragedy is full of these leviathan images. Hannibal, in Lee's *Sophonisba*, is

> . . . like some rolling Whale, who as he laves,
> With his bright Armoury gilds the Waves,
> Dashes the frighted Nation from his side. . . .
>   (III. i)

The villain of Crowne's *The Ambitious Statesman* (1679) sees himself floundering in the shallows 'like a great whale' (I. i). Most extreme of all is the splendid description of the wicked Pope in Settle's *The Female Prelate* (1679):

> Draw me, some Painter,
> This Church Leviathan, draw him at full length;
> In some deep Ocean, bottomless as Hell,
> And wide as Worlds for his vast Bulk to move in;
> Paint his each breath a Storm, each Rowl a Tide,
> And every gust from his impetuous Nostrils
> A Mountain Sea. . . .   (II. i)

Buckingham was not insensible to the tragic whale. He introduces it into *The Rehearsal*, during the course of an argument between Volscius and Prince Prettyman. Bayes, the author of the parody play, is particularly proud of the image: 'As far a fetched fancy . . . 'y gad, as ever you saw' (IV. ii).

Except for the essential silliness of the love-honour dilemmas into which his characters get themselves, Orrery's plays had been relatively restrained. Certainly, their language was cold and formal. It was not long, however, before rant and bombast at a pitch that would have silenced Tamburlaine made their way into heroic tragedy. Tamburlaine's pampered jades of Asia and his slaughter of the gods had, of course, been objects of parody throughout the Elizabethan period. The excesses of characters like Dryden's Maximin or Lee's Roxana, on the other hand, exist beyond parody:

> But by the Gods (by *Maximin*, I meant)
> Henceforth I and my World
> Hostility with you and yours declare.
> Look to it, Gods; for you th' Agressors are.
> Keep you your Rain and Sun-shine in your Skies,
> And I'le keep back my flame and Sacrifice.
> Your Trade of Heav'n shall soon be at a stand,
> And all your Goods lie dead upon your hand.
> (*Tyrannic Love*, V. i; vol. II, pp. 391–2)

It is, as more than one critic has pointed out, impossible to make verse like this any more ludicrous than it already is. It is like the Restoration advance from the great man as lion to the great man as whale; a limit has been reached, an extreme, which already topples over into the grotesque. Parody retreats before Maximin's final reduction of the gods to small shopkeepers busy with the 'trade of heaven' for the good reason that it recognizes itself. There is nothing left for it to do.

Tamburlaine's rant had been a measure both of the man and of the ambitions of an age. The speech of characters like Maximin represents a mere straining after excess for its own sake. No genuine emotions inform it; it is a calculated expedition into hysteria, literary, contrived, linked with no reality of the time, capable of providing the theatre audience with nothing more than an agreeable sort of *frisson*. As such, it blends perfectly with the horrors of Restoration tragedy: the violent deaths, the sudden disclosure of instruments of torture, the loving description of bodies racked and torn. The horrors of good Elizabethan and Jacobean plays had possessed a structural as well as an emotional purpose: one need only think of the blinding of Gloucester, or of the severed finger in Middleton's *Changeling* which teaches Beatrice-Joanna that murder is not a clean and bloodless abstraction. Even the deaths of Bajazet and his wife in *Tamburlaine* were meaningful in their effect upon Zenocrate. In Restoration tragedy, on the other hand, the blood which inundates the stage, in defiance of neo-classical principles, is purely gratuitous. At the very end of Settle's *Empress of Morocco*, curtains draw back to reveal the villain of the play impaled on iron spikes. There is no reason for this discovery, except that it means to exact a delighted shudder from the audience. In terms of the tragedy itself, which is in effect over, the scene is completely unnecessary, mere Grand Guignol.

*   *   *

Constancy, love and pleasure, virtue and honour, marriage, and the relations of parents and children are issues over which comedy and tragedy divide as sharply as they do over those of 'poetic justice' and excess. The comedy gallant flatly disbelieves in constancy, although at the end of the play he may be willing to try. The remarks of Etherege's Dorimant, when he is upbraided by Mrs. Loveit for transferring his affections to Bellinda, are typical: 'What we swear at such a time may be a certain proof of a present passion, but to say truth, in Love there is no security to be given for the future' (II. ii. 216). This is the credo of the rake, a curious but not unattractive mixture of energy and regret. Rochester, the Dorimant of real life, had touched upon it too:

> Nimph, unjustly you inveigh;
> Love, like us, must Fate obey.
> Since 'tis Nature's Law to Change,
> Constancy alone is strange.

Light, graceful, disillusioned, these weather-vane images of love seem more sad than outrageous.

They have many equivalents in tragedy.

> If to new persons I my Love apply,
> The Stars and Nature are in fault, not I . . .
> I can no more make passion come or go,
> Than you can bid your *Nilus* ebb or flow.
> 'Tis lawless, and will love, and where it list:
> And that's no sin which no man can resist.

Out of context, it might be Dorimant in rhyme. Yet in the tragedy itself, Dryden's *Tyrannic Love* (IV; vol. II, p. 369), the speech has a very different effect. Maximin, whose sentiments these are, is no less than five times a murderer in the course of the play. His philosophy of the necessary waywardness of passion is part of his villainy; he advances it, in fact, to justify himself in brutally disposing of a beautiful and constant wife, at the same time that he tries to violate the chastity of the profoundly unwilling St. Catherine of Alexandria.

The heroes of Restoration tragedy speak of constancy in very different terms. Thus, in the second part of Dryden's *Conquest of Granada* (1671), the lovely and unscrupulous Lyndaraxa tries to gain the affections of Almanzor. His first love, as she reminds him, is now totally unattainable since she has, in obedience to her father's wishes, married Almanzor's rival and enemy, the King of Granada. In a roughly similar situation in Shadwell's comedy *Epsom-Wells* (1672), the hero embraces temptation immediately: 'Is it reasonable that a man that has a good stomack should refuse Mutton to day, because he expects Quails to morrow?' (I; vol. II, p. 119). But not Almanzor:

> Fair though you are—
> As Summer mornings, and your Eyes more bright
> Than Starrs that twinckle in a winters night;
> Though you have Eloquence to warm, and move
> Cold age and praying Hermites into Love;

Though *Almahide* with scorn rewards my care;
Yet; than to change, 'tis nobler to despair.
My Love's my Soul; and that from Fate is free:
'Tis that unchang'd; and deathless part of me.
(*Conquest of Granada, Part II*, III. iii; vol. III, p. 128)

It is the exact reversal, the conscious contradiction, of Rochester's
'Love, like us, must Fate obey', and of the realism of the comedy gallants.

Like their creators, these gallants were often caught reading Epi-
curus, Lucretius and Hobbes. Restoration comedy is filled with vaguely
Hobbesian appeals to Nature as the proper guide to conduct, descrip-
tions of pleasure as an obligation, of the gratification of the senses as a
rival religion to the one preached from church pulpits. Ramble, in
Crowne's comedy *The Country Wit* (1676), asserts that

> The world is Nature's house of entertainment, where men of wit
> and pleasure are her free guests, tied to no rules and orders. . . .
> However 'tis in other affairs I am for reducing love to the state of
> nature; . . . no propriety, but every man get what he can. . . . When
> a pretty young woman lies in the possession of an old fellow, like
> a fair fertile province under the dominion of the Turk, uncultivated
> and unenjoy'd, no good Christian but ought to make war upon
> him.   (II; vol. III, pp. 44–5)

Ramble's views here are essentially those of Settle's Empress of Morocco,
just after she has been caught enjoying herself with one of her coun-
cillors.

> Is it not pity now—
> That Grave Religion, and dull sober Law
> Should the high flights of sportive lovers awe?
> Whilst for the loss, of what's not worth a Name,
> The slight excursions of a wanton flame,
> You must your Ruin meet, and I my Shame.
> And yet we must not at our Dooms repine,
> Because Law and Religion are divine.
>   Yes, they're Divine; for they're so overgood
> I'm sure they ne'er were made by Flesh and Blood.
>   (III. i)

Ramble is sympathetic and a truewit; the Empress of Morocco is a
figure of pure, Baroque evil. Her championship of the natural appetites

against the restraints of law and religion leads her directly into the boast, amply justified by the events of the tragedy:

> Let single murders Common hands suffice,
> I scorn to kill less than whole Families.
>
> (V. i)

In Restoration tragedy, the thoughts and actions of those characters who correspond to the comedy truewits are controlled unequivocally by abstract ideas of Virtue and Honour—not in any sense by the psychology of Hobbes. 'What less than Death could I to Honour give?' inquires a young prince in Lee's *Sophonisba*, and stabs himself because a few minutes earlier he had been unjustly suspected of having seduced the lady he adores. His friends are grieved by this suicide, but they understand it. Honour, Virtue and Love are the three incontrovertible absolutes of tragedy, and the words themselves are rarely absent from the lips of the characters. Only the creatures of darkness sneer:

> The points of Honour Poets may produce;
> Trappings of life, for Ornament, not Use:
> Honour, which onely does the name advance,
> Is the meer raving madness of Romance.
>
> (*Aurengzebe*, II. i; vol. IV, pp. 113–4)

Thus a wicked lord tries, and fails, to corrupt Dryden's hero Aurengzebe. The virtuous man 'does but act a part, and shews not his own Nature, but his art' asserts another villain (in Sir Robert Howard's *Vestal Virgin* (ed. 1665), Act II), only to find his words disproved by the implacable probity of his victims.

Comedy, of course, reverses the situation. Men and women who appeal loudly to Virtue and Honour are almost invariably hypocrites. Olivia, in *The Plain-Dealer*, is a typical example and so, later in the century, is Lady Plyant in Congreve's *Double-Dealer*. Cant of this kind is primarily a feminine failing, but it may also be adopted by men, usually gallants who find this style of address indispensable in dealing with certain women. 'Now you have been seen with me . . . my concern for your honour will make me so feverish and disordered, that I shal lose the taste of all the happiness you give me':—so Etherege's Mr. Courtall tries to free himself from the tedious company of Lady Cockwood (*She Wou'd if She Cou'd*, III. i. 177). In her reply, she calls him 'heroick Sir', a reference to tragedy which is not accidental. More often, however, the gallant simply confronts the fair hypocrite with the truth. He may even, like Mrs. Behn's gallant Wilding, re-define the words virtue and honour in order to break down the defences of the lady: 'All the Desires of mutual Love are virtuous. Can Heav'n or Man be angry that you please Your self, and me, when it does wrong to none?' (*The City Heiress*, IV. i). Wilding's remark has its significant real-life echo: the two maxims of Rochester's morality, as he himself told Bishop Burnet, were 'that he should do nothing to the hurt of any other, or that might prejudice his own health. . . . All pleasure, when it did not interfere with these, was to be indulged as gratification of our natural Appetites.'

As for family ties and the institution of marriage, comedy and tragedy again stand at opposite poles. A standard situation in tragedy shows the unhappy heroine forced to deny herself to the man she adores because her father insists, quite unreasonably, that she marry another. The king's son is frequently unable to wed his love because his lecherous old father has taken a fancy to the girl himself. In the latter instance, the unfortunate young man may try to prevent the girl from being actually dishonoured but he cannot, even though threatened with death or perpetual imprisonment, actually proceed against his tyrannical parent. The question posed by the indignant heroine of Arrowsmith's comedy *The Reformation* (1673), whether a father can rightfully think that 'because he had the pleasure to get us, we are bound to be his slaves?' (III. ii), presupposes a firm negative in terms of comedy, an affirmative in tragedy.

> I Freely at his feet my Life will throw;
> Life is a debt we to our Parents owe,

says a character in *The Empress of Morocco* (I. i), learning that his father, in a jealous rage, has condemned both himself and his mistress to death. Only the wicked and the unchaste deny the authority of age in the 'serious' drama.

Violent disagreement between parents and children over the question of arranged marriages had, of course, been a staple of comedy since the time of Menander. It appears throughout the Elizabethan period, as witness the imbroglio in *A Midsummer Night's Dream*, or in *The Winter's Tale*. Yet disobedient children had also figured prominently, and by no means distastefully, in Elizabethan tragedy: Desdemona, Romeo and Juliet. We are inclined, in fact, to think of Ophelia's subservience to her father's will against the dictates of her own heart as a fatal weakness of character, tragic in its consequences. It was French neo-classicism which made resistance to the parental will not only undesirable, but positively culpable. French comedy of the late seventeenth century, although it makes use of the traditional theme of parent and child disagreement, is totally unlike its Restoration equivalent in that it insists, even when such insistence is difficult, upon filial respect. The requirements of decorum force Molière into some curious manœuvres. When Orgon, in *Tartuffe*, tells his horrified daughter Mariana that she must marry his grotesque favourite, she is silent. It is the maidservant Dorine who declares on the spot that such an idea is horrible and later, when Mariana has avowed tearfully that a father's authority is too great to contradict, concocts a plot to free her. In *Le Malade Imaginaire*, it is again the maid Toinette who speaks for Argan's oppressed daughter Angelique in similar circumstances, and invents a means of outwitting her father. In *Le Bourgeois Gentil-homme*, Lucile, the daughter of M. Jourdain, is so innocent of the scheme which unites her with her lover despite the snobbish objections of her father that she almost wrecks the contrivance at the last moment. Julie, in *Monsieur de Pourceaugnac*, sanctions but takes no direct part in the humiliation of the suitor forced upon her. When, in *L'Avare*, the children of a tyrannical parent do actually speak their minds and them-selves strike for freedom, they are treated so bitterly by the dramatist that the exception virtually proves the rule.

Decorum, then, could be observed in comedy as well as tragedy. Certainly, the undisguised contempt for the older generation, the hostility towards parents, the fear of age displayed by the heroes and heroines of Restoration comedy cannot be explained away on the grounds of the pressure of comic form. In their savagery and single-mindedness such attacks represented, as English dramatists well knew, a radical departure from the tradition of Elizabethan comedy, as well as from the practice of Molière and of contemporary tragedy. Marriage itself was an issue over which a somewhat similar division occurred. In Molière, as in Shakespearean comedy, the joining of hands at the end of the play represented the end of the story. If only the lovers could reach that point, despite the obstinacy of fathers and the machina-tions of rivals, everything would be all right. No questions were to be asked regarding the future; everyone lives happily ever after as a matter of course. Restoration comedy, on the other hand, queries this whole convention. The truewits and their ladies are painfully aware that the institutionalisation of love may be its death, that time and habit are terrible enemies. They must marry if they are to possess one another at all, yet they confront this solution at the end of the play with a dubiety which, in Elizabethan comedy, had been reserved only for clowns and fools: for Launce and his slovenly milkmaid, Touchstone and Audrey. Dorimant and Harriet, Millamant and Mirabell, describe marriage as the risk they take, not as the end of the story.

Needless to say, such an attitude is totally foreign to tragedy. There, the dangers and violence of the plot engage the lovers' attention wholly. A passing fit of jealousy on the part of the hero is the only psychological disturbance allowed. Comedy scepticism, the insistence of Dorimant and his like that expectation is sweeter than fruition, that a woman must not yield readily, but linger out the chase as long as possible, is left to the villains.

> No; 'tis resistance that inflames desire,
> Sharpens the Darts of Love, and blows his Fire.
> Love is disarm'd that meets with too much ease;
> He languishes, and does not care to please.
> And therefore 'tis your golden Fruit you guard
> With so much care, to make possession hard.

So the old Emperor in Dryden's *Aurengzebe* (II. i; vol. IV, p. 105) assaults the idealism of Indamora. Only the unregenerate characters in tragedy suspect that marriage may outlast love, that time annihilates passion. The despicable King of Granada in Dryden's *Conquest* speaks pure comedy sentiments:

> Marriage, thou curse of love; and snare of Life,
> That first debas'd a Mistress to a Wife!
> Love, like a Scene, at distance should appear;
> But Marriage views the gross–daub'd Landscape near.
> (*Conquest of Granada, Part II*, III. i; vol. III, p. 115)

Heroes like Almanzor or Aurengzebe prepare to marry in a very different and utterly confident spirit:

> The very hope is a full happiness;
> Yet scanty measures what I shall possess.
> Fancy it self, ev'n in enjoyment, is
> But a dumb Judge, and cannot tell its bliss.
> (*Aurengzebe*, V. i; vol. IV, p. 159)

*   *   *

On all of these specific issues over which comedy and tragedy divide, it is remarkable how much conviction the comedy attitudes carry with them when they appear in tragedy. For all the villainy of the speakers, they are vivid and persuasive as the eulogies of virtue and honour rarely are. This is particularly true with Dryden; in fact, it has often been suggested that plays like *Tyrannic Love* and the *Conquest of Granada* are really satires on the heroic mode in which the realism of the wicked characters represents Dryden's own point of view. This idea will not stand up against the evidence of the prefaces or of Dryden's other essays on drama. Nor is it really credible in the light of the plays themselves. Heroic drama is a far more complicated and serious phenomenon than such a notion would imply. It is more just, perhaps, to say that the comedy attitudes drew strength from the Restoration world itself. The heroic attitudes, on the other hand, were (for all the wish-dreams of the ladies) mere artificial constructions, bloodless, frail, impossible to believe in. The most real thing about them, aside from the theatrical and musical display which they occasioned, was the idea of tragedy itself: the conviction of Dryden and others that, despite the preference of the age for comedy, tragedy was the truly significant form. Surely, with attention to the practice of the ancients and a certain limited deference to the Elizabethans, a great tragic drama could be created by poets conscious of its worth and possibilities as never before. In fact, a still-birth was all that resulted, but this failure was not really the fault of the dramatists. The playhouse, the structure of the audience, the quality of the age all presented problems with which only comedy could deal. Hence the frequency with which comedy attitudes appear, under various disguises, in a tragedy which frowned upon a straightforward mingling of the *genres*. And hence the disproportionate, and sometimes embarrassing, authority of their voice.

It was, however, an ephemeral authority. The division between Restoration comedy and tragedy, a division both extreme and unique in theatrical history, was too uncomfortable to last long. After 1676, the two forms gradually moved closer together. Comedy, abandoning the balance of Etherege, became increasingly harsh and nihilistic. It rejected its own earlier attitudes and ideals. Tragedy, for its part, settled into an endless series of variations upon Aurengzebe's statement: 'When I consider life, 'tis all a cheat.' A common sense of weariness, of the purposeless character of all human activity, comes to unite the comedies and tragedies of the 1680's. It is not merely that heroism itself now seems to the tragic protagonists as silly as it always had to the comedy gallants:

> He who cuts the throats of men for glory,
> Is a vain savage fool; he strives to build
> Immortal honours upon man's mortality,
> And glory on the shame of human nature,
> To prove himself a man by inhumanity.
> He puts whole Kingdoms in a blaze of war,
> Only to still mankind into a vapour;
> Empties the world to fill an idle story.
> In short, I know not why he shou'd be honour'd,
> And they that murder men for money hang'd.
> (Crowne, *The Ambitious Statesman*, II; vol. III, p. 177)

Death becomes a positive value in tragedy, a consummation devoutly to be wished, bestowed upon virtuous characters almost as though it were a happy ending. Heroes like Almanzor, in earlier tragedy, had faced the prospect of annihilation without flinching, but they did not rush towards it with positive expressions of pleasure. The weary and disgusted lovers of post-heroic tragedy, on the other hand, often seem to look forward to a union in the grave, rather than in the marriage-bed.

In the work of a dramatist like Otway, who wrote both comedy and tragedy, the eventual synthesis of the eighteenth century is prefigured. *The Soldier's Fortune* (1680) and *The Atheist* (1683) are comedies filled with undisciplined passion, with a harshness and nihilism by no means alien to Wycherley's *The Plain-Dealer* (1676) but also strikingly close to the pessimism and death-wish of Otway's own tragedies. The pathos, the morbidity and generalised sense of disillusion which mark *The Orphan* (1679) have their analogues in the bitter destinies of Otway's comic characters. Otway's most famous tragedy, *Venice Preserv'd* (1682), has more backbone than *The Orphan*, lent it partly by imitation of Shakespeare and partly by its involvement with current political reality. Yet as a whole, the tragedy is nihilistic. Both the Venetian establishment and the conspirators who would overthrow it are hopelessly corrupt. There is nothing to choose between them, and no other alternative. Injured and persecuted by the senators, poor Jaffeir throws in his lot with the revolutionaries, only to find that with the single exception of his friend Pierre they are bloodthirsty and vicious, motivated by jealousy and thoughts of personal gain. When one of them tries to violate his wife, Jaffeir breaks down and discloses the plot to the Senate, asking in return that the lives of Pierre and certain others among the conspirators be spared. The Senate promises smoothly—and then proceeds to torture and kill them all. There is nothing left for Jaffeir to do at this point except to kill Pierre in order to spare him the indignity of torture, and then to kill himself. For both of them, death is welcome.

> This vile World and I have long been jangling,
> And cannot part on better terms than now.
> (IV; vol. III, p. 60)

Death, in fact, is the only positive value remaining in the world. Certainly, any possible society is rotten to the core. The good cannot prosper, and even the private relationships of the few virtuous (Jaffeir and Pierre) are so bedevilled by misunderstanding, and by a kind of feverish emotionalism, that they are more destructive than anything else. Very little really is left, except for the tears, the racked feelings of Pierre, Jaffeir and his wife and—Otway hoped—the audience.

By 1700, the Restoration breach between comedy and tragedy had been effectively healed. There were some exceptions, of course: wistful attempts to return to the comic form of Etherege, tragedies which incorporated older heroic modes. For the most part, however, in language, setting, manner of presentation, acting style and direction of appeal, comedy and tragedy were no longer opposites. They reflected the same world. That the attitudes of drama were now, essentially, those which tragedy had promulgated so unconvincingly throughout the Restoration proper is only superficially surprising. As the composition of the audience altered, the temper of the century changed, those attitudes towards old age, marriage, constancy, virtue and honour which had seemed so artificial in tragedies of the 1660's and 1670's came to reflect the real convictions of playgoers. Comedy moved gradually from the nihilism of Otway to the sentimentality of Cibber; tragedy from the all-pervading death-wish of plays like *Venice Preserv'd* to the gentle pathos of Rowe. A play like Steele's *The Conscious Lovers* (1722) represents the ultimate reconciliation of the two forms. The attitudes of tragedy, once so inimical, now form the basis for comedy; only in the trivial levity of the servants does one hear, as from a great distance, the voices of Dorimant and Harriet. In this senile marriage of opposites, the real greatness of Restoration comedy was finally lost.

Note

Biography. John Dryden (1631–1700) was born in the vicarage of Aldwinkle All Saints in Northamptonshire. He was educated at Westminster and Trinity College, Cambridge. In 1663, Dryden married Lady Elizabeth Howard, eldest daughter of the Earl of Berkshire. His *Annus Mirabilis*, a poem on contemporary events in heroic style which included praise of Charles II and ended with a prophecy of England's greatness as a 'famed emporium', was published in 1667, and he was created poet laureate in the following year; he became historiographer in 1670. Dryden refused to take the oaths at the Revolution and lost his laureateship and an office in the Customs he had enjoyed since 1683; his last years were chiefly occupied in translations from Juvenal, Virgil, Horace, Ovid and others; he also paraphrased tales from Chaucer, Boccaccio and Ovid. He was buried in Westminster Abbey.

Plays. Dryden wrote or collaborated upon nearly thirty plays. His first was *The Wild Gallant* at the Theatre Royal in 1662/3; this was a prose comedy and was followed by the tragi-comedy with rhymed verse, *The Rival Ladies* of 1664. Next came the first of the heroic tragedies, *The Indian Emperor; or, The Conquest of Mexico by the Spaniards* (Theatre Royal, 1665); this was a sequel to *The Indian Queen* (1663/4), a tragedy in which he had collaborated with Sir Robert Howard. Later heroic tragedies were *Tyrannic Love* (1669), *The Conquest of Granada* (in two parts, 1670/1) and *Aurengzebe* (1675); these were in rhymed verse. His comedies included *Marriage à la Mode* (Lincoln's Inn Fields, 1672), *The Spanish Friar* (1679/80), and *Amphitryon* (1690). His first attempt at opera was *Albion and Albanius* (1685); this was followed by *King Arthur* (1691). The tragedy, *Don Sebastian*, was his first play after the Revolution. His last play was the tragi-comedy, *Love Triumphant* (1693). His blank-verse alteration of Shakespeare's *Antony and Cleopatra* was performed in 1777, entitled *All for Love; or, The World well Lost.*

Scholarship and Criticism. Bonamy Dobrée's *Restoration Tragedy* (1929) has done much to foster appreciation of Dryden's plays. M. van Doren's *John Dryden* (rev. ed., 1931) is a good introduction, and Johnson's *Lives of the Poets* (1779–81) is still helpful. L. E. Bredvold, *The Intellectual Milieu of John Dryden* (new ed., 1956), is an admirable account of his thought. A recent biography is by K. Young (1954). One of D. Nichol Smith's Clark Lectures, *John Dryden* (1950), is on the plays. Articles on the plays include S. C. Osborn, 'Heroical Love in Dryden's Heroic Drama', *P.M.L.A.* (1958); T. H. Fujimura, 'The Appeal of Dryden's Heroic Plays', *P.M.L.A.* (1960); A. C. Kirsch, 'Dryden, Corneille, and the Heroic Play', *Modern Philology* (1962), and 'The Significance of Dryden's Aureng-Zebe', *E.L.H.* (1962); and J. A. Winterbottom, 'Stoicism in Dryden's Tragedies', *J.E.G.P.* (1962).

D. W. Jefferson has discussed 'The Significance of Dryden's Heroic Plays' in *Proceedings of Leeds Philosophical and Literary Society* (1940) and 'Aspects of Dryden's Imagery' in *Essays in Criticism* (1954).

For modern editions of Dryden, see notes to Chapters V and VI.

VII

'All, all of a piece throughout'

Thoughts on Dryden's Dramatic Poetry

D. W. JEFFERSON

*

It has become customary to see a poet's writings as 'all of a piece throughout', the significant uses of words and images in one work reinforcing, with variations, the effect of similar uses elsewhere. This approach works perfectly with Dryden. He was a poet of regular imaginative habits. Taken as a whole his poetry presents an economy within which each individual passage of sentiment or imagery is enhanced for us by our recognition of its kinship, first, with the other passages nearest to it in mood, but finally with everything else that is Dryden. These relationships of passage to passage are easy and flexible, as befits Dryden's temperament. Thematic patterns suggest themselves, but it would probably be unwise to try to define them closely. Any unity that emerges is personal and too elusive for abstract formulation.

Don Sebastian (1689), now generally regarded as his best play, provides some good examples of Dryden at his habitual game. It is a tragedy, with a powerful religious element;[1] but, as we know from *The Hind and the Panther* and other works, religion was a subject that tempted him to indulge his fancy. We may begin by considering a number of passages on themes relating to heaven which modify the solemnity of the central action. In the first scene between Sebastian and Almeyda (they are captives at the Emperor of Barbary's court) the latter sees death as the solution to their unhappy fate, and expresses her scepticism concerning the Christian prohibition against suicide:

> Divines but peep on undiscover'd Worlds,
> And draw the distant Landshape as they please:

---

[1] Bruce King has written convincingly on this aspect in 'Don Sebastian. Dryden's Moral Fable', *Sewanee Review* (1962), pp. 651–70.

> But who has e'er return'd from those bright Regions,
> To tell their Manners, and relate their Laws?
> I'll venture landing on that happy shoar
> With an unsully'd Body, and white Mind;
> If I have err'd, some kind Inhabitant
> Will pity a stray'd Soul, and take me home.
>
> (II; vol. VI, p. 59)

The idea of heaven as a place in which one might be at a loss is taken up, more pessimistically, by Sebastian, who is urging her to be united with him in love before they die:

> Our Souls for want of that acquaintance here,
> May wander in the starry Walks above,
> And, forc'd on worse Companions, miss our selves.
>
> (II; vol. VI, p. 59)

In a later scene, after their union has been rapturously consummated, the lovers are confronted by the wicked emperor, Muley-Moluch, who threatens to kill Sebastian and ravish Almeyda:

> ALMEYDA: How can we better dye than close embrac'd,
> Sucking each others Souls while we expire?
> Which so transfus'd, and mounting both at once,
> The Saints deceiv'd, shall by a sweet mistake,
> Hand up thy Soul for mine, and mine for thine.
> EMPEROR: No, I'll untwist you:
> I have occasion for your stay on earth:
> Let him mount first, and beat upon the Wing,
> And wait an Age for what I here detain.
> Or sicken at immortal Joys above,
> And languish for the Heav'n he left below.
>
> (III; vol. VI, p. 69)

Again heaven is depicted, in Almeyda's speech, as pleasantly fallible. The emperor introduces a different note. Sebastian's upward flight is seen in palpable, physical terms, and the joys of the blest are cynically disparaged. It might be argued here, if one were anxious to vindicate Dryden's adherence to decorum, that Almeyda's pretty sentiments are in keeping with her role in the drama—she is a tender convert, young and unschooled in the faith—and that Muley-Moluch's are equally in keeping with his; but our pleasure in these exchanges has little to do with such considerations. The justification is unnecessary. It is also perhaps inadequate, since the play of fancy pleases us at a non-dramatic level, and may deflect attention from the drama.

Before we turn to other places in *Don Sebastian* where heaven's supremacy is slightly compromised, it is worth while to note a few passages from earlier plays which have a close affinity with those already cited. Torrismond, the hero of *The Spanish Friar*, says in a moment of discouragement:

> Sure my lot
> By some o'er-hasty Angel was misplac'd
> In Fate's Eternal Volume!
>
> (II; vol. V, p. 144)

But there are much earlier and more interesting parallels in the speeches of Berenice, Maximin's empress, in *Tyrannic Love* (1669). They occur in scenes with Porphyrius, who is in love with her. Dryden's plays are full of debates in which ladies of varying degrees of amiability or otherwise—the ruthless Lyndaraxa, the gentle Indamora—reject the entreaties of their desiring lovers. However amiable the lady may be, the slight note of complacency accompanying the well-turned refusal (in couplets) is liable to give a flavour to the situation that adds to the reader's pleasure but raises questions about Dryden's intention and also about possible interpretations by Restoration actresses. Berenice's attitude is quite free from coquetry. She loves Porphyrius: honour and the marriage vow, as she admits, are the only obstacles. But her description of the spiritual substitute she promises him owes some of its charm to associations with speeches in other plays where the lady offers friendship or a sister's love in response to the lover's famished protestations. Here the effect has a special piquancy. Were she not understood to be a ghost Berenice's approaches as she pictures them would be sexually quite provocative:

> PORPHYRIUS: And would you rather chuse your death, than me?
> BERENICE: My earthy part—
> Which is my Tyrant's right, death will remove,
> I'le come all Soul and Spirit to your Love.
> With silent steps I'le follow you all day;
> Or else before you in the Sun-beams, play:
> I'le lead you thence to melancholy Groves.
> And there repeat the Scenes of our past Loves:
> At night, I will within your Curtains peep;
> With empty arms embrace you while you sleep;

In gentle dreams I often will be by;
And sweep along, before your closing eye.
All dangers from your bed I will remove;
But guard it most from any future love.
And when at last, in pity, you will dye,
I'le watch your Birth of Immortality:
Then, Turtle-like, I'le to my Mate repair;
And teach you your first flight in open Air.

(III; vol. II, p. 359)

It is the almost humorous prettiness of the image in the last two lines
that reminds the reader of Almeyda's speeches. The similarity is closer
in Berenice's later promise:

If I dye first I will—
Stop short of Heav'n, and wait you in a Cloud;
For fear we lose each other in the crowd.

(V; vol. II, p. 389)

Liberties of a rather different kind are taken in the other *Don Sebastian*
passages about heaven. Describing his efforts to kill Sebastian in battle,
his former friend, the renegade Dorax, makes the extravagant statement that he would willingly have been slain himself:

That, catching hold upon his flitting Ghost,
I might have robb'd him of his opening Heav'n;
And drag'd him down with me, spight of Predestination.

(I; vol. VI, p. 32)

An image of heaven as unreliable in its control of events occurs in one
of Almeyda's utterances, in the scene where the emperor orders
Sebastian to be taken away and killed:

But is there Heav'n, for I begin to doubt;
The Skyes are hush'd; no grumbling Thunders roul . . .
Eternal providence seems overwatch'd,
And with a slumb'ring Nod assents to Murther.

(III; vol. VI, p. 72)

The villainous Benducar attributes the uncertainty of his own position
before the insurrection to vacillation on the part of heaven; and the
vacillation is expressed in elementary terms:

This hour my Lott is weighing in the Scales,
And Heav'n, perhaps, is doubting what to do.

(IV; vol. VI, p. 85)

Immediately after Sebastian and Almeyda have consummated their love, and Sebastian is in a kind of stupor of bliss that unfits him for facing further crises, he uses an entertaining image of the sleepers awakened at the Last Judgement:

> Not the last sounding, cou'd surprize me more,
> That summons drowzy Mortals to their doom,
> When call'd in haste, they fumble for their Limbs,
> And tremble unprovided for their charge:
> My Sense has been so deeply plung'd in Joys,
> The Soul out-slept her hour . . .   (III; vol. VI, p. 68)

No one but Dryden would have represented so tragic a lover as virtually gorged with sexual delight; and the use of words like 'drowsy' and 'fumble' in the account of the last awakening is typical. He was fond of words like 'rubbish', 'luggage', 'grumble', 'puddle' and 'lump', introducing them often into passages otherwise quite elevated.[2] This speech is a curious licence, but one to which Dryden was accustomed; and, oddly, the gravity of the main action is not compromised by so near an approach to drollery.

At the end of the play, when Sebastian's union with Almeyda is discovered to have been incestuous, the thought of suicide seizes him; and he despises the slowness of heaven's dispensations:

> He [i.e. Dorax *alias* Alonzo] knows, that men, abandon'd of their hopes
> Shou'd ask no leave, nor stay for sueing out
> A tedious Writ of ease, from ling'ring Heav'n
> But help themselves, as timely as they cou'd,
> And teach the fates their duty.   (V; vol. 6, p. 125)

In Dorax's description of Sebastian's crime heaven is depicted as susceptible to nervous shock:

> . . . such a Crime,
> As frighten'd nature, made the Saints above
> Shake Heav'n's Eternal pavement with their trembling,
> To view that act . . .   (V. i; vol. VI, p. 126)

---

[2] Almeyda says to Sebastian:

> Leave then the luggage of your Fate behind . . .
>   (II; vol. VI, p. 58)

And later:

> Mine is a flame so holy and so clear,
> That the white taper leaves no soot behind . . .
>   (II; vol. VI, p. 60)

Both are quite serious speeches and occur in the most solemn part of the play, but we are conscious of a similarity to other speeches that are more openly amusing. It seems that the idea of heaven, for Dryden, had to have a twist, whatever the context.[3] With these examples in mind we may expect *The State of Innocence*, Dryden's operatic version of *Paradise Lost* not to disappoint us, and it does not. The twist may be only slight, his treatment of the theme of the work being generally dignified, but the choice of image in the following passage asserting the unshakeable consistency of heaven has the mark of Dryden upon it:

> Heav'n sleeps not; from one wink a breach wou'd be
> In the full Circle of Eternity.   (I; vol. III, p. 428)

And the archfiend sometimes sounds a blatant note. His revengeful intention is conveyed in language that makes it seem shockingly practicable:

> T'o'erleap the Etherial Fence, or if so high
> We cannot climb, to undermine his Skie,
> And blow him up, who justly Rules us now.
>   (I; vol. III, p. 427)

Dryden achieves one of his more obvious strokes of comedy in Satan's gibe at the relaxed discipline of the heavenly hosts:

> Seraph and Cherub careless of their charge,
> And wanton, in full ease now live at large;

---

[3] There is a faint hint of the subversive even in the splendid scene in *The Hind and the Panther* where the price of man's salvation is announced and the heavenly hosts seem for a moment to be at a loss:

> Millions of millions at a distance round,
> Silent the sacred Consistory crown'd,
> To hear what mercy mixt with justice cou'd propound.
> All prompt with eager pity, to fulfill
> The full extent of their Creatour's will:
> But when the stern conditions were declar'd,
> A mournfull whisper through the host was heard,
> And the whole hierarchy with heads hung down
> Submissively declin'd the pondrous proffer'd crown.
>   (Part II, ll. 501–09)

'Submissively declin'd' is a neat stroke. But the solemnity of the whole is somehow not impaired.

> Unguarded leave the passes of the Skie,
> And all dissolv'd, in Hallelujahs lie.
>
> (I; vol. III, p. 428)

More blatant still are the tirades of Maximin in *Tyrannic Love*. But here the theme is a pagan heaven, viewed by a brutish tyrant, and Dryden can go to extremes:

> What had the Gods to do with me or mine?
> Did I molest your Heav'n?—
> Why should you then make *Maximin* your Foe,
> Who paid you Tribute, which he need not do?
> Your Altars I with smoak of Gums did crown:
> For which you lean'd your hungry nostrils down.
> All daily gaping for my Incense there,
> More than your Sun could draw you in a year.
>
> (V; vol. II, p. 391)

Passages like these come within a category familiar to readers of Dryden: the disgruntled speech in which the ways of heaven are bluntly questioned. The best of Dryden's characters are liable, in moments of great vexation, to speak in this vein, but the villains do so more outrageously. The fact that Dryden can sometimes let himself go on this theme, obviously enjoying it, is relevant to our response to the milder and prettier images of heaven's foibles and aberrations.

Don Sebastian would not occur to one as the play most likely to abound in Dryden's characteristic wit; and, of course, it contains much less than *Aurengzebe*. The surprising thing is that it contains as much as it does. *Aurengzebe*, and the other works of the rhymed heroic play type, have no serious content. Everything is emotionally and morally neutral; the rhetoric can at any moment become absurd, and nothing is spoilt. But Dryden turned away from such writing after *Aurengzebe*, and *All for Love* (1677) marks a new beginning, a conversion to blank-verse tragedy. *All for Love* contains relatively little of his wit, but in *Don Sebastian*, for all its deeply felt seriousness, this subversive element found an outlet again. Is it in any way integrated with the rest of the play, or must we accept it as quite gratuitous? We must not expect too much, but nowhere is the integration more effective than in the character of Dorax who, as Sebastian's passionate enemy—formerly his dear friend—is important in the main action but is also, in his role as a sardonic *émigré*, a mouthpiece for witticisms in a caustic version of the

Dryden manner. In the early part of the play he describes the battle in which he had hoped to slay Sebastian, and makes contemptuous references to the worthlessness of his actual opponents:

> I spitted Frogs, I crush'd a heap of Emmets,
> A hundred of 'em to a single Soul,
> And that but scanty weight too . . .
>
> I kill'd not one that was his Makers Image;
> I met with none but vulgar two-leg'd Brutes . . .
>   (I; vol. VI, p. 31)

This echoes the note of several passages in *Aurengzebe*, for example, the exchange between the emperor and Morat, in which 'subjects' are dismissed as 'the Vulgar, a scarce animated Clod' and 'the little Emmets with the humane soul', and many other places in his works where what I have elsewhere termed 'body-soul' imagery is used. In earlier articles on Dryden, I have stressed the central importance of his comic or near-comic images of the creation or generation of the human species and of the relation between soul and body, in association with other images of similar tendency. Without saddling Dryden with a Hobbist or an anti-Hobbist position one can say that he enjoyed the distorting effect of current materialist views on the traditional conception of man's spiritual status. In many cases the grotesque image occurs in a reference to an absurd or villainous character, or in a speech where a personage of this kind expresses his depraved attitude to others or to life in general. The depraved attitude is also a humorous attitude, congenial to Dryden's temperament, and there can be no doubt of his peculiar pleasure in formulating it, in season and out of season. It is liable to occur, as a modifying element, in such Christian works as *The Hind and the Panther*. Since the creatures referred to in these images are either, by some aberration, the work of heaven, or specifically accounted for in another way, we have here an imaginative link with the heaven-images already noted. But the Dorax passages are too formidable to illustrate the generally entertaining quality of this vein of imagery in Dryden. He continues in this manner in a speech to the Mufti, where he attributes to him an insulting view of the laity:

> We know your thoughts of us that Laymen are
> Lag Souls, and rubbish of remaining Clay,
> Which Heav'n, grown weary of more perfect work,

> Set upright with a little puff of breath,
> And bid us pass for Men.   (II; vol. VI, p. 50)

His invectives against Mustapha and his rabble contain similar ingredients:

> Away ye skum,
> That still rise upmost when the Nation boyls:
> Ye mungrill work of Heav'n, with humane shapes,
> Not to be damn'd, or sav'd, but breath, and perish . . .
>   (IV; vol. VI, p. 105)

In studied contrast to this is the emperor's admiring comment on
Sebastian and Almeyda when they are brought in as prisoners:

> Ay; These look like the Workmanship of Heav'n;
> This is the porcelain clay of human kind,
> And therefore cast into these noble moulds.
>   (I; vol. VI, p. 35)

There are better passages of 'body-soul' imagery than these in
Aurengzebe, but *Don Sebastian* contains a superb one in which the
emperor confesses to a spiritually clogged condition such as only
Dryden's imagination could have conceived. Benducar explains it, in
terms no less characteristic, as the result of his gloating in advance over
the rape of Almeyda:

> EMPEROR: . . . A kind of weight hangs heavy at my Heart;
>   My flagging Soul flyes under her own pitch;
>   Like Fowl in air too damp, and lugs along,
>   As if she were a body in a body . . .
> BENDUCAR: . . . Your Soul has been beforehand with your Body,
>   And drunk so deep a Draught of promis'd bliss,
>   She slumbers o'er the Cup.   (IV; vol. VI, pp. 88–9)

Muley-Moluch is one of Dryden's grotesque villains, and the images
are therefore in order; that is, if we accept a grotesque villain in a play
with so serious a central theme. But there is an odd similarity between
this passage and that already quoted in which Sebastian, after his night
of love with Almeyda, confesses to being still very much under the
influence and generally stupefied:

> My Sense has been so deeply plung'd in Joys,
> The Soul out-slept her hour.
>   (III. i; vol. VI, p. 68)

Where sexual passion is concerned the good characters as well as the bad in Dryden may express themselves rather blatantly. If all his passages on this theme were stretched out in a line, from the most brutal to the most beautiful, the effect would not be so much one of sharp cleavages and gulfs of dissimilarity, as of gradation, with piquant, unexpected overlappings and incongruous groupings. Inflamed lust may have its lurid grandeur, heroic love its element of sensual stupefaction, and boundless bliss is an idea that can approach the brink of comedy. Aurengzebe, though impossibly correct in his dealings with his father and, in general, a most virtuous hero, is consumed with gluttonous sensuality towards Indamora:

> Oh, I could stifle you with eager haste!
> Devour your kisses with my hungry taste!
> Rush on you! eat you! wander o'r each part,
> Raving with pleasure, snatch you to my heart!
> Then hold you off, and gaze! then, with new rage
> Invade you, till my conscious Limbs presage
> Torrents of joy, which all their banks o'rflow!
> So lost, so blest, as I but then could know!
>> (IV; vol. IV, p. 141-2)

The Dryden who (as he admitted) enjoyed translating Lucretius' account of sex, took pleasure in associating his heroes with intercourses of peculiar turbulence and duration. Aurengzebe dreams of 'An Ages tumult of continu'd bliss'. Torrismond, in *The Spanish Friar*, envisages a similar prolongation of delight with Leonora:

> The sweetest, kindest, truest of her Sex,
> In whose Possession years roule round on years,
> And Joys in Circles meet new Joys again:
> Kisses, Embraces, Languishing, and Death,
> Still from each other, to each other move
> To crown the various seasons of our Love . . .
>> (IV. ii; vol. V, pp. 181-1)

Better known is Antony's rapturous description of his years of love with Cleopatra:

> One day past by, and nothing saw but Love;
> Another came, and still 'twas only Love;
> The Suns were weary'd out with looking on.
>> (II; vol. IV, p. 212)

In some of these passages the 'body-soul' theme can be sensed as implicit: man's nature submits, most willingly, to a shocking, amusing travesty of itself. But Dryden knew how to control these implications, or cut them out. In *All for Love*, where the accent is on simple heroic splendour, he usually excludes the subversive elements; though in the place where Antony imagines himself making love to Cleopatra in the face of the most august publicity, splendour and comedy are merged:

> Let *Caesar* spread his subtile Nets, like Vulcan;
> In thy embraces I would be beheld
> By Heav'n and Earth at once
>   . . . I would love on,
> With awful State, regardless of their frowns,
> As their superior god.
> There's no satiety of Love, in thee;
> Enjoy'd, thou still art new; perpetual Spring
> Is in thy armes . . .   (III; vol. IV, p. 217)

If Dryden were taxed for making Sebastian's love so sensual, a special justification could easily be found. Sebastian is a noble and tragic figure, but he is a sinner, and his night of love with Almeyda constitutes the crime for which he must later suffer. His bemused stupefaction could then be claimed as in keeping with the moral of the play. A similar comment could be made of his speech later in the action, when, in his despair, he refers to his 'glorious guilty night' in terms recalling one of Dryden's quasi-comic *motifs*: rational man's envy of the brutes:

> . . . one moment longer,
> And I shou'd break through Laws Divine and Humane
> And think'em Cobwebs, spred for little man,
> Which all the bulky herd of nature breaks.
> The vigorous young world was ignorant
> Of these restrictions . . .[4]   (V; vol. VI, p. 129)

It is a morally irresponsible speech and could be claimed as dramatically apt—that is, if questions of decorum preoccupy us. But with echoes of

[4] Cf. Arimant's complaint:
> Or make thy Orders with my reason sute,
> Or let me live by Sense a glorious Brute . . .
>   (*Aurengzebe*, III; vol. IV, p. 115)

other irresponsible speeches in our heads, speeches in which similar ideas are more wantonly or more elaborately developed, we may be less interested in dramatic justification than in the inveterate Dryden note. Dryden's plays are full of pleasing speeches in which depravity finds arguments for itself. Nourmahal's opulent appeal to her stepson, Aurengzebe, with whom she is infatuated, comes to mind at this point:

> And why this niceness to that pleasure shown,
> Where Nature sums up all her joys in one;
> Gives all she can, and, labouring still to give,
> Makes it so great, we can but taste and live:
> So fills the Senses, that the Soul seems fled,
> And thought it self does, for the time, lie dead.
>   (IV; vol. IV, p. 131)

Dryden liked the theme of incest, as may be gathered from his handling of the story of Cinyras and Myrrha in Ovid's *Metamorphoses*.

Muley-Moluch's speeches of lust recall the 'illustrious depravity' of the tyrants in earlier plays. There are some powerful images of rape, which is his sole preoccupation:

> . . . rugged Lions love,
> And grapple, and compel their savage Dames.
>   (II; vol. VI, p. 56)

In one of his portentous threats to Almeyda he declares that he

> Wou'd hunt thee bare-foot, in the mid-day Sun,
> Through the parch'd Desarts, and the scorching Sands,
> T' enjoy thy Love, and once enjoy'd to kill thee.
>   (II; vol. VI, p. 57)

Later he promises to 'engender poison' with her:

> Joyn Hate with Hate, add Venom to the Birth;
> Our Off-spring, like the seed of Dragon's Teeth,
> Shall issue arm'd, and fight themselves to death.[5]
>   (II; vol. VI, p. 57)

---

[5] It is characteristic of Dryden that Lucifer, in *The State of Innocence*, should entertain the thought of possessing Eve:

> I could (so variously my passions move)
> Enjoy and blast her in the act of love.
>   (III; vol. III, p. 439)

It was hardly in Dryden's nature to create a villain who was not comic.
Muley-Moluch is in the tradition of Maximin, which goes back
through Marlowe's Barabbas to the Herods of the medieval stage.
There is, of course, nothing in *Don Sebastian* quite on the scale of
Maximin's more absurd tirades ('Free-will's a cheat in any one but me'
or 'What! miracles, the tricks of Heaven, to me?') or the intemperate
outbursts of Morat and the emperor in *Aurengzebe*. But for a tyrant in
a solemn tragedy Muley-Moluch goes quite a long way in this direction.

In speeches expressing or flattering the insolence of despots Dryden,
naturally, draws upon the political theories of the century, and he
travesties them. His tyrants, after all, belong to Mexico, ancient Rome,
India or Barbary, not seventeenth-century England, so any licence is
permissible. They are as inflated with egoism as his rhetoric and wit can
make them. One of his habits is to give to depraved characters images
of undeserved dignity; or, rather, to modify a dignified image so that
it expresses a brutal or empty pomp. He had special, ominous uses for
images that, in the poetry of other writers, would have conferred
honour upon the characters associated with them. For example, an
ancient tree sometimes occurs as an image of power or regal sway, but
with sinister or ridiculous associations. In one of Morat's invectives
against his father, the emperor, trees are poisonous:

> Could you shed venom from your reverend shade,
> Like Trees, beneath whose arms 'tis death to sleep.[6]
> > (*Aurengzebe*, IV; vol. IV, p. 137)

An oak image in *Don Sebastian* conveys the idea of brute unresponsive-
ness. Muley-Moluch is vindicating unyielding tyranny ('What's
Royalty, but pow'r to please my self?'):

> Weak Princes flatter when they want the power
> To curb their People; tender Plants must bend:
> But when a Government is grown to strength,
> Like some old Oak, rough with its armed Bark,

---

[6] Charinus, Maximin's son, views the encroachments of Porphyrius in similar
terms:

> He blasts my early Honour in the bud,
> Like some tall Tree the Monster of the Wood:
> O're-shading all which under him would grow,
> He sheds his venim on the Plants below.
> > (*Tyrannic Love*, I; vol. II, p. 338)

It yields not to the tug, but only nods,
And turns to sullen State.[7]   (II; vol. VI, p. 46)

The image of a river of blood in association with the exploits of the ambitious appears in several places. The three passages that follow are from works performed in 1665, 1675 and 1689 respectively, and are remarkably similar in view of these intervals of time. The first, from *The Indian Emperor*, occurs in a smart, fairly prolonged debate between Cortez and the Mexican ladies on the theme of love and honour:

> CYDARIA: Lay down that burden if it painful grow;
>   You'l find, without it, Love will lighter go.
> CORTEZ: Honour, once lost, is never to be found.
> ALIBECH: Perhaps he looks to have both passions Crown'd:
>   First dye his Honour in a Purple Flood,
>   Then Court the Daughter in the Father's Blood.
>   (II; vol. I, p. 292)

The turn of imagery ironically understates the unpleasant implications, and indeed gives the proposed behaviour of the hero a pretence of decorum. The passage in *Aurengzebe* refers to the warfare between the four princes, sons of the emperor:

> *Indus* and *Ganges*, our wide Empires Bounds,
> Swell'd their dy'd Currents with their Native's wounds:
> Each purple River winding, as he runs,
> His bloudy arms about his slaughter'd Sons.
>   (I; vol. IV, p. 89)

In both cases the heroic couplet helps to formalise the shocking scene. In fact, it is so formalised as not to be a human scene at all; and this is in keeping with the nature of the rhymed heroic plays, as works superbly empty of human feeling. But the splendid neutrality of the imagery does operate, in some measure, as a moral preservative. The exclusion of human feeling is stylistically so absolute as to invite recognition as such. Dryden handles the theme with great ease. His style is discreet and florid at the same time, and puts a smooth surface on the ferocities of this exotic world. With a slight modification the images

----

[7] He reminds one a little of Shadwell:

> Thoughtless as Monarch Oakes, that shade the plain,
> And, spread in solemn state, supinely reign.
>   (*MacFlecknoe*, ll. 27–8)

could become comic. The parallel passage on the first page of *Don Sebastian* lacks the neatness and stylistic detachment of its predecessors, not being in couplets, but there is an echo of the same effect. The lurid, as in the other examples, becomes rhetorically pleasing; it is on its way to being amusing; and this prepares us for later speeches in which there will be a comic twist:

> Thus, *Moluch*, still the Favourite of Fate
> Swims in a sanguine torrent to the Throne.
> As if our Prophet only work'd for him . . .
>
> (I; vol. VI, p. 29)

The comic twist *is* present in the lines, too august to be true, in which Benducar reassures Muley-Moluch that his secret thoughts (that is, his lust for Almeyda) have not been detected:

> EMPEROR: And think'st thou not it was discover'd?
> BENDUCAR: No.
> The thoughts of Kings are like religious Groves,
> The Walks of muffled Gods: Sacred retreat,
> Where none but whom they please t'admit, approach.
>
> (II; vol. VI, p. 45)

Dryden's images of fire operating upon metal, used frequently to express some aspect of a strong man, hero or tyrant, show some notable similarities and variations. The savage Morat admits the effect of love on his metallic nature:

> Love softens me; and blows up fires, which pass
> Through my tough heart, and melt the stubborn Mass.
>
> (V; vol. IV, p. 147)

And Almanzor, hitherto a stranger to this sentiment, acknowledges that Almahide has caused a change in him:

> There's something noble lab'ring in my brest:
> This raging fire which through the Mass does move,
> Shall purge my dross, and shall refine my Love.
>
> (*Conquest of G.*, *Pt. I*, III; vol. III, p. 56)

Maximin makes a similar confession about the effect upon him of St. Catharine:

> This Iron heart, which no impression took,
> From Wars, melts down, and runs, if she but look . . .
>
> (III; vol. II, p. 352)

But Muley-Moluch is tougher in the scene where Almeyda, pleading for Sebastian's life, clutches his knees. He enjoys the contact, but the effect on *his* metallic nature does not help her cause:

> A secret pleasure trickles through my Veins:
> It works about the inlets of my Soul!
> To feel thy touch; and pity tempts the pass;
> But the tough mettle of my heart resists;
> 'Tis warm'd with the soft fire, not melted down.
>
> (III; vol. VI, p. 71)

To be hugged by Almeyda, and see Sebastian die, will be a double pleasure. A rather different metal image was used in the dying speech of Montezuma:

> Still less and less my boyling Spirits flow;
> And I grow stiff as cooling Mettals do . . .
>
> (*Indian Emp.*, V; vol. I, p. 334)

In any Dryden play where priests appear we can be sure that there will be some anti-clerical talk. Serapion's prophetic speech in the first Act of *All for Love* is greeted by Alexas as

> A foolish Dream,
> Bred from the fumes of indigested Feasts
> And holy Luxury.   (I; vol. IV, p. 192)

And, later in the play, when he enters ready to utter a final pronouncement of doom, Alexas refers to him as the 'holy Coward'. Dominic in *The Spanish Friar*, the 'holy Stallion', is an obvious anti-clerical creation. The 'puffing friar' who marries Sebastian and Almeyda is described in comic terms and, after he is no longer needed, he departs with a 'holy leer'. The Mufti is ridiculed by the emperor and by Dorax. The emperor calls him a 'druggerman [i.e. dragoman] of heaven', commends him satirically for his 'religious ruddy countenance', and demands a truce to fasting; while Dorax calls him a 'heavenly demogogue', and insults him in witty speeches of considerable elaboration, chiefly on the subject of his political meddling:

> Content you with monopolizing Heav'n,
> And let this little hanging Ball alone;
> For give you but a foot of Conscience there
> And you, like *Archimedes*, toss the Globe.
>
> (II; vol. VI, p. 50)

It is evident that, apart from the somewhat elementary comic sub-plot in prose, *Don Sebastian* contains a considerable range of ingredients that do not contribute to the effect of tragedy and moral seriousness. Can they be related to the tone of the main theme? This question was asked earlier. The answer lies partly in one of Dryden's most interesting qualities as a poet: his capacity to achieve occasionally an unequivocal seriousness without actually throwing off the imaginative equipment that is elsewhere chiefly active in the modifying or subversion of seriousness. The most solemn passages in *Don Sebastian* have a toughness in their gravity, a sturdy freedom from pretence, that makes them of a piece with the wittier parts of the play. How finely Sebastian states the Christian view of suicide! Yet he does not state it with any more Christian acceptance or understanding than one would expect of a Dryden hero. The attitude is stoical, almost phlegmatic:

> *Brutus* and *Cato* might discharge their Souls,
> And give'em Furlo's for another World:
> But we, like Centry's, are oblig'd to stand
> In starless Nights, and wait the pointed hour.
>
> (II; vol. VI, p. 59)

With a slight change in diction or imagery, such as one might almost have expected, the speech could have taken its place among those referred to earlier: that is, the disgruntled utterances of sympathetic characters to whom the laws of the universe seem a little unreasonable. In the splendid scene of reconciliation between Dorax (the 'Lucifer' figure in Bruce King's interpretation) and Sebastian, there is no mitigation of the rougher and harsher aspects of the renegade's nature, penetrated to the heart though he is with the recognition of his failure. Sebastian describes how Henriquez, the hated rival, met his end:

> SEBASTIAN: . . . He dy'd in Fight:
> Fought next my person; as in Consort fought:
> Kept pace for pace, and blow for every blow;
> Save when he heav'd his Shield in my defence;
> And on his naked side receiv'd my wound.
> Then, when he could no more, he fell at once:
> But rowl'd his falling body cross their way;
> And made a Bulwark of it for his Prince.
> DORAX: I never can forgive him such a death!
> . . . .

I should have fallen by *Sebastian's* side.
My Corps had been the Bulwark of my King.
His glorious end was a patch'd work of fate,
Ill sorted with a soft effeminate life;
It suited better with my life than his:
So to have dy'd, mine had been of a piece,
Spent in your service, dying at your feet.
                              (IV; vol. VI, pp. 110–11)

The harshness of Dorax, which makes him formidable in invective, is also part of his tragedy. Even when he intervenes later to save Sebastian from self-murder, he has to do it harshly: he has no other manner. Against this background of an unfortunate temperament expressing itself in unhappy decisions, his repentance and reconciliation with Sebastian are most moving. Such scenes are rare in dramatic literature, and *Don Sebastian* achieves a high position largely on the strength of it. It would be too much to claim for Dryden that the play is a dramatic unity, and that its wit and imagery are assimilated throughout to its dramatic purpose. Dryden as a dramatist is nearly always working on two levels. The public, theatrical side of his task, which he performs effectively but often without inspiration, is not wholly wedded to the more private poetic or satirical side. But *Don Sebastian* has another kind of unity, such as we find in works like *The Hind and the Panther*. The mixture of elements, whatever it may or may not achieve dramatically, expresses Dryden; and for that reason it is satisfying. What may seem incongruous and therefore out of keeping from one point of view is right from another, because delight in incongruity is essential to Dryden. When his sense of incongruity cuts across the particular decorum expected of the heroic or the tragic the modern reader can afford to write off the dramatist in favour of the poet and wit.

Note

Allardyce Nicoll's *History of English Drama*, vol. I (1955), is the standard work on theatres and theatre practices in the Restoration; there are sections on the audience, scenery and actors and actresses, and appendices give details of individual theatres and reprint important documents illustrating the history of the stage.

Two books by Montague Summers should also be consulted, *The Restoration Theatre* (1934) and *The Playhouse of Pepys* (1935), and L. Hotson's *The Commonwealth and Restoration Stage* (1928). The rules of acting associated with Betterton were set forth in *The History of the English Stage from the Restoration to the Present Time . . . Compiled from the Papers of T. Betterton by E. Curll* (1741); but this should perhaps be cautiously considered as a retrospective view of Betterton's art, rather than a sure proof of common practice; its author was probably Curll or William Oldys. Important extracts from this work together with more than thirty other contemporary accounts of plays in performance during the Restoration will be found in A. M. Nagler, *A Source Book in Theatrical History* (1952 and 1959).

A new and full record of dramatic performances is due to appear in Part I of *The London Stage*, ed. E. L. Avery.

Richard Southern's *Changeable Scenery* (1952) records and explains the Restoration practices.

J. H. Wilson, *All the King's Ladies* (1958), is an account of the actresses of the period.

VIII

Restoration Acting

HUGH HUNT

*

THE patents granted by the king to Thomas Killigrew and Sir William Davenant in 1660 stipulated that not only should they be allowed to build their own playhouses and form their own companies, but they should henceforth only permit women to play women's parts to the end that plays might 'be esteemed not only harmless delights but useful and instructive representations of human life'.

The high hopes expressed in the Royal Warrants were realised in a somewhat ironic sense. One wonders whether the official who drew them up, knowing the frailty of his royal master, had his tongue in his cheek. But the introduction of actresses in the place of boy actors together with the introduction of movable scenery were the two most significant conventions adopted by the resurrected theatres and were to have far-reaching results on the style of performance. Neither of these conventions can strictly be called novelties to the English stage. Scenic elements, housed behind proscenium frames together with machines to change them, had graced with elaborate splendour the court masques devised by Inigo Jones. French acting companies employing actresses had been seen on the public stages in the pre-Commonwealth period, and that alliterative Puritan, William Prynne, reported with pleasure that 'they were hissed, hooted, and pippin-pelted off the stage'. Even in the dark years of the Puritan Commonwealth, Sir William Davenant had prevailed on the authorities to allow him to present private performances of opera, and in *The Siege of Rhodes* (1656) both an actress and scenery made their appearance. The significance of the adoption of these two conventions by the acting companies licensed by Charles II lies in the fact that they were adopted as a rule and not as a rarity.

The time was ripe for the substitution of actresses for boy actors.

The voice of Puritanism was temporarily muffled; feminism both in costume and social influence had never achieved such freedom, and a considerable percentage of the new audience had grown accustomed to seeing actresses in the French theatre during the exile of the king. The new actresses had, however, to be selected and trained for the stage. And, although it seems likely that the first professional British actress may have made her appearance as early as November or December 1660, in the part of Desdemona, it was some years before the full influence of women made itself felt. But even in the earliest days when the newcomers to the stage had little more than their youth and beauty to rely on, it is clear that their impact on the public was considerable. The play-going public during the years following the emancipation from Puritanism was a minute fraction of society confined almost entirely to those who frequented the court with an occasional country cousin up for a visit to town and, of course, the inevitable prostitutes, or vizard-masks, who plied their trade in the galleries and boxes. The majority of the merchant classes, even if they were of the Royalist party, were nervous of frequenting this exotic and unfamiliar meeting place of fashionable society with its strange dress and manners and its disdainful attitude to the homely citizens. This small, exclusive audience would have been incapable of supporting the two patent playhouses had there not been a strong attraction to induce them to do so. One of those inducements was the appearance of actresses. It is, therefore, not to be wondered at that the companies exploited the charms of their female recruits to the full, and exercised the greatest care in their selection; not without success both with regard to their future histrionic powers and to their immediate physical attractions.

The problem of recruitment must have been considerable. First, because none of the candidates had previous experience of acting; not even in an amateur capacity. Secondly, because no lady of education and breeding would deign to accept a job on the stage. This entailed training the raw recruits in manners, deportment and elocution in order to meet the demands of acting parts that were almost exclusively aristocratic. From the little that is known of the family or social origins of the first actresses, it would seem that the principle was to choose them from an impecunious middle stratum of society which might be expected to have some pretensions to literacy and refinement, such as the daughter of a 'decayed knight', like Charlotte Butler, or of a notary, like Mrs. Shadwell, or Mrs. Pepys' personal maid, whose mother was a widow with genteel connections. Some may have been gentlemen's bastards, like Moll Davis, or orphans, like Mrs. Barry who, having been brought up in the household of Sir William Davenant, would have been steeped in the traditions of the stage. Probably the exceptions were the totally illiterate cockney wenches, like Nell Gwynn. But there were other attributes which the new managers must have looked for in making their selection. Little time was available for preliminary training; once the first actresses had appeared on the stage to the considerable delight of spectators like Pepys, it was clearly impossible to carry on with the boy actors without considerable losses at the box office. Consequently, quickness of wit, a good sense of mimicry, an immediately engaging manner and a pert and impudent approach could do much to compensate for inexperience. It is precisely these characteristics which Nell Gwynn, Moll Davis and many of their sisterhood must have possessed, that appear most frequently in the parts written for young ladies of Restoration comedy. It must not be forgotten that the dramatists of the new age had only two companies to whom they could sell their plays; indeed from 1682 to 1695, during which period the two theatres were amalgamated, there was only one. As a result playwrights were forced to write plays with the particular characteristics of the actors and actresses in mind, and this gave rise to a certain similarity of characterisation both in tragedy and in comedy throughout the period. This tendency was emphasised by the audience's attitude towards the players. Association between the private life of the players and their stage impersonations became inevitable in so small a world of theatre; doubly inevitable when the private lives of the players—more especially of the actresses—were so intimately entangled with those of the audience.

As a result of the success of the new actresses—success which was not only dependent on the possession of histrionic talents—the career of an actress became attractive to ladies whose main concern was the acquisition of a rich husband or 'keeper'. Husbands were hard to obtain in a society which placed greater emphasis on social and financial advantages in matrimonial arrangements than on mutual affection, but potential 'keepers' abounded. The determined and skilful female practitioners of this age-old profession could beguile the lecherous admirers who thronged the green rooms and wings into providing handsome settlements. The success of Mrs. Davenport who, after some difficulties and an irregular marriage ceremony, managed to persuade Parliament into forcing the Earl of Oxford in 1662 into granting her a handsome pension, was more than matched in subsequent years by a whole series of successes of this kind with the most renowned and powerful of the land, culminating in the triumphs of Moll Davis and Nell Gwynn with the king himself. Whilst it can be rightly said that such affairs had nothing to do with theatrical art, they had an important bearing on the whole attitude of the audience towards the theatre and of the theatrical companies towards their public. There is no need to pursue the salacious stories of the lives of most, though not all, of the actresses; we can accept the ample evidence that the tiring rooms of the playhouses were commonly used to pave the way for future adventures.

The clinching of an affair backstage was amply prepared for on the stage, where sex-stimulation was incorporated not only into the texts of the plays, but in the acting style itself. Bawdry and sensual situations were nothing new to English drama; the plays of the Jacobean and Carolean stages had exploited every aspect of situations which might be expected to stimulate the jaded palates of their patrons. What was new was the realism given to sensuality by the appearance of real women on the stage. Pepys had already seen *The Scornful Lady* by Beaumont and Fletcher with a boy player in the lady's part, but when in 1661 he saw it again 'now done by a woman', he recorded with delight that it 'makes the play much better than ever it did to me' (*Diary*, 12 Feb., 1661).

This new dimension of sensual realism which was now available to the dramatist allowed him greater freedom to develop situations which had hitherto been denied him. As a result, the Restoration drama was able to explore the whole territory of sex with far greater realism than had been possible with a 'squeaking boy' to shatter the illusion. It was an opportunity the dramatists, more especially in their comedies, were not slow to seize upon. Every opportunity was taken to display the beguiling ways of the female; sex-play was openly favoured to an extent which would make even a modern audience blush, and the female form was exhibited for the deliberate purpose of provocation. The costume of the early Restoration period was particularly suited for exhibiting the upper part of what Steele later called 'the structure of the fair sex', but not only could the stage display the upper part, it could also display the lower part as well. The old plays, that had perforce to fill out the repertoire of the early Restoration theatres, contained many situations in which a girl was disguised as a boy. This was a useful convention in the pre-Restoration period to overcome the unreality of the boy player in female attire. On the Restoration stage the tables were turned, and instead of a boy, pretending to be a girl, dressed as a boy, a real girl was dressed as a boy. To a contemporary audience the display of a woman's legs from the knee downwards provides no particular 'kick'; to the Restoration gallants the public display of a woman's calf and ankle was little less than a 'bombshell'.

In all our high-flown talk about style in the theatre we are inclined to ignore that one of the most potent forces of theatrical entertainment is the influence of sex in arousing our sympathies and promoting our involvement. The question of what can be accepted as art and what is purely vulgar is a matter of taste, and taste can change from age to age; but there can be no denial that much of what took place on the Restoration stage and was an integral part of theatrical style is, to our taste, pure vulgarity.

The exploitation of sex through the development of the 'breeches parts', as the male impersonations were called, was carried to extremes. Not only did the new dramatists write 'breeches parts' into their plays, but the managers took every opportunity to introduce them into prologues, jigs and epilogues, or to cast women in men's parts, like the celebrated Peg Woffington as Sir Harry Wildair, and on more than one occasion whole plays were performed by women. All this disguising may seem to us to be pure artifice unrelated to reality, but in fact in this stylistic convention as in others the Restoration stage was merely a mirror of the practices of society. The ladies of Charles's court frequently dressed up as men for mad-cap escapades. Fashionable ladies would adopt male disguise for visiting their lovers, and even the bourgeois Pepys records a hilarious party at which he and two of his male guests dressed as women and his wife's maid 'put on a suit of Tom's like a boy, and mighty mirth we had'.

The pursuit of sex which dominated the stage was followed with equal vigour in the auditorium, where the courtesans and common whores plied their trade with such open impudence and in such numbers that it was almost impossible for a virtuous woman to visit the playhouse without her intentions being suspect. What happened behind the scenes, on the stage, and in the auditorium was no different from what happened in the Mall, in the parks, in the coffee-houses and in the court itself. After twenty years of sexual repression, during which the natural instincts of men and women had been hypocritically cloaked under the saintly garb of Puritanism, human instincts had broken out in a riot of sensuality, which has known no parallel in our social history. The society that patronised the playhouses was one in which extra-marital sex relations were normal behaviour. Women had become as free in their relations as men and had achieved, by means of sexual freedom, a degree of equality which was not to be repeated until the 1920's.

The Comedy of Sex, which has been more genteelly called the Comedy of Manners, and which, almost without exception, is the theme of all Restoration comedy from Dryden to Farquhar, was played in a realistic style, not an artificial one. This does not mean that artifice was not an important aspect of acting as it was of life: but both the comedies and their acting were, within the given conventions of Restoration stage-craft, imitations of life; they were not artificial inventions. What was represented on the stage, however flagrant it may seem to us today, was no exaggeration of what happened in life—albeit in the life of a very small section of society. Nor was the wit, the repartee, the precision of language and the elegance of manners that expressed this display of sex an exaggeration of reality. The society that frequented the playhouses and whose style of life was mirrored in the comedies was, as we have said, a court society many members of which had absorbed by personal contact something of the elegance and wit of the French salons where precious language, repartee and wit were essential qualifications for admission. This Parisian aristocratic style of address with its particular code of subject matter and its emphasis on the niceties of phrasing and pronunciation was duly anglicised without losing much of its gallic gallantry and became the fashionable language of British upper-class society. The high-flown mode of address is displayed by Melantha in *Marriage à la Mode* in her constant search for new words to furnish her daily conversation; for, as she says 'Let me die, if I have not run the risk already, to speak like one of the vulgar . . .' or in its more gallicised form in the conversation of Monsieur de Paris in *The Gentleman Dancing Master* who scorns the plain-speaking Englishman who cannot 'swear a *French* Oatè, nor use the polite *French* word in his Conversation . . . but speaks base good *Englis*, with the commune homebred pronunciation'. As Dryden contends repartee is the charm of conversation, and the soul of comedy. To acquire this conversational art became the necessary sign of good breeding. So what the audience saw and heard on the stage in this Comedy of Sex was life as it was—a mirror held up to nature.

It is our failure today to recognise this reality of Restoration style, or else our prudery, which leads us to shy away from it. It was this sort of whitewashing attitude that led Lamb in the *Essays of Elia* to conclude that Restoration comedies were a 'fairy land'—'the Utopia of gallantry'—and to state that he could 'never connect those sports of a witty fancy in any shape' . . . with an 'imitation in real life'. It is an attitude that has led some directors to cloak their productions with an air of unreality in which scenery, costumes, fans and snuff-boxes assume such importance that reality is overlooked. To a great extent this reality of style was brought about by the introduction of actresses 'to the end that plays might be esteemed . . . useful and instructive representations of human life'; for it was the actresses who were not only largely responsible for reviving the popularity of the theatre, but who gave to the style of acting a reality which it had never acquired before.

*   *   *

Just as the novelty of the actress was filtered through to the public playhouses of the Restoration from the private playhouses of the Carolean stages by way of Davenant's opera, *The Siege of Rhodes*, so, too, was the novelty of 'scenes'. In Rutland House, the private residence of Sir William Davenant, the first English opera was presented in the month of September 1656; for political reasons it was announced as 'A Representation by the Art of Prospective in Scenes, and the Story sung in Recitative Musick'. The scenes framed by a frontispiece, or proscenium arch, were painted by John Webb, the pupil and collaborator of Inigo Jones, who was later to be employed in the Restoration playhouses. Thus the stream of theatrical style, both with regard to the employment of actresses and the use of scenes, flowed directly from the court masques of the pre-Restoration stage through the Commonwealth 'Representations' to the public theatres of 1660. Whatever elaborations of machinery and refinements of scenic techniques may have been later introduced from France, it was the English traditions themselves which led directly to these novelties on our public stages.

To call the new scenery realistic, as we understand the term today, would be ludicrous. The scenes themselves which were formed by the bringing together of two painted canvas flats or shutters running in grooves were framed by side wings and borders. They were, in fact flat pictures or panoramas on which rooms, prisons, streets, landscapes and, when occasion demanded it, battles and crowds were painted. Richard Southern, whose book *Changeable Scenery* is a mine of information on this subject, concludes that there were four grooves carrying the shutter-like scenes in the two fully developed Restoration playhouses. These grooves were spaced so as to allow room between each set of scenes for setting furniture and for assembling actors in a tableau, such as a company assembled round a dining table. By drawing the two halves of the scene apart such discoveries were revealed against the succeeding scene. Not all these 'discoveries' were flat paintings running in grooves; 'relieve' scenes, consisting of cut-out ground-rows set one behind the other, provided vistas extending to a back-scene which was set up in a recess behind the space occupied by the grooves themselves, thus giving an illusion of great depth to the scenic area. A distant vista could also be revealed by drawing aside the upper portions of a scene which, when painted as a cloud formation, could discover succeeding cut-outs of billowing clouds terminating in a distant vision of an enthroned deity, or a heaven filled with allegorical figures.

Such elaborate scenic displays together with the use of traps in the stage floor to bring up set-pieces from below or to provide descents into the nether regions, as well as flying devices, added greatly to the spectacle, but can hardly be said to have contributed to realism in the naturalistic sense; nor were they so intended.

Just as the charms of the actresses were exploited to induce the small audience to make frequent visits to the theatre, so were the spectacular scenes. Rivalry between the two patent playhouses in scenic 'shows' was intense, and on more than one occasion an eye-catching spectacle in one playhouse resulted in the emptying of the other. In opera, tragedy and heroic plays, the scenes were not only elaborate and, consequently, expensive (the scenes of one opera alone cost £800—a considerable sum), they must have been, on occasions, extremely beautiful. In Act V of Shadwell's opera, *Psyche*, the scene changes to a heaven:

'In the highest part is the Palace of *Jupiter*; the Columns and all the Ornaments of it of Gold. The lower part is all fill'd with *Angels* and *Cupids*, with a round open *Temple* in the midst of it. This *Temple* is just before the *Sun*, whose Beams break fiercely through it in divers places: Below the Heav'ns, several Semi-circular Clouds, of the breadth of the whole House, descend. In these Clouds sit the

Musicians, richly Habited. On the front-Cloud sits *Apollo* alone. While the Musicians are descending, they play a *Symphony* till *Apollo* begins, and sings.

The full flavour of Baroque taste bursts forth in this description.

Spectacular scenery, however, was generally confined to operas, tragedies and heroic plays; comedies and revivals of pre-Restoration plays were normally performed in whatever scenery the theatres possessed. This was hardly surprising since a failure might only run one night, and even a success could not be expected to run for more than eight to ten performances in a season. This limitation of the available scenery was a factor to be taken into account by the author of a comedy and affected the style in which plays were conceived and constructed. It cannot, then, be argued that spectacular or original scenery was characteristic of Restoration staging. What was characteristic, and is highly important from the point of view of contemporary staging, was the relation of the scenery to the action.

Before considering this relationship a word must be said about the use of the front curtain and of the all-important forestage area.

Apart from some early experiments with painted curtains in the pre-Commonwealth masques, a front curtain was unknown in British theatrical tradition. To the mind of the Restoration player the front curtain, which he inherited from the French and Italian theatres, was merely a cover for the stage; the raising of which was the signal for the play to commence. It was not used to conceal changes of scenery, nor to denote a passage of time, nor to provide full-stops in the action. Once raised the curtain did not fall again until the epilogue had been spoken. Exceptions to this rule were sometimes made in opera which was derived directly from the continental traditions, but the dropping of the curtain during a play was, I suggest, considered in very much the same way as the French neo-classical theatre regarded a breach in the rules of the unities of action, time and place—it was bad stage-craft. The Earl of Orrery, who used the front curtain for the discovery of tableaux in some of his plays, was severely satirised for this practice by Buckingham in *The Rehearsal*. This deliberate refusal to punctuate the action by using the front curtain was not merely a quaint convention, nor was it due to failure to realise its possibilities as a means of concealing a scene-change. It would be ridiculous to suggest that the players were too stupid not to realise that the use of the curtain for this purpose in the operas might also serve for the same purpose in the plays. The point that the players were making in refusing to use the curtain, as we use it today, was a deliberate stylistic point; namely that the action of a play is a continuous action which must flow onwards without breaks within each act in exactly the same way as it did on the open stage of the Elizabethan period, or as it does in the cinema. Scene changes, then, had to take place within sight of the audience and were not allowed to halt the action.

The method the players employed was the use of the sliding scenes operating in the grooves, and this simple and swift way of changing the location could not only take place within full view, but its operation provided, just as it does in a pantomime transformation scene, an important part of the entertainment. Apart from the visual entertainment provided by this 'play of the moving scenery', the more important stylistic point of the flow of the action was emphasised by the use of the forestage and its doors.

The Restoration forestage, as shown in Wren's design for the second Theatre Royal, which took the place of the former building destroyed by fire in 1672, was serviced by two doors on each side. There is evidence that during the early part of the period there were three doors a side leading on to the forestage. These doors were the main entrances to the stage, and entry through the scenes was sufficiently rare to require a stage-direction to this effect to be included in the prompter's script. The size of the forestage itself, which in Wren's design is seventeen feet deep, was almost equal to the entire area that lay behind the proscenium arch and which housed the scenery and the grooves. Thus the stage was divided into two areas, the one serving the scenery and the other the action. The action area, or forestage, was not only provided with its own entrances, but also with its own lighting system. The footlights, or 'floats', which could be raised or lowered in a trough located in the front of the forestage to control their intensity, were the main source for lighting the actors' faces. Chandeliers located above the forestage, or within the scenic area, provided supplementary lighting, but were by themselves inadequate for displaying facial mimicry. Similarly any candles or oil lamps located in the wings of the scenic area were only adequate for lighting the scenery. Consequently almost the whole action of the play took place on the forestage, and when the action required that actors be discovered within the scenic area at the drawing apart of the sliding scenes, a stage-direction usually bids them 'to come forward'. The action area was, like the Elizabethan platform stage, a neutral area; it was not considered necessary for an actor to leave this area if the action required him to be present at the end of one scene and also at the beginning of the next one. Instead of the actor leaving the room, the room left the actor, revealing him in a new location. In these cases the stage direction '*manet*' usually takes the place of the familiar '*exit*'.

The flexibility provided by the sliding scenes behind the proscenium arch and the neutral acting area in front of it offered the playwright far greater opportunities to manœuvre his action through a variety of locations without overtaxing the imagination of his audience than either the older conventions of the Elizabethan stage or our contemporary proscenium stage when it is used to house box-settings. From the point of view of our contemporary productions of Restoration plays the vital point is to preserve this flexibility and to maintain the continuous flow of the action; both are an integral part of the style of the plays themselves. Too often contemporary directors either destroy the unity of each act by breaking it up into a sequence of heavily built scenes, separated from each other by pauses filled out with recorded music; or—what is no less harmful—adapt the text so as to allow a variety of locations to be played in the same set. To preserve the stylistic requirements of the 'play of the moving scenery' and its relation to the action we do not, of course, have to reproduce the conventions of grooves and sliding scenes. The convention of changing the scenery in view of the audience by means of modern stage-devices is now a commonplace in Shakespearian productions, and we have discarded our reliance on naturalistic box-settings. But wherever possible the contemporary director should, I think, construct or make use of a forestage and doors if he is to recapture the flavour of the acting style in which the play was intended to be performed.

*   *   *

The principles of the acting style were taught in the 'nurseries', or acting schools, maintained by the two acting companies. In these the older actors were the tutors, and Betterton himself was awarded fifty guineas a year for this work. Private coaching was also given, and John Wilmot, Earl of Rochester, is said to have transformed Elizabeth Barry in six months of intensive training from a complete failure who was three times rejected by the Duke's Company into one of the greatest actresses of her age. Needless to add that in the course of training he is also said to have made her his mistress.

The basic training of a Restoration player covered speech, singing, dancing, stance, gesture and walking; all were equally important. Walking or standing on the stage may seem to the layman to require no training, but to the acting student this often proves the most difficult lesson to master. Never more so than to the young players of the Restoration who had to learn all the arts of deportment in order to emulate a society in which the upper classes were immediately recognisable by a strict code of mannerisms. These mannerisms included the mincing steps, later known as the stage 'strut', the typical stance with chest thrust forward and hips forced back, the prescribed elegancies of the curtsy and the bow, the manipulation of the long tragedienne's train, usually held up by a page, the various symbolic uses of the fan, the veiled looks and languid glances, or 'doux yeux', which signalled the lover, and the 'black disorder'd Look' of the villain.

The acme of theatrical style was centred in tragic acting. Here the set of rules attributed to Betterton emphasise the importance placed on control of the voice, and the tragedian's success was judged in particular by his ability to rouse enthusiasm through the delivery of the great tirades, commonly known as 'rants'. Musical speech was assiduously cultivated, and was generally known as the 'heroic tone'. This tone, or series of tones, was codified in Betterton's rules which had to be learned by rote. The young player had to learn to

express love by a gay, soft, charming Voice, his Hate, by a sharp, sullen and severe one; his Joy, by a full flowing and brisk Voice, his Grief, by a sad dull and languishing Tone; not without sometimes interrupting the Continuity of the Sound with a sigh or Groan, drawn from the very inmost of the Bosom.

To these tones were added a whole range of gestures. The tragedian was required to point to his head and his heart to indicate reason and passion, to raise his eyes and hands upwards when invoking the Gods, to extend his arms forward with palms extended to indicate horror or surprise. In short his arms, hands, head and features seem to have been in almost continual motion, 'For indeed', said Betterton, 'Action is the Business of the Stage, and an Error is more pardonable on the right, than on the Wrong side.'

Today it would be impossible to induce our actors to adopt such mannerisms, and even more impossible to expect our audiences to accept them. The path of naturalism has been trodden too far, and only in opera or ballet can we accept symbolic acting. Peter Brook's recent revival of Otway's *Venice Preserved* made little attempt to recapture the style of Restoration tragic acting, but although the production had much merit, one felt it belonged to the Elizabethan or Jacobean period, rather than to the age of Dryden and Congreve. If a director is bold enough to attempt to bridge the wide gap between the Baroque style and the taste of a modern audience, it is clear that a great deal of study would have to be given to the question of acting style. It is a sad fact that the acting student today is given too little training in musical speech and graceful gesture and, consequently, he has little basis on which to develop Restoration style. An overdose of contemporary naturalism coupled with a mistaken belief that acting is necessarily based on psychology has resulted in an all-too-ready condemnation of the emotional appeal of the grand manner, which is commonly derided as 'ham' acting. The French theatre with its strong neo-classic traditions and wealth of fine tragic drama has been careful to ensure that its student-actors are trained to speak the verse of Racine and Corneille in a way which, with intelligent direction, will illuminate without anachronism the style of the epoch of Louis XIV to a contemporary audience.

Between the styles of tragic acting and comic acting there was a wide gulf fixed; the one was frankly artificial, the other sought to provide an imitation of life. The two styles are effectively juxtaposed in Dryden's *Marriage à la Mode*. But whilst the tragic conventions could be lampooned, as they are in Buckingham's satire, *The Rehearsal*, the real art of the stage, at least in the view of the Restoration actors, lay in the tragic rather than the comic style. Amongst actors, Grammont explained, it was

> a standing and incontrovertible principle, that a tragedian always takes the place of a Commedian; and 'tis very well known the Merry Drolls who make us laugh are always placed at the lower end of the table, and in every Entertainment give way to the Dignity of the Buskin.

But, whilst it was easier for the 'Merry Drolls' of the Restoration companies to imitate life than for the tragedians to master the difficult techniques of their artificial conventions, we must not forget that the life they imitated was not our life. The modern actor will require just as much training to acquire the essentials of the comic style as he will to acquire the essentials of the tragic; both are equally foreign to him. Once again the emphasis of our dramatic training on contemporary naturalism and especially on psychological realism are against him.

When we talk of realism in relation to Restoration style, either in the matter of scenery or comic acting, we must not confuse what we mean by the theatrical realism of the epoch with what we mean by theatrical realism today. Both forms are real in that they are true to the spirit of their period, but both are theatrical since their truth is expressed through their respective theatrical conventions. Archaic reproduction of theatrical conventions is not the business of a live theatre; but illumination of the truth, or realism, of the playwright's intention is very much its concern. Congreve is the most realistic of the comic playwrights of his period, but the realism he aimed at is not expressed in terms of psychological realism, though his attitude towards sex and marriage is entirely realistic. His characterisation may have been based on observation of life, but it was an imitation of the externals only; to this extent Restoration comedy is truly named the Comedy of Manners. It is the technical mastery of these manners, and manners includes phrasing, timing and diction, that requires the attention of our teachers of acting, but technique is only the bare bones of style. I mentioned earlier that it is the fault of some directors to cloak their productions with an air of unreality in which scenery, costumes, fans and snuff-boxes assume such importance that reality is overlooked. The director and the actor will only be able to breathe life into the style of Restoration plays if they can make the audience feel that what they see and hear on the stage is a true reflection of life as it was lived and as it was understood. To do this requires more than the bare bones, it also requires an instinctive understanding of the stage of the period and its relation to the audience who frequented it.

Note

Scholarship and Criticism. Hazelton Spencer's *Shakespeare Improved; the Restoration Versions in Quarto and on the Stage* (1927) is a general survey and a useful introduction. More will be learnt from the studies of theatre practice listed in the Note for Chapter VIII, and from two works of stage-history, G. C. D. Odell, *Shakespeare from Betterton to Irving* (1920), and the useful compendium of details theatrical and gossipy in ten volumes, John Genest, *Some Account of the English Stage from 1660* (Bath, 1832).

Allardyce Nicoll has written a Shakespeare Association Pamphlet, *Dryden as an Adapter of Shakespeare* (1922), which is a clear and brief introduction to both Dryden's adaptations and others.

Two chapters of W. M. Merchant's *Shakespeare and the Artist* (1959) are of special importance: 2, on 'The Later Seventeenth Century', considers the staging of Shakespeare in the period and, in particular, assembles and interprets evidence of French and Italian influences; and 3, on '*Timon of Athens* and the Visual Conceit', considers Shadwell's *Timon* in relation to Shakespeare's. J. R. Brown's 'Three Adaptations', in *Shakespeare Survey* (1960), considers the production of *The Enchanted Island* at the Old Vic in 1959 in relation to *The Tempest*.

Texts. Shadwell's plays were edited by M. Summers (1927); quotations in this chapter are from that edition. Dryden is quoted from Summers' edition, as in other chapters. Tate's *Lear* is quoted from Summers' useful collection of *Shakespeare Adaptations* (1922). Davenant's *Macbeth* has recently been edited from the Yale MS. by C. Spencer (Yale, 1961). Other plays are quoted in this chapter from original editions.

IX

Shakespeare 'Made Fit'

W. MOELWYN MERCHANT

*

MUCH of the opprobrium for tampering with the texts of Shakespeare's plays at the Restoration has fallen on Nahum Tate, poet laureate. The many charges resolve themselves in the main under two indictments, to neither of which could Tate plead not guilty but of which, in justice we must recognise, he was on the whole less guilty than many of his fellows: in the first place, Shakespeare's text was 'made fit' for the Restoration stage, rewritten and made contemporary in matter and manner, by principles it is not always easy to understand; it is indeed difficult to justify Macbeth's speech in Davenant's version:

> He after life's short feavor, now sleeps well.
>
> (III. iii. 24)

And in the second place they were refurbished, set within the changed conditions of the new theatres. This process was of varying intensity, and Shadwell, one of the chief refurbishers, was impelled at one moment of tender conscience to record:

> There came Machines, brought from a Neighbour Nation;
> Oh, how we suffer'd under Decoration!

Nahum Tate was involved in three of these adaptations, of *King Lear*, *Richard the Second* and *Coriolanus*, and, perhaps from their long vogue in the theatre, they have added the term 'Tatification' to our dramatic vocabulary. His visual reordering of the play was, however, quite modest; his handling of Shakespeare's words was grosser but deserves more critical examination than it is normally given. It may be helpful to approach his work obliquely by way of another field of adaptation, his collaboration with Nicholas Brady on a metrical version of the Psalms. Here he was working within an established tradition and the results are illuminating. There are failures of taste and too frequent verbosity; the twenty-third Psalm, which provided so many moving versions from the sixteenth to the eighteenth century, is flatly pedestrian. But the two which have been reprinted most frequently in our hymn books, 'As pants the hart for cooling streams' and 'Through all the changing scenes of life', have a direct simplicity which anticipates the dignity of Isaac Watts in the next generation. Our sung versions are in fact abridgements, but even in the longer and clumsier original text of 1696 (commended for use by the Bishop of London in 1698) there are interesting dramatic echoes. 'As pants the hart for cooling streams' is a rendering of the evocative 'Like as the hart desireth the water-brooks' of Psalm 42. Our hymn books omit Tate's version of verses three and four and for just reason. The Prayer Book version reads:

My tears have been my meat day and night: while they daily say unto me, Where is now thy God?

Now when I think thereupon, I pour out my heart by myself: for I went with the multitude, and brought them forth into the house of God.

This is reduced by Tate to the unhappily dramatised:

Tears are my constant Food, while thus
insulting Foes upbraid.
'Deluded Wretch, where's now thy God?
and where his promis'd Aid?'
I sigh when e'er my musing Thoughts
those happy days present,
When I with Troops of pious Friends
thy Temple did frequent.

For all its falsity of tone this has a moment of allusive success when the Prayer Book version, 'went with the multitude', becomes 'with Troops of pious Friends', recollecting Macbeth's isolation from all that still old age should expect, as 'troops of friends'. It is proper to remember that Nahum Tate collaborated more than once with Purcell, providing him with lines which called out some of his noblest music. Much must be forgiven a writer who opened the way for Dido's lament, 'When I am laid in earth'; nor is it an insignificant contribution to our hymnody which can carry very frequently the simple grace of quatrains like these:

Why restless, why cast down my Soul?
hope still, and thou shalt sing

The Praise of him who is thy God,
        thy Health's eternal Spring.[1]

Blundering clumsiness and failure of taste may blur the aims of these
Restoration dramatists in their treatment of Shakespeare, but the whole
of their work cannot be dismissed as contemptible. Their motives
were not simple and were quite adequately documented in dedications
and prefatory notes. There were men of integrity and some distinction
among these revisers and it seems unwise critical practice to dismiss in
one gesture writers of such diversity of standing as Dryden, Shadwell,
D'Urfey, Davenant, Tate and Gildon. The tone of a prefatory apologia
is rarely that of an arrogant meddler, even when we cannot assent to
Shadwell's claim for his *Timon*: 'I can truly say, I have made it into a
Play.' Nor need we suppose that there is condescension in his noting
'the inimitable hand of *Shakespear* in it, which never made more
Masterly strokes than in this' (vol. III, p. 194). Some injustice has in
fact been done to their motives by quoting their brasher claims in
isolation. Nahum Tate's dedication of his *King Lear* deserves in this
respect some closer attention. It is customary to quote from it a single
sentence as an indication of Tate's presumption:

> I found the Whole to answer your Account of it, a Heap of Jewels,
> unstrung, and unpolish'd; yet so dazling in their Disorder, that I
> soon perceiv'd I had seiz'd a Treasure.

This sentence is set in a quite substantial dedication to Thomas Boteler,
which opens with an apology for reviving the play 'with Alterations'
and attributes his boldness to his 'Zeal for all the Remains of *Shakespear*'. This is followed by three considerations which had clearly been
much meditated by Tate before he embarked on his alterations. The
first concerns the dilemma of having to match the style of his interpolated scenes with Shakespeare's. That he found it necessary to make
the attempt (despite his inevitable failure) depends on a judgement
which the temper of his age must have made difficult:

> *Lear's* real and *Edgar's* pretended Madness have so much of *extrava-
> gant Nature*, (I know not how else to express it,) as cou'd never have

---

[1] The Bishop of London's commendation of 'Tate and Brady' speaks of its
'Judgement *and* Ingenuity' which '*may take off that unhappy Objection, which has
hitherto lain against the* Singing Psalms'. If we remind ourselves of the most
popular of the earlier versions, of 'Sternhold and Hopkins', we may see the
substance in his permission to use this new version in the diocese of London.

started, but from our *Shakespear's* Creating Fancy. The Images and Languages are so odd and surprizing, and yet so agreeable and proper, that whilst we grant that none but *Shakespear* cou'd have form'd such Conceptions; yet we are satisfied that they were the only Things in the World that ought to be said on these Occasions.

That is very fairly said, especially in the central critical phrase 'agreeable and proper'. To find congruity and propriety in the language Shakespeare uses for states of madness required some detachment in an early minor Augustan. Nor does his practice deny his judgement. Lear on the heath opens in his madness with some modification of Shakespeare:

> Blow Winds, and burst your Cheeks, rage louder yet,
> Fantastick Lightning singe, singe my white Head;
> Spout Cataracts, and Hurricanos fall,
> 'Till you have drown'd the Towns and Palaces
> Of proud ingratefull Man.

Lear's next speech begins uncertainly with a concession to 'taste' in its first two lines but proceeds substantially with the accelerated tempo of his madness:

> Rumble thy fill, fight Whirlwind, Rain and Fire;
> Not Fire, Wind, Rain, or Thunder are my Daughters:
> I tax not you, ye Elements, with Unkindness.

The second consideration in the dedicatory epistle concerns the preoccupation of the Restoration with symmetry in the plot and with appropriate motivation:

'Twas my good Fortune to light on one Expedient to rectifie what was wanting in the Regularity and Probability of the Tale, which was to run through the Whole, as *Love* betwixt *Edgar* and *Cordelia*; that never chang'd Word with each other in the Original. This renders *Cordelia's* Indifference, and her Father's Passion in the first Scene, probable. It likewise gives Countenance to *Edgar's* Disguise, making that a generous Design that was before a poor Shift to save his Life.

It must be frankly confessed that there is little in the text to justify this alteration. Tate rarely handles their dialogue without bathos and the return of Cordelia from France to the heath scene produces passages of dramatic embarrassment. Tate is on stronger ground, by the critical

canons of his age, in the third consideration which issues from this
love of Edgar and Cordelia; for 'this Method necessarily threw me on
making the Tale conclude in a Success to the innocent destrest Persons'. This is a complex matter. 'Innocent' in this context is a question-
begging term, involving a moral calculus which Shakespeare deliberately sets aside. Its validity is best tested in the quite economically
written passage with which Tate compasses the change. Lear reflects
on the fate of Edmund, Goneril and Regan:

> LEAR: Ingratefull as they were, my Heart feels yet
>   A Pang of Nature for their wretched Fall;—
>   But, *Edgar*, I defer thy Joys too long:
>   Thou serv'dst distrest *Cordelia*; take her Crown'd;
>   Th' imperial Grace fresh blooming on her Brow;
>   Nay, *Gloster*, thou hast here a Father's Right,
>   Thy helping Hand t'heap Blessings on their Heads.
> KENT: Old *Kent* throws in his hearty Wishes too.
> EDGAR: The Gods and you too largely Recompence
>   What I have done; the Gift strikes Merit dumb.
> CORDELIA: Nor do I blush to own my Self o'er-paid
>   For all my Suff'rings past.
> GLOSTER: Now, gentle Gods, give *Gloster* his Discharge
> LEAR: No, *Gloster*, thou hast Business yet for Life;
>   Thou, *Kent*, and I, retir'd to some cool Cell
>   Will gently pass our short Reserves of Time
>   In calm Reflections on our Fortunes past.

The sterile neatness of this passage provides a conclusion for the central
tragic figures which Shakespeare reserves for those minor characters
who, humbly and with some passivity, wait on providential shaping—
as in the humility of Edgar's

> The weight of this sad time we must obey,
> Speak what we feel, not what we ought to say:
> The oldest hath borne most, we that are young,
> Shall never see so much, nor live so long.

The tentative finality of those closing couplets of the play is scarcely
echoed in Tate's conclusion, in which Edgar moralises from Cordelia's
happy fate:

> Thy bright Example shall convince the World
> (Whatever Storms of Fortune are decreed)
> That Truth and Vertue shall at last succeed.

Tate was clearly insecure even with the theoretic justification for the happy ending and appealed to the perpetual criterion of 'good theatre' ('Yet was I wrack'd with no small Fears for so bold a Change, 'till I found it well receiv'd by my Audience') and even this practical matter required authority. This he found in Dryden, in the Preface to *The Spanish Friar*, which he quotes at some length:

> Neither is it of so Trivial an Undertaking to make a Tragedy end happily, for 'tis more difficult to save than 'tis to kill: the Dagger and the Cup of Poyson are always in Readiness; but to bring the Action to the last Extremity, and then by probable Means to recover All, will require the Art and Judgment of a Writer, and cost him many a Pang in the Performance.

This consideration of Tate's *Lear* which, with some modification by other adapters in the eighteenth century, displaced Shakespeare's play for a century and a half, has taken us to the core of the critical dilemma in Dryden's day. Shakespeare remained the incomparable dramatist; much of his work, as it was divided between the copyright theatres, remained relatively untouched and was, so far as we can judge, staged with modest means. Yet, in varying degrees, many different criteria of dramatic propriety impelled Dryden and his contemporaries to modify Shakespeare's text: the influence of the French classical theatre with its concern for muted action; concern for the Aristotelian canons; the conviction that language had progressed to a greater refinement since Shakespeare's day; a shift in the ethics of personal relationships and in the emotional tones in which they were expressed; a revaluation of the nature of decorum and urbanity. We are led to some critical confusion in assessing the weight which the adapters gave to these very diverse matters, for they were capriciously applied. Racine would have approved the urbanity with which certain moments of violence were removed, while Tate, Shadwell and Davenant were capable of a gratuitous violence, especially in descriptive language, which would have coarsened *Titus Andronicus* or the *Spanish Tragedy*. In certain of the plays we are impressed by the economy with which the plot is manipulated; in others the unities are set aside as freely as in Shakespeare and without his creative justification. Few of these dramatists had the stature to match Dryden's skill or integrity, so that we are left with the uneasy conviction that making Shakespeare 'fit' was a logical necessity for the emerging Augustan temper, while few or none had the sustained tact or insight to carry through the necessary consistent adaptation.

Meanwhile another practical revolution, in the craft of theatrical presentation, complicates the issue still further. This problem must be reduced to broad outlines so that some of the issues may emerge from the debatable detail. It is still customary to attribute much of the scenic elaboration of the Restoration to French influences acquired during the exile of the English court in the Commonwealth period; the dramatists were themselves self-conscious in their repudiation of the new-fangled imports, Elkanah Settle in 1697 claiming, in his dedication of *The World in the Moon*, that he had '*thrown away all our old* French *Lumber . . . and set theatrical Painting at a much fairer Light*', while Shadwell confesses that in the operatised versions of Shakespeare, we 'for your pleasures traffick'd into ffrance' (Epilogue to *The Tempest* adaptation). Addison extends the accusation to borrowings from Italy in condemning, in the Italians' own phrase, 'the *Fourberia della Scena, The Knavery or Trickish Part of the Drama*'. But this argument from the corruption of French and Italian influences is double-edged. Throughout the Restoration there was a conscious attempt to assert the unbroken tradition in acting and scenic painting, which linked their age with Shakespeare's, despite the closing of the theatres and the subsequent return of the court from contact with continental practice. There is substance in their plea; but the assertion of this continuity involves the recognition that in Shakespeare's own day masque and entertainment were closely related to Mannerist and early Baroque trends on the Continent; that Inigo Jones echoed the work of Parigi in Florence and that the Restoration 'Art of Perspective' was already present in the cloths and shutters with which Inigo Jones gained depth in his scenes. Nor ought it to be necessary any longer to point to the scenic sophistication of a great deal of Shakespeare's own art, and not only in the late plays for the indoor theatres, but early, in the masque interludes of his plays at the Globe, throughout *A Midsummer Night's Dream*, in the Masque of Hymen in *As You Like It* and, most maturely, in the Masque of the Senses in *Timon of Athens*. The tact with which these are embraced by the plot, and the terseness of their 'libretti' which conceals the length and elaboration which music and setting would give them, has led to an undervaluing of these moments in Shakespeare. But it is an historical failure to neglect their anticipation of elements in the Restoration theatre.

At this point—and before passing to a closer look at other Restoration versions of Shakespeare—it is the merest justice to the adapters to see their work as part of a continuous tradition which has lasted to our own day. They were neither exceptional nor unique vandals, with no progeny. When alteration of the text in response to the demands of a new taste in writing and theatre setting had reached a momentary conclusion in the age of Cibber, a new occasional use was found for Shakespeare's writing during Garrick's ascendancy, as a quarry for brief interludes. The most interesting in its implications was *The Sheep-Shearing, or Florizel and Perdita* hacked out of the fourth act of *The Winter's Tale* by M'Namara Morgan in 1754, an exercise made possible by regarding the pastoral movement in the play as an isolated action, with no relevance to the theme of innocence and purification in the third and fifth acts. This kind of dismemberment was comparatively rare but in the nineteenth century the play took up another relation, foreshadowed at the Restoration, that of opera libretti. In particular Verdi deserves much closer attention than he has been normally accorded as a critical interpreter of Shakespeare. To consider this at its sharpest: Boito's insertion into the libretto of *Otello* of the explicit clarity of Iago's 'Credo' changes the whole focus and stress of the plot, making lucid and explicable a diabolic relationship which Shakespeare deliberately leaves allusive and questionable. The necessary compression of an opera libretto forces expedients of this kind on the librettist, and when the music isolates a limited number of interpretative themes to set against each other, the original play loses its complexity and the moral and personal issues take on the qualities of a morality. The revival of Verdi's *Macbeth* this year (1963) by the Welsh National Opera Company raises this issue in a new and illuminating way. Piave's libretto has been newly translated from the Italian by John Moody who directed the current production. Whether in Italian or English, Verdi's massive structure reduces the issues to the career of a dominating Lady Macbeth who receives far subtler treatment than her husband. But Moody's translation boldly returns to Shakespeare's words whenever possible, and produces moments of intense tragedy. One occurs at the brooding sombreness of Banquo's ironic reflection on the dimmed 'candles' of the stormy night, 'there's husbandry in heaven'; here the conjunction of Shakespeare's own line and the dark music of Verdi produces a complexity beyond that of the Italian version. We esteem these operas and we have had another of great distinction in our own day, in Britten's *Midsummer Night's Dream*.[2] In some respects they carry 'adaptation' much further than the seventeenth-century works we are considering, shifting the matter into a wholly new medium. It seems to me valuable to refer back from these nineteenth- and twentieth-century works to the 'operatic versions' of the Restoration, not so much in such works as *The Fairy Queen*, as in such interesting hybrids as Gildon's *Measure for Measure* (to be considered below) where Shakespeare and Purcell meet.

New media in the twentieth century have carried the process of adaptation still further. Cinema and television have had their rare but significant successes, not when they have imitated the functions of the theatre but when they have exploited the technique of their own medium in true adaptation. An early *Macbeth* on television superbly exploited the exploratory lens of the camera in the opening contact with Macbeth, three gaunt hands traversing the screen at the triple hailing by the witches. The same intimacy of detail was reached by the peculiar quality of television, at the insidious whispering of Lady Macbeth, a quality of temptation difficult to achieve in the wider territory of the stage. A similar technique of detailed exploration was achieved in the witty scene of Viola's first meeting with Olivia in the Russian film of *Twelfth Night*. In most English stage versions only a moronic Viola would fail to distinguish the courtly 'lady of the house' from the kitchen wench which is the usual disguise of the young gentlewoman Maria. But in the Russian film Viola stands bewildered before identically dressed court ladies; Olivia is recognised only by the dropping of her handkerchief immediately picked up for her by her lady-in-waiting. Such an effect is possible on the stage but the wit is intensified at those valid moments of translation into a new and more intimate medium.

A still further degree of adaptation, well beyond the bounds of Restoration practice, has been seen on our stage in the ballet versions, notably the *Hamlet* of Robert Helpmann. Here the peculiar mimetic qualities of the medium, its broad stylisation of the themes, led to a morbid intensification of the mental processes of Hamlet, a creation out of the Shakesperian material more radically new than even Boito's Iago.

[2] Considered in *Stratford-upon-Avon Studies 3: Early Shakespeare*, 'M.N.D.: a Visual Re-creation', pp. 182–3. It has recently been announced that Britten is considering a *Lear*, a project considered but unrealised by Verdi.

We should in honesty cite *Kiss me, Kate* and *The Boys from Syracuse* as a still further extension of Restoration principles into the entertainment of our own day. To indulge our indignation at the indignities to which Shakespeare's text was subjected by Dryden and his fellows, while enjoying more recent quarryings from the mine, is probably to display a too elastic discrimination. Shakespeare has a remarkable quality of surviving any public performance and we should probably not be too jealously exercised on behalf of his integrity. When we cavil at frank adaptations for the Restoration stage or in later opera, ballet or 'musical', we perhaps underestimate the degree of adaptation inherent in any new performance, that subtle adaptation to the dimensions, the insight and the psychological make-up of the actors in the uniqueness of each new production. Every successive revolution in theatre design, each change in the conventions and techniques of acting contributes its creative moment in the progressive realisation of the Shakespearian text. It is as well that we write with less moral reprehension of any departure from our conception of the place of interpretation; the open stage, the proscenium arch, the camera's intrusive eye or the conventions of the French Baroque theatre, are all neutral agents of the living text.

As we explore the Restoration experiment, then, we should suspend our judgements, derived from generalisations, of that subtle adaptation exercised by theatre history. Even more must we suspend our own scholarly antiquarianism which stands firm for the criteria of the Jacobean stage and is appalled by the irreverence of Augustan improvers. Dryden, Shadwell and Tate had none of our reverence for the text—though few of them claimed a greater 'liberty of prophesying' in interpreting that text than a Guthrie or Peter Brook in our own day. We shall be on safer ground for the moment if we return to these adaptations, looking at them by the light of their own principles of theatre-craft and social criticism.

We shall do the most manifest justice to this work by beginning with Dryden. His handling of the Shakespearian text in three major adaptations, of *Antony and Cleopatra*, *The Tempest* and *Troilus and Cressida*, is of a piece with the main body of his dramatic criticism, and his careful prefaces to the adaptations provide the most reasoned apologia for this aspect of dramatic history. One of the most striking qualities of the introductions provided by the Dedications and Epistles to the Reader is their unassertive consistency and the unforced respect they accord

Shakespeare, despite the greatly changed critical canons with which, at the Restoration, they measured dramatic writing. We cannot expect dramatic criticism of distinction from Tate, D'Urfey or even Shadwell, but if there is to be justification or (at the most moderate) explanation, for this body of rewriting, it must be found in the work of Dryden, at once the first dramatist and critic of his generation.

Dryden began his adaptations with *The Tempest*, performed in 1667 and published in 1670. (We leave consideration of the elaborately 'operatised' *Tempest* of Shadwell, based on Dryden's text in 1674, until later.) Dryden's introduction, giving an account of his debt to Davenant, has a manifest unease throughout. The first approach to Shakespeare's text is to repair its symmetry and the relations of the original characters:

> *Davenant* . . . soon found that somewhat might be added to the Design of *Shakespear*, of which neither *Fletcher* [in *The Sea Voyage*, 1647] nor *Suckling* [in *The Goblins*, 1646] had ever thought: and therefore to put the last hand to it, he design'd the Counterpart to *Shakespear's* Plot, namely, that of a Man who had never seen a Woman, that by this means those two Characters of Innocence and Love might the more illustrate and commend each other.

This is clearly a very considerable reinterpretation, not solely prompted by the desire for classical symmetry. The relation of innocence to a fallen world is a potent theme in the last plays; the marvelling of Miranda at the potentiality of a redeemed world (even if her invocation of a 'brave new world' is a momentary irony, going beyond the evidence) is consistent with the pastoral innocence of Perdita, her passionate and uncorrupt sensuality ('quick and in my arms') and her complex relation with living and growing things. For Davenant and Dryden to have intensified this, by balancing Miranda's innocence with that of a 'Man who had never seen a Woman', is wholly to invoke Eden, a totally pre-lapsarian state. Pursued consistently it destroys the spiritual irony of Miranda's judgement on 'such people' in her vision of a new world, and destroys also the significance of the return to the old order; for neither Miranda nor Perdita—nor their elders—remain in the pastoral paradise. In fact Davenant's 'somewhat added to the Design of *Shakespear*' was pursued with no such consistency and the verbal relations of the two innocent creatures who had seen none of the opposite sex are pursued with a bawdy verve which changes the scenes to the tone of a Wycherley comedy.

It is not easy to pursue the principles by which the adaptation was followed through. Symmetry was clearly a main consideration and it is carried into the minor relationships of Caliban, who is given a *sister*, Sycorax; of Ariel, who is given a pastoral lover, Milcha; and Miranda, whose relationships are further complicated by a sister, Dorinda. It is not surprising then, from the tone with which these variations are achieved, that Prospero's transition from visionary magic to the conduct of daily affairs is also greatly changed and that 'We are such stuff as dreams are made on' is omitted from the text. It is clear that Dryden was not easy in his collaboration with Davenant and there is an air of deprecation in his acknowledgement of some of Davenant's contributions:

> The Comical parts of the Saylors were also his Invention, and for the most part his writing, as you will easily discover by the style.

It is difficult to do justice in a brief summary to the achievement in Dryden's *All for Love* (1678), the most massive and the most successful of the adaptations. Here the alterations are so consistent and thoroughgoing that they produce a major work, independent of the Shakespearian original. But we should nevertheless do an injustice to the total body of Restoration adaptations if we set aside their solitary masterpiece because of its singular integrity. Tate and Gildon exhibited the same aim; they were simply not of Dryden's stature.

The most striking change from Shakespeare is in the structure and duration of the scenes, particularly in the middle reaches of the play. For the cinematic *montage* of Shakespeare's brief scenes Dryden substitutes tableaux, the nearest approach of English drama to the statuesque of Racine. There are moments in Shakespeare's *Coriolanus* when we find a similar confrontation of classical ideals personified in persons who, for the moment, achieve symbolic dignity; Milton's *Samson Agonistes* is constructed wholly in this manner, with the opposition of single individuals in a conflict of principles. But Milton failed to assimilate the classical form to the theatric movement of western drama—if that was in any way his intention. But Dryden succeeds in the process, involving himself in so doing, in a pleasant irony of theatre history. The flexibility of Jacobean setting enabled Shakespeare to maintain throughout the play the utmost subtlety in asserting the rival ideals of Rome and Alexandria against each other. This antithesis of the two cities is excluded by Dryden's adherence to the unity of place, and in this consistency of setting. Dryden goes beyond even the Jacobean convention of delocalisation; in a very real sense the stage itself, rather than a conventional Alexandria, is the conscious setting of the play. The successive entrances of Roman and Egyptian protagonists to confront each other make little if any demand on our feeling for locality; their points of view clash on an undifferentiated arena. This is of course not to say that décor was unimportant in *All for Love*; one significant detail, the elaborate death of Cleopatra, crowned and enthroned in dignity, is the regular *mise-en-scène* for the closing movement of the play both in Dryden's version and Shakespeare's.

The Preface has a very direct statement of Dryden's canons and intention. The 'moral' is clear, 'for the chief persons represented, were famous patterns of unlawful love; and their end accordingly was unfortunate'. He is equally clear in his statement of the play's formal values: 'The Fabrick of the Play is regular enough as to the inferior parts of it; and the Unities of Time, Place and Action, more exactly observ'd than, perhaps, the English Theater requires.' Much more interesting is the tact with which he judges what we might call the emotional architecture of the play. Where Shakespeare is organic in the slow growth of the relationships within his play, allowing consistency and inconsistency to play off against each other as the theme and the characters develop, Dryden judges with more 'contrivance', with a more mechanically judicious sense of propriety and expedience:

> The greatest errour in the contrivance seems to be in the person of *Octavia*; For, though I might use the priviledge of a Poet, to introduce her into *Alexandria*, yet I had not enough consider'd, that the compassion she mov'd to her self and children, was destructive to that which I reserv'd for *Anthony* and *Cleopatra*; whose mutual love being founded upon vice, must lessen the favour of the Audience to them, when Virtue and Innocence were oppress'd by it.

More impressive than even this objective observation of his own achievement is the generosity with which he acknowledges the stature of Shakespeare:

> In my Stile I have profess'd to imitate the Divine *Shakespeare*; which that I might perform more freely, I have disincumber'd my self from Rhyme. Not that I condemn my former way, but that this is more proper to my present purpose. I hope I need not to explain my self, that I have not Copy'd my Author servilely: Words and Phrases must of necessity receive a change in succeeding Ages: but 'tis almost

a Miracle that much of his Language remains so pure; and that he who began Dramatique Poetry amongst us, untaught by any, and, as *Ben Johnson* tells us, without Learning, should by the force of his own Genius perform so much, that in a manner he has left no praise for any who come after him . . . Yet I hope I may affirm, and without vanity, that by imitating him, I have excell'd myself throughout the Play; and particularly, that I prefer the Scene betwixt *Anthony* and *Ventidius* in the first Act, to any thing which I have written in this kind.

That the 'Stile' was by no means uniformly Shakespeare's becomes most obvious at those moments when he is most conscious of his original. Shakespeare gave to Enobarbus, at 'the barge she sat in', his subtlest handling of North's Plutarch; in Dryden this is given to Antony and becomes

> Her Gally down the Silver *Cydnos* row'd,
> The Tackling Silk, the Streamers wav'd with Gold,
> The gentle Winds were lodg'd in Purple sails:
> Her Nymphs, like *Nereids*, round her Couch, were plac'd;
> Where she, another Sea-born *Venus*, lay.
>
> (III; vol. IV, p. 221)

The death of Cleopatra is the passage which earns closest study. It is prefaced by Antony's long debate on love and innocence, the counterpoise to the opening confrontations of love and honour. But at the meeting of Antony and Cleopatra the emotional tension appears at first to need an external aid, which Dryden gives it in half-allusions to other tragedies of Shakespeare, in Antony's echo of Hamlet in his request to Ventidius:

> Wilt thou not live, to speak some good of me?
> (V; vol. IV, p. 255)

or in his reversal of Macbeth's sense of deprivation:

> While hand in hand we walk in Groves below,
> Whole Troops of Lovers Ghosts shall flock about us.
> (V; vol. IV, p. 258)

But the transformation of the Shakespearian tone comes at Cleopatra's end. For Shakespeare's

> Come, thou mortal wretch,
> With thy sharp teeth this knot intrinsicate
> Of life at once untie,

Dryden substitutes two successive images of theft and sleep, less complex in themselves than Shakespeare's 'knot intrinsicate . . . untie' and
reaching a more direct but less potent antithesis:

> Welcom, thou kind Deceiver!
> Thou best of Thieves; who, with an easie key,
> Dost open life, and, unperceiv'd by us,
> Ev'n steal us from our selves: discharging so
> Death's dreadful office, better than himself;
> Touching our limbs so gently into slumber,
> That Death stands by, deceiv'd by his own Image,
> And thinks himself but Sleep.
>
> (V; vol. IV, p. 260)

The manner has dignity but calls out little of the ambiguity with which
we follow the tragedy of Shakespeare's Cleopatra.

Dryden's third and last adaptation of Shakespeare, *Troilus and
Cressida, Truth Found too Late* appeared a year after *All for Love*, in
1679. There is a moderate and perceptive Preface which justifies the
adaptation on largely moral grounds, and indicates, even more clearly
than *All for Love*, the gap in insight and perception between the
dramatic intentions of the Jacobean and Restoration playwrights at
their most serious.

> The Author seems to have begun it with some fire; the Characters of
> *Pandarus* and *Thersites*, are promising enough; but as if he grew
> weary of his task, after an Entrance or two, he lets 'em fall: and the
> latter part of the Tragedy is nothing but a confusion of Drums and
> Trumpets, Excursions and Alarms. The chief persons, who give
> name to the Tragedy, are left alive: *Cressida* is false, and is not
> punish'd. Yet after all, because the Play was *Shakespear's*, and that
> there appear'd in some places of it, the admirable Genius of the
> Author; I undertook to remove that heap of Rubbish, under which
> many excellent thoughts lay wholly bury'd. Accordingly, I new
> model'd the Plot; threw out many unnecessary persons; improv'd
> those Characters which were begun, and left unfinish'd: as *Hector*,
> *Troilus, Pandarus* and *Thersites*; and added that of *Andromache*. After
> this, I made with no small trouble, an Order and Connection of all
> the Scenes; . . . no leaping from *Troy* to the *Grecian* Tents, and
> thence back again in the same Act; but a due proportion of time
> allow'd for every motion: . . .
>
> The whole Fifth Act, both the Plot and the Writing are my own
> Additions.

This is a convenient epitome of Restoration principles in the whole project of adapting Shakespeare. Proper deference is accorded the original; Dryden is not alone in his classical reprehension of the closing scenes, for modern producers and actors express equal, if unjustified unease; Dryden makes a clear issue of the *genre* which had been left in doubt in the folio—for him the play is clearly a tragedy. It is moreover, as left by Shakespeare, a tragedy of moral confusion, with a false Cressida left unpunished. For the rest, we find principles clearly enough demonstrated elsewhere in Dryden and in Nahum Tate: a clarified characterisation to point moral antitheses, and a moderate application of the unity of place. If this were all we should have a repetition of the approach of *All for Love*, a refinement on Tate's *Lear*. But the addition and the clarification imposed by the newly written fifth Act goes a great deal further, and is probably the most decisive moment in these Restoration versions. For in one lucid Act it destroys the complex and ironic ambiguities in the shaping of the matter of Troy from Chaucer and Henryson to Shakespeare. For the tensions between courtly love and the bitter conclusion of Henryson's Cressida, Dryden substitutes the suicide of Cressida as a heroic demonstration of her faithfulness, achieving in one unjustifiable moment, both a degree of 'poetic justice' for her infidelity and a swing of moral sympathy for the expiation. The loss is perhaps greater than in any other direction. By the very lucidity of the solution the sickness of soul in Shakespeare's version, the disenchantment with human intention, is excluded, together with the other degree of moral clarity which accompanies disenchantment. The insight of a Parolles at the moment of humiliation, the saving humility of Angelo at his self-discovery, these are given with a difference in the final rebellious revelation of Shakespeare's Troilus:

> If beauty have a soul, this is not she;
> If souls guide vows, if vows be sanctimonies,
> If sanctimony be the gods' delight,
> If there be rule in unity itself,
> This is not she. O madness of discourse,
> That cause sets up with and against itself:
> Bifold authority, where reason can revolt
> Without perdition, and loss assume all reason
> Without revolt. This is, and is not, Cressid.
>
> (V. ii. 138)

And this is achieved by a dramatic understatement of Cressida's quality, which is left poised between wantonness, perfidy and simple weakness; nor does Shakespeare require Henryson's bitter coda in the final end of Cressida. All this is pruned away in Dryden's direct manipulation of moral consequence.

One moment however remains almost isolated in its complete dramatic propriety. While Dryden is still engaged in adapting the Shakespearian text and before the radical additions of Act V, he achieves a simplicity rare in Restoration tragedy and the more poignant in its isolation from the dignified rhetoric of the play. At the moment when Cressida and Diomedes have been overheard in their love-making by Troilus and Ulysses, Troilus has only one bemused question in response to the treachery:

Was *Cressida* here?

It is one of the finest moments in the Restoration theatre. It is perhaps difficult to share Hazelton's Spencer's enthusiasm for this version as a whole:

In the hands of a sweet and dignified Cressida, an accomplished tragedian as Troilus, and a coolly insolent stage villain as Diomedes, the final scene must have acted admirably. If I were an actor, I would rather play Dryden's Troilus than Shakespeare's;

but it is certainly neither a mean nor an impertinent adaptation, even if the issue in Shakespeare in sour inconclusion, with its insight into a particular and corrosive evil, has been excluded from Dryden's version.

Nahum Tate was not Dryden's equal as an adapter but he has an undeserved reputation as a mere botcher. It is true that he can produce moments of involuntary comedy out of high tragedy; Cordelia, brought back from France with her *confidante*, Arante, to take part in the elemental conflict on the heath, comforts her companion with her own stoicism:

ARANTE: Look, here's a Shed; beseech ye, enter here.
CORDELIA: Prethee go thy self, seek thy own Ease,
Where the Mind's free, the Body's delicate;
This Tempest but diverts me from the Thought
Of what would hurt me more—   (Act III)

with its appropriate cue, *Enter Two Ruffians*.

We need not return to Tate's reworking, except to recall the principles on which he relied; first, in the exercise of that poetic justice which
motivated Dryden's *Troilus* he produced an ending which may con-
found us, but is not merely contemptible; it is based rather on a deeply
felt if mistaken and inadequate notion of the equity of things. In the
second place, his *Lear* is another in the series of political comments
which Shakespeare was made to subserve in these Restoration versions.
Dryden's *Troilus* became in part tractarian: 'Let subjects learn obedience
to their Kings'; similarly, in the Preface to *Lear*, the clergy of England
are admonished against pursuing their Whiggish ways, a disloyalty
to the established order which contributes to a disintegration like that
of Lear's England in Acts III and IV. This political comment inspires
the many versions of the history plays for the next three-quarters of a
century and is the mainspring of Tate's *The Ingratitude of a Commonwealth, Or the Fall of Caius Martius Coriolanus*, in 1682. This is a violent,
tasteless adaptation, designed by its author to reflect 'the busie Faction
of our own time':

> The Moral therefore of these Scenes being to Recommend Sub-
> mission and Adherence to Establisht Lawful Power.

The end of the play is an offensive mixture of madness, rape and violent
death, of which Tate himself realises that there is no aesthetic justification, protesting rather:

> Where is the harm of letting the People see what Miseries Common-
> Wealths have been involv'd in, by a blind Compliance with their
> popular Misleaders.

This ambiguous motive for altering his original throws a little light on
a central modification in his *Lear*. It is not customary in any criticism
of this adaptation to connect the three major changes from Shakespeare's structure as modifications of one fundamental attitude. It is
usual to attribute the return of Cordelia in the middle reaches of the
play to a desire to enlarge the leading actress's role; to ascribe the
cutting of the Fool (who was not to return for a century and a half)
to the classical separation of comedy and tragedy; and to give a plain
Restoration reading to the enlargement of the amours of Edmund. In
fact all three contribute to the same final warping of the play and
Tate's failure to understand Shakespeare's handling of a particular
corruption, a failure precisely analogous with Dryden's in his *Troilus*

and Cressida. To omit the Fool is not simply to excise unseemly comedy from the tragic scene; it is rather to omit profound sexual comment on the sickness of Lear. We must of course admit that neither Tate nor the Restoration were unique in this kind of blind warping of Shakespeare's intention; the customary reduction of Polonius to the status of a boring but harmless bumbler is to reduce the impact of Denmark's 'rottenness' in the characters of Hamlet and Ophelia. To introduce at the same time into *Lear* a sentimental corrective in the love of Edgar and Cordelia, and to reduce Edmund's demonic destruction of Goneril and Regan to the level of mere intrigue, entirely alters the complexity of Shakespeare's Edmund, reducing both the subtlety of his relation with Gloucester and the moment of pride in his end:

Yet Edmund was beloved.

The stature of Edmund is wholly dwarfed when this quality is lost in exchange for the Restoration realism of Tate's interpolated setting:

A Grotto. Edmund *and* Regan *amorously Seated, listening to Musick.*
(Act IV)

'Love' in this version is reduced from its manifold quality and value in Shakespeare's *Lear* to a simple antithesis between innocent and redemptive love in Cordelia and an adulterous and destructive passion in Edmund. For the infinite mutations of possessiveness, compassion, lust and the exchange of charities in Shakespeare we have in Tate a neat and manipulated counterposing of two forces. Once more it was no capricious version of the original but an attempt to apply neoclassic canons where the stature of the material made them irrelevant.

'Yet I can truly say, I have made it into a Play'; Shadwell's claim for his handling of *Timon* is, throughout all this refurbished material, the basic defence for rewriting work in which they always recognised 'the inimitable hand of Shakespeare'. But his was a hand of 'Masterly Strokes', of the casual gesture of genius which produced single moments of dramatic intensity but fundamentally lacked the power of orderly, finished creation. Dryden, Shadwell, Tate and Davenant all attempted in their way to rectify this 'irregularity', to clear the rubbish from the jewels of Shakespeare's scenes. Their failure was inevitable and the return in the nineteenth and twentieth centuries to an increasing respect for Shakespeare's text places the work of the Restoration in an increasingly unfortunate light. But to one aspect of their work, related to the versions we have considered but distinct from them, scarcely any attempt has been made to do critical justice. For the 'operatised versions' of Shakespeare after 1660 have always been dismissed as a more brutal travesty of his work than even the *Lear* or *Coriolanus* of Nahum Tate. But the masque in Shadwell's *Timon*, his version of *The Tempest*, the reshaping of *A Midsummer Night's Dream* as *The Fairy Queen* and the curious conflation of Shakespeare and Purcell in Gildon's *Measure for Measure or, Beauty the Best Advocate*, deserve attention as a group, as the only serious attempt before our own century to shape a *genre* which may in any real sense be called 'operatic'. It was an unhappy accident that the dramatic genius of Purcell flourished at a moment when it was thought necessary to reform the structure of Shakespeare's plays; for Purcell had the ability to collaborate with writers of very diverse talent, from Dryden to Settle and Lee, and it was unfortunate that he was not given the clearest occasion for setting a Shakespearian plot as an opera. Dryden, speaking of Purcell's part in his comedy, *Amphitryon*, recognises his standing in the new form:

> What has been wanting on my Part, has been abundantly supplyed by the Excellent Composition of Mr. *Purcell*; in whose Person we have at length found an *English-man*, equal with the best abroad.

With the performance of *King Arthur* in 1691, the text by Dryden and the music from 'the Artful Hands of Mr. *Purcel*', the opera reached its most just balance of dignity in the text and the music, and less flawed in its words than much of the greater *Dido and Aeneas*. The ambiguous association of Purcell's name with Shakespeare's (in a reference which appears to be to Shadwell's *Timon*) indicated an uneasy relationship. Granville's *Jew of Venice* in 1701 has some prefatory verses which include:

> Shakespeares sublime in vain entic'd the Throng,
> Without the Charm of Purcels Syren Song.

The masque in Shadwell's *Timon* is, in fact, the best point at which to examine this relationship. In 1678 *The History of Timon, The Man Hater* was produced at Dorset Garden, with the masque at Timon's first feast extended to a full-length masque of Cupid and Bacchus, the music being by Purcell. Downes wrote of it: 'The Musick in't well Perform'd, it wonderfully pleased the Court and City.' From this commendation we are tempted to assume that the masque has dominated the performance, at least in the memory of the audience, and it is true that with its classical structure it becomes a set piece to entertain the guests. But in fact, Shakespeare's *Timon* had already a most elaborate entertainment at this point, of far greater weight and significance than the length of the text alone on the page would indicate. Indeed Shakespeare's masque here fulfils more of the Baroque ideal of the union of word, music and décor in a significant whole than the later elaboration of Shadwell; for this is a 'Masque of the Senses', both an elaboration and a focusing of Shakespeare's concern with the visual conceit and the function of poet and painter in the first half of the play. Cupid establishes the subject:

> Haile to thee worthy *Timon* and to all that of his Bounties taste: the five best Sences acknowledge thee their Patron, and come freely to gratulate thy plentious bosome.

> Th'ear, taste, touch, and smell, pleas'd from thy Table rise:
> They onely now come but to Feast thine eies.

After this opening movement, '*Maskers of Amazons*' dance, and their performance is followed by a concerted dance with the guests, a dance in two movements:

> *The Lords rise from Table, with much adoring of Timon, and to show their loves, each singles out an Amazon, and all Dance, men with women, a loftie straine or two to the Hoboyes, and cease.* (I. ii)

Here then is an elaborate dramatic structure in four movements, as elaborate as anything in the Restoration and more organically related to the theme of *Timon*.

Four years earlier than *Timon*, in 1674, Shadwell's *Tempest* had produced a tighter unity of scenic elaboration with the fundamental structure of Shakespeare's play. For Shakespeare had provided for the visual excitement of a shipwreck and a masque in the penultimate scene of the play. In place, however, of the token formality of sight and sound in the opening shipwreck in Shakespeare's *Tempest*, Shadwell has an elaborate scenic prologue; he requires a 'scene'

> *which represents a thick Cloudy Sky, a very Rocky Coast, and a Tempestuous Sea in perpetual Agitation. This Tempest (suppos'd to be rais'd by Magick) has many dreadful Objects in it, as several Spirits in horrid shapes flying down amongst the sailers, then rising and crossing in the Air.*
> (I. i; vol. II, p. 199)

When this 'scene' has been removed the essentially Palladian structure of the stage set is revealed:

> When the Lights return, discover that Beautiful part of the Island, which was the Habitation of Prospero; 'Tis compos'd of three Walks of Cypress-trees, each Side-walk leads to a Cave, in one of which Prospero keeps his Daughters, in the other Hippolito: The Middle-Walk is of a great depth, and leads to an open part of the Island.   (I. ii; vol. II, pp. 202–3)

This neo-classical symmetry in setting, echoing the symmetry of the characterisation which Shadwell imposed upon the Shakespearian original ('a man who had never seen a woman', Hippolito balancing Miranda), leads the expectation of the audience to its fulfilment in the elaboration of the magic banquets and the considerable extension of Shakespeare's masque of Ceres and Iris:

> Neptune, Amphitrite, Oceanus and Tethys, appear in a Chariot drawn with Sea-Horses; on each side of the Chariot, Sea-Gods and Goddesses, Tritons and Nereides.   (V; vol. II, p. 265)

In the course of this spectacle the scene changes, concluding with the release of Ariel, 'flying from the Sun'. This is elaborate, but like its original, Shadwell's Tempest is of a piece, the spectacle an extension of the magic theme, even if the exaggeration of this material provided by Shakespeare leads to moments of banality.

The case is different with the better known Fairy Queen of 1692. Here the entertainments between Acts are inset, essentially spectacular in every sense, and bearing no relation whatever to the bulk of the play, based on A Midsummer Night's Dream.[3] Gildon's Measure for Measure, or Beauty the Best Advocate closes this series of adaptations and ingeniously unites the 'operatic' techniques hitherto rather tentatively employed. The work as it was produced in Lincoln's Inn Fields in 1699 (published in 1700) had a complicated history. In December 1689 Purcell had written The Loves of Dido and Aeneas to a libretto by Nahum Tate for Josias Priest's Academy in Chelsea; it was a balletic masque, for Priest directed dance in the London theatres. When Charles Gildon adapted Measure for Measure ten years later, he incorporated Dido and Aeneas as entr'acte material, an operation which appears to resemble the essentially spectacular devices of The Fairy

---

[3] This version is examined in Stratford-upon-Avon Studies 3: Early Shakespeare (1961), 'M.N.D.: a Visual Re-creation', pp. 166–9.

Queen. But Gildon is in fact much more successful than most of the earlier adapters. Despite the disarming description on the title-page:

> Written *Originally* by Mr. *Shakespear*:
> And now very much Alter'd; with *Additions*
> of several *Entertainments* of MUSICK

Gildon, in the Prologue, is scornful of contemporary botching:

> No more let Labour'd *Scenes*, with Pain, be Wrought,
> What least is wanting in a *Play*, is *Thought*.
> Let neither *Dance*, nor *Musick* be forgot,
> Nor *Scenes*, no matter for the *Sense*, or *Plot*.
> Such things we own in *Shakespears* days might do;
> But then his Audience did not Judge like you.

a sentiment echoed by the Epilogue delivered by Shakespeare's Ghost:

> My *Plays*, by *Scriblers*, Mangl'd I have seen;
> By Lifeless *Actors* Murder'd on the *Scene*.

But Gildon has himself to buy the time for *Dido and Aeneas* by a drastic rewriting of Shakespeare. The formal intellectuality of Shakespeare's opening, 'of government the properties to unfold', is sacrificed for a plunging entry into the plot, with a brisk exchange between Lucio and Balthazar and we are quickly led to both the passion of Angelo and the first of Purcell's 'Entertainments'. Angelo questions his lust ('Can Vertue win us more to Vice, than Vice?') but suppresses his self-examination:

> No Vicious Beauty cou'd with Practis'd Art,
> Subdue my Heart like Virgin Innocence.
> I'll think no more on't but with Musick chase
> Away the Guilty Image.

The opening of *Dido* has the foreboding aria,

> Ah! *Belinda* I am prest,
> With Torment not to be Confest,

and the whole scene can be heard as a comment on Angelo's condition. He responds to it:

> This Musick is no cure for my Distemper;
> For, every note, to my Enchanted Ears,
> Seem'd to Sing only *Isabella's* Beauty . . .
>   Let her Brother Live.

> Thieves, for their Robbery, have Authority,
> When Judges steal Themselves.

The Second Entertainment is heard by Angelo as a closer comment on his love and on his stratagems. Dido is held in the Cave of the 'Weyward Sisters' and the scene ends with a dance and the Echo Song 'In our deep vaulted Cell'. Angelo commits himself to the seduction of Isabella:

> All will not do: All won't devert my Pain,
> The Wound enlarges by these Medicines,
> 'Tis She alone can yield the Healing Balm.
> This Scene just hits my case; her Brothers danger,
> Is here the storm must furnish Blest Occasion:
> And when, my Dido, I've Possess'd thy Charms,
> I then will throw thee from my glutted Arms,
> And think no more on all thy soothing Harms.

This is crude stuff but it comes to a moving moment almost of justification at the Third Entertainment. In *Dido* this is the Act in which Aeneas and his 'Saylors' determine their leaving Carthage. Dido's lament, 'When I am laid in earth', is followed by the most acceptable transition in Gildon's adaptation:

> CHORUS: With drooping Wings you Cupids come,
>   Soft and Gentle as her Heart,
>   Keep here your Watch and never part
> ANGELO: I see my Ev'ning Star of Love appear . . .
>   Wou'd you ought with me?
> ISABELLA: I come my Lord on the same humble suit . . .

If Shakespeare's text is to serve an operatic form, especially one which, in the manner of the seventeenth century—and until Mozart's day—united a terse spoken play with passages of music in solo and chorus, this *Measure for Measure* comes as near success as an inferior writer can achieve. This is one of the problems throughout any consideration of these Restoration versions, that rarely did the literary competence of the adapters match their pretensions in handling the original text.

It is difficult to make a critical summary of our attitude to this material. There are three distinct problems involved which enter into a consideration of every Restoration version in varying proportions. First, there is the matter of theatre history, the changed function of décor and of music in the period after 1660. It is possible to exaggerate the degree of change and to forget the continuity with the age of Shakespeare which so much of this work demonstrates. But in the hands of the clumsy, the settings deserved the censure of Cibber in the next generation:

> It was no wonder that the sensual supply of sound and sight grew too hard for sense and simple nature, when it is considered how many more people there are that can see and hear than can think and understand.

The second critical problem has been obvious throughout, that apart from Dryden and, on rare occasions, some of the other adapters, the writers were simply not competent at the craft they professed. This has blurred the third issue, which is of some importance. England participated only very partially in the Baroque: Purcell, Vanburgh and Wren, *Dido*, Blenheim and St. Paul's, these would be ambiguous figures and achievements in any European consideration of the Baroque, yet from Crashaw through the Augustan age, continental Baroque in word, music and the other arts, had to be reckoned with as a neighbour influence. Those Restoration versions of Shakespeare, of which *The Fairy Queen* is the best example, which pursued a mechanical mixture of play and inset 'entertainment', were a denial of the Baroque ideal, the organic relation of all the arts in one dramatic act, whether that be opera, a princely entertainment in a court, or the union of architecture, word and music in the operatic liturgy of a Baroque church. By these criteria, the 'operatic' versions of Shakespeare, which drew to an end in 1700 with Gildon's *Measure for Measure*, may have been mediocre failures but it is an exercise of critical decency to recognise their *genre* and to assess the temper and the ideals against which their failure must be judged.

Note

Biography. William Congreve (1670–1729) was born near Leeds, of an ancient family. His father commanded the garrison at Youghal and so he was educated at Kilkenny School and Trinity College, Dublin; a fellow student at both places was Swift. He entered the Middle Temple in London but did not pursue his studies; he published a novel, *Incognita*, in 1692, and his first play, *The Old Bachelor*, was performed at Drury Lane in January 1693, with immediate success. *The Double Dealer* (1693), *Love for Love* (1695) and his one tragedy, *The Mourning Bride* (1697), established him firmly in literary London; he was given government sinecures and enjoyed friendship and admiration. *The Way of the World* (1700) was comparatively a failure on its first performance at Lincoln's Inn Fields; it was his last play. His works were published in three volumes in 1710. He died a bachelor, after years troubled with gout.

Modern Editions. The complete works have been edited by M. Summers (1923) and the plays in one volume in the Mermaid series. But the best edition, from which quotations in this chapter are taken, is B. Dobrée's two volumes in the World's Classics: *The Comedies* (1925) and *The Mourning Bride, Poems & Miscellanies* (1928).

Scholarship and Criticism. Three books published in the first decades of this century have been especially influential: J. Palmer, *The Comedy of Manners* (1913); Bonamy Dobrée, *Restoration Comedy* (1924); and Kathleen M. Lynch, *The Social Mode of Restoration Comedy* (1926).

J. C. Hodges, *William Congreve, the man; a biography from new sources* followed a renewed interest in 1941, and so did two contrasted essays by L. C. Knights and Virginia Woolf, both written in 1937 and reprinted, respectively, in *Explorations* (1946) and *The Moment* (1947).

In more recent years there has been a controversy about the worth of Restoration comedy centring on Congreve: F. W. Bateson, 'Elementary, My dear Hotson', and 'Second Thoughts . . . L. C. Knights and Restoration Comedy', *Essays in Criticism* (1951 and 1957); and John Wain, 'Restoration Comedy and its Modern Critics' in *Essays in Criticism* (1956) and reprinted in *Preliminary Essays* (1957). Clifford Leech's 'Congreve and the Century's End' in *Philological Quarterly* (1962) is written in the knowledge of this debate. Kathleen M. Lynch published *A Congreve Gallery* in 1951.

X

The Comedies of William Congreve

KENNETH MUIR

*

WILLIAM CONGREVE'S reputation as a dramatist, which was at a low ebb during most of the nineteenth century, rose to its height after the 1914–18 war. This was partly due to Nigel Playfair's demonstration, aided by the genius of Edith Evans, that the plays could still give enormous pleasure to modern audiences, and partly to the influence of several critics—John Palmer, Bonamy Dobrée, Kathleen Lynch—who gave us intelligent interpretations of the Comedy of Manners. But during the last thirty years Congreve's reputation seems to have declined. L. C. Knights' essay (1937), which was somewhat hostile, has been more influential than Virginia Woolf's more generous essay written in the same year. Bloomsbury's appreciation of Congreve was unfairly reckoned to his discredit. The most recent estimate, by G. Wilson Knight in *The Golden Labyrinth* (1962), damns him with faint praise. Yet it can hardly be denied that Congreve remains incomparably the best writer of comedy between Shakespeare and Shaw, and we may suspect that those critics who profess to find him boring are more willing to be thought impervious to wit than lenient to immorality.

Congreve's first published work, the novel *Incognita* (1692), may be appropriately mentioned in a discussion of his plays because, as he pointed out,[1] the plot is carefully constructed, and because Congreve already displayed a remarkable talent for dialogue and a perfection of style unique in a writer scarcely out of his 'teens. The style of the dialogue may be illustrated by a single passage:

> Ah! Madam, (reply'd *Aurelian*) you know every thing in the World but your own Perfections, and you only know not those, because

[1] 'Preface to *Incognita*', in *The Mourning Bride, etc.*, ed. Dobrée, p. 6: 'I resolved in another beauty to imitate *Dramatick* Writing, namely, in the Design, Contexture and Result of the Plot. I have not observed it before in a Novel.'

'tis the top of Perfection not to know them. How? (reply'd the Lady) I thought it had been the extremity of knowledge to know ones self. Aurelian had a little over-strain'd himself in that Complement, and I am of Opinion would have been puzzl'd to have brought himself off readily: but by good fortune the Musick came into the Room and gave him an opportunity to seem to decline an answer, because the company prepared to dance: he only told her he was too mean a Conquest for her wit who was already a Slave to the Charms of her Person. She thanked him for his Complement, and briskly told him she ought to have made him a return in praise of his wit, but she hoped he was a Man more happy than to be dissatisfy'd with any of his own Endowments; and if it were so, that he had not a just Opinion of himself, she knew her self incapable of saying any thing to beget one.

(pp. 18–19)

The Old Bachelor was performed in the following year, and Dryden and Southerne are said to have helped Congreve prepare it for the stage, Dryden saying that it was the best first play he had ever seen. In some ways, as we might expect, it is immature. The Fondlewife scenes, amusing as they are, have too little connection with the main plots of the play, and nearly three acts intervene between Bellmour's agreement to seduce Laetitia and his carrying the plan into execution. We are given only a belated and insufficient reason for the brutal mockery of Heartwell by Araminta and Belinda, who appear elsewhere to be good-natured. Most of the characters are mere types, taken over from previous plays. Captain Bluffe, the braggart soldier, has a long ancestry. Bellmour might have appeared in almost any comedy of manners. Sylvia resembles Mrs. Loveit in The Man of Mode; Araminta, played by Mrs. Bracegirdle, is comparatively colourless; and Heartwell, the old bachelor himself, might have stepped out of a Wycherley play. Vainlove, the hero, is more successful; and if he owes something to Dorimant, he is observed with greater detachment. His name is itself a criticism of his character, and Congreve was clearly alive to its absurdities. He has been so successful with women that he is sickened by his conquests. When Sharper tells him he has 'a sickly peevish Appetite', that he can 'only chew Love and cannot digest it', he replies:

Yes, when I feed my self—But I hate to be cramm'd—By Heav'n there's not a Woman, will give a Man the Pleasure of a Chase: My Sport is always balkt or cut short—I stumble over the Game I would

pursue—'Tis dull and unnatural to have a Hare run full in the
Hounds Mouth: and would distaste the keenest Hunter.   (IV. v)

This accounts for the way in which he hands over his conquests to
Bellmour and for his callous treatment of Sylvia, who is regarded as
unworthy even of Heartwell. The situation is not romanticised. Lucy
remarks that Vainlove is 'the Head Pimp to Mr. *Bellmour*' (III. vi). It
is only Araminta's refusal to capitulate that maintains Vainlove's interest in her. Sharper tells Heartwell: 'That's because he always sets out
in foul Weather, loves to buffet with the Winds, meet the Tide, and
sail[2] in the Teeth of Opposition' (I. iv). It is clear from the dialogue
with Bellmour in III. iii that Vainlove wants the impossible:

BELLMOUR: Thou dost not know what thou would'st be at; whether
   thou would'st have her angry or pleas'd. Could'st thou be content
   to marry *Araminta*?
VAINLOVE: Could you be content to go to Heav'n?
BELLMOUR: Hum, not immediately, in my Conscience not heartily!
   I'd do a little more good in my Generation first, in order to
   deserve it.
VAINLOVE: Nor I to marry *Araminta* 'till I merit her.
BELLMOUR: But how the Devil dost thou expect to get her if she
   never yield?
VAINLOVE: That's true, but I would—
BELLMOUR: Marry her without her Consent; thou'rt a Riddle be-
   yond Woman.

Vainlove is a prisoner of the sexual conventions not merely of the
drama but of the age. The conflict between the sexes in which both
parties struggle for mastery, in which the conquered is despised, and
in which the man therefore forfeits most of the satisfaction of victory,
is exposed by Congreve and indirectly satirised.[3] The crowning revelation of Vainlove's neurosis is his reception of the forged letter in which
Araminta not merely forgives him for stealing a kiss but confesses her
love. He tells Sharper that Araminta is lost—lost to him, because she has
lost his love—that her love is 'an untimely fruit', and that he will snub her:

'Tis fit Men should be coy, when Women woo.   (IV. v)

[2] 'fail', ed. Dobrée.
[3] Congreve avoids the tragic implications of the theme, which were exploited
by Richardson and Laclos. Lovelace and Valmont both fall in love with their
victims, too late to save themselves or their victims, but soon enough to know
that they have damned themselves.

At the end of the play, when he formally proposes to Araminta, sacrificing his pride at last, she refuses to give a definite answer because, as Bellmour explains, 'she dares not consent for fear he shou'd recant'.

The most interesting character in the play, however, is Belinda, who may owe something to Melantha in *Marriage à la Mode* and who looks forward to Millamant, but who is a splendid creation in her own right. She is described before she appears as 'too proud, too inconstant, too affected and too witty, and too handsome for a wife'. Bellmour admits 'she is excessively foppish and affected' and he pretends that his main interest is in her fortune (I. iii). When we meet her in the second act, she pretends she is not in love, and she rails at Araminta for having 'raved, talked idly, and all in Commendation of that filthy, awkward, two-leg'd Creature, Man'. She mocks at Bellmour's 'poetical' wooing, and urges him to adore her in silence. In the last act she tells him:

> O my Conscience, I cou'd find in my Heart to marry thee, purely to be rid of thee—At least, thou art so troublesome a Lover, there's Hopes thou'lt make a more than ordinary quiet Husband.

She is afraid—and this is the explanation of her pretended scorn of men —that courtship is 'a very witty Prologue to a very dull Play' and that she will get from her husband 'only Remains, which have been I know not how many times warm'd for other Company, and at last serv'd up cold to the Wife'. This chord was to be struck by all Congreve's later heroines, and there is nothing original in the sentiment. But the great triumph in the presentation of the character is the way Congreve contrives to give her a distinctive rhythm and turn of phrase, as when she quotes Cowley's 'both the great Vulgar and the small' and adds: 'Oh Gad! I have a great Passion for *Cowley*—Don't you admire him? . . . Ah so fine! So extreamly fine! So everything in the World I like.' Even finer—extremely fine—a passage that reveals Congreve as already a great writer of comic dialogue, is the speech she makes after she has been jolted to a jelly in a hackney-coach. Araminta tells her that her head is 'a little out of order', and Belinda replies:

> A little! O frightful! What a furious Phyz I have! O most rueful! Ha, ha, ha: O Gad, I hope no body will come this way, 'till I have put my self a little in repair—Ah! my Dear—I have seen such unhewn Creatures since—Ha, ha, ha, I can't for my Soul help thinking that I look just like one of 'em—Good Dear, pin this, and I'll tell you—Very well—So, thank you, my Dear—But as I was telling you

—Pish, this is the untoward'st Lock—So, as I was telling you—How d'ye like me now? Hideous, ha? frightful still? or how?

(IV. viii)

Congreve's next play, *The Double Dealer*, was produced in the following year. When it was published it appeared with Dryden's famous epistle in which he saluted his young rival as the equal of Shakespeare, the superior of Jonson and Fletcher, combining the merits of Etherege, Southerne and Wycherley, and concluding with an appeal:

> But You, whom ev'ry Muse and Grace adorn,
> Whom I foresee to better Fortune born,
> Be kind to my Remains; and oh defend,
> Against your Judgment, your departed friend.

Certainly the play represents a great advance: the plot is well constructed, the characters are well drawn, the dialogue is more continuously brilliant. But, despite Dryden's eulogy, the play has seldom been revived. Its relative unpopularity may be due to the feeling that the villainy of Maskwell and the outrageous passions of Lady Touchwood blend awkwardly with the satirical comedy of the Froths and the Plyants.[4] Another objection to the play was raised by Congreve's first critics—Maskwell's soliloquies. Congreve in his Epistle Dedicatory defends the use of soliloquy; but he evades the real objection. At the beginning of Act V Maskwell deliberately talks to himself of his love for Cynthia so as to be overheard by Lord Touchwood. Yet Congreve tells us that if a character 'supposes any one to be by, when he talks to himself, it is monstrous and ridiculous to the last degree'. A third criticism which may be made of the play is the improbability of Maskwell's plot to marry Cynthia while she believes she is marrying Mellefont. Congreve had used a similar device in *The Old Bachelor* where Sir Joseph Wittol marries Sylvia in mistake for Araminta; and he was to use it again in *Love for Love*, somewhat more plausibly, where Tattle, meaning to marry Angelica, finds himself married to Mrs. Frail who thought she was marrying Valentine.

The play, however, is not seriously damaged by these faults. The plot is exciting. The schemes of Mellefont to foil his aunt, and the counter-schemes of Lady Touchwood and Maskwell, keep the audience in

[4] In a recent revival at the Liverpool Playhouse the producer sought to overcome this difficulty by the disastrous expedient of burlesquing the serious scenes.

suspense until the last few minutes of the play. In Lady Touchwood's
incestuous passion for Mellefont and her determination to be revenged
on him for rejecting her advances, we are almost in the same world
as Racine's tragedies. She wishes first to disinherit him by bearing
Maskwell's child, then to prevent his marriage to Cynthia by accusing
him of attempted rape, and finally to ruin him after blackmailing him
into complying with her desires. Yet she is right in thinking that her
violent passions have more excuse than the cold-blooded lechery and
treachery of Maskwell, 'a sedate, a thinking Villain, whose black Blood
runs temperately bad'.

The comic scenes are carefully dovetailed into the serious intrigue.
Lady Plyant's willingness to be seduced by Mellefont is a comic
parallel to Lady Touchwood's incestuous desires, and her actual seduction by Careless is a by-product of Mellefont's scheme to win her to
his side. 'She's handsome, and knows it; is very silly, and thinks she has
Sense, and has an old fond Husband' (I. iii). Sir Paul, indeed, dotes
upon her so much that he is completely enslaved, though seldom or
never allowed to touch her. The Froths are fools of another kind. Lord
Froth, the solemn coxcomb, thinks it beneath his dignity to laugh; and
Lady Froth, 'a pretender to Poetry, Wit and Learning', writes execrable
verses and is easily seduced by the 'pert coxcomb', Brisk.

> BRISK: The Deuce take me, I can't help laughing my self, ha, ha, ha;
> yet by Heav'ns I have a violent Passion for your Ladyship,
> seriously.
> LADY FROTH: Seriously? Ha, ha, ha.
> BRISK: Seriously, ha, ha, ha. Gad I have, for all I laugh.
> LADY FROTH: Ha, ha, ha! What d'ye think I laugh at? Ha, ha, ha.
> BRISK: Me I'gad, ha, ha.
> LADY FROTH: No the Deuce take me if I don't laugh at my self; for
> hang me if I have not a violent Passion for Mr. *Brisk*, ha, ha, ha.
>
> (IV. vi)

It is the absurdities of the Froths and the Plyants that make Cynthia
hesitate about marriage: all through the play her sense and sensibility
are contrasted with the aberrations of the other women; and she is
given a soliloquy, significantly placed at the end of an act, which
enables Congreve to comment through her mouth:

> 'Tis not so hard to counterfeit Joy in the Depth of Affliction, as to
> dissemble Mirth in Company of Fools—Why should I call 'em

Fools? The World thinks better of 'em; for these have Quality and Education, Wit and fine Conversation, are receiv'd and admir'd by the World—If not, they like and admire themselves—And why is not that true Wisdom, for 'tis Happiness: And for ought I know, we have misapply'd the Name all this while, and mistaken the Thing: Since

> If Happiness in Self-Content is plac'd,
> The Wise are Wretched, and Fools only Bless'd.
>
> (III. xii)

Congreve tells his readers in the Epistle Dedicatory that 'It is the Business of a Comick Poet to paint the Vices and Follies of Human-kind'; and in his answer to Jeremy Collier (who had criticised *The Double Dealer*) he showed that his view of comedy was classical:

> *Comedy* (says *Aristotle*) is an Imitation of the worse sort of People . . . He does not mean the worse sort of People in respect to their Quality, but in respect to their Manners . . . But the Vices most frequent, and which are the common Practice of the looser sort of Livers, are the subject Matter of Comedy . . . the Business of Comedy is to delight, as well as to instruct: And as vicious People are made asham'd of their Follies or Faults, by seeing them expos'd in a ridiculous manner, so are good People at once both warn'd and diverted at their Expence.
>
> (*Amendments; Mourning Bride*, p. 408)

Congreve therefore lashed the follies of Sir Paul and Lord Froth, the folly and immorality of their wives, the ungovernable passions of Lady Touchwood, and the hypocrisy and wickedness of Maskwell; but, as in all his comedies, he depicts also a pair of lovers who (at least in comparison with the circle in which they move) deserve their happiness.

In *Love for Love* Congreve follows the same pattern, except that he excludes examples of monstrous wickedness and concentrates on the follies and sexual irregularities of his characters—the superstition of Foresight, the adultery of his wife, the simplicity of Miss Prue, the frailty of Mrs. Frail, the vanity of Tattle, the egotism and arbitrariness of Sir Sampson Legend, the satirical humour of Scandal. Ben is used, as Sir Wilfull Witwoud was later to be used, partly as a means of showing up the artificiality of society and partly as the target for good-natured satire on his uncouth ways and nautical vocabulary. Valentine himself has been a rake: he is about to be disinherited by his father for his extravagant way of life, and he has at least one bastard. He has therefore to undergo probation and to prove to Angelica that he is constant in his love and not merely anxious to secure her fortune.[5]

Valentine's pretended madness enables Congreve to extend the range of his satire to cover the law, trade, religion, the court and friendship. It also enables him to be more poetical than he had allowed himself to be in his previous comedies, or than he was able to be in *The Mourning Bride*. One of the most beautiful passages in all his works, spoken to Angelica but not applicable to her, is the speech beginning:

> You're a Woman,—One to whom Heav'n gave Beauty, when it grafted Roses on a Briar. You are the Reflection of Heav'n in a Pond, and he that leaps at you is sunk. You are all white, a Sheet of lovely spotless Paper, when you first are born; but you are to be scrawl'd and blotted by every Goose's Quill.   (IV. xvi)

Those who praise Congreve's style are liable to be labelled 'style-fanciers' and it is, of course, impossible to divorce style and content—a mistake, incidentally, into which Dobrée never fell. What is really remarkable about Congreve's prose is its variety. Its rhythms are always those of colloquial speech, and its vocabulary and idiom always suit the character who is speaking. Many dramatists succeed in distinguishing some of their characters by giving them tricks of speech; but Congreve is unique among dramatists since the Restoration in his ability to distinguish all his characters in his last two plays by their manner of speech. This is a quality of which too little has been made. Of course, as he tells us, 'the distance of the Stage requires the Figure represented to be something larger than the Life' (*Comedies*, p. 6); and, he might have added, more eloquent than they would be in real life. Even his fools are sometimes witty, as Pope saw; but Congreve defended himself from the charge that they speak out of character by pointing out that:

> The saying of Humorous Things, does not distinguish Characters; For every Person in a Comedy may be allow'd to speak them. From a Witty Man they are expected; and even a *Fool* may be permitted to stumble on 'em by chance.   (*Comedies*, p. 2)

[5] Four of Congreve's heroines have fortunes their lovers do not wish to forfeit, and one of the main themes of *The Way of the World* is the protection of Mrs. Fainall's fortune.

Witwoud, for example, 'a fool with a good memory', is shown striving to be witty by churning out fashionable similitudes, but his memory furnishes him with at least one genuinely witty remark. So, in *Love for Love*, the nautical idiom of Ben—he uses thirty nautical images on his first appearance—the astrological patter of Foresight, the high-pitched fopperies of Tattle, the adolescent gaucherie of Miss Prue, the down-to-earth wit of Jeremy are all perfectly distinguishable without the need of speech-prefixes. The prose is essentially dramatic: it needs to be spoken, and the actor who keeps Congreve's rhythms automatically registers his points.

In *Love for Love* even the minor characters are alive, whereas in *The Double Dealer* the important character of Lord Touchwood had been somewhat wooden. In another respect *Love for Love* shows an advance on Congreve's previous plays and, indeed, it is this quality which has made some critics place it above *The Way of the World*: it acts even better than it reads. From the theatrical point of view, there is not a weak scene in the play, from the exposition by Jeremy and Valentine to the marriage of Tattle and Mrs. Frail. Such scenes as the exposure of Tattle, the quarrel between Sir Samson and Foresight, Ben's abortive courtship of Miss Prue, Scandal's pretence that Foresight is ill, and Valentine's pretended madness are inevitably successful on the stage; and the way Mrs. Frail turns the tables on her sister is one of the most effective scenes in the whole range of English comedy:

MRS. FORESIGHT: . . . You never were at the *World's-End*?

MRS. FRAIL: No.

MRS. FORESIGHT: You deny it positively to my Face.

MRS. FRAIL: Your Face, what's your Face?

MRS. FORESIGHT: No matter for that, it's as good a Face as yours.

MRS. FRAIL: Not by a Dozen Years wearing.—But I do deny it positively to your Face then.

MRS. FORESIGHT: I'll allow you now to find fault with my Face; for I'll swear your Impudence has put me out of Countenance:— But look you here now,—where did you lose this Gold Bodkin? —Oh Sister, Sister!

MRS. FRAIL: My Bodkin!

MRS. FORESIGHT: Nay, 'tis yours, look at it.

MRS. FRAIL: Well, if you go to that, where did you find this Bodkin? —Oh Sister, Sister!—Sister every way.

(II. ix)

Fanny Burney admitted that the play was 'fraught with wit and entertainment', but she assumed that no lady could approve of it. Its defence was put into the mouth of the robust Captain:

'What, I suppose it is not sentimental enough!' cried the Captain, 'or else it is too good for them; for I'll maintain it's one of the best comedies in our Language, and has more wit in one scene than there is in all the new plays put together.'   (*Evelina*, Letter XX)

The Way of the World, Congreve's last and best play, was not so immediately successful as *Love for Love*, and it is not difficult to see why. The first act is slow, and there is a great deal of discussion of characters we do not meet until later in the play, Millamant not appearing until the middle of Act II and Lady Wishfort, who provides the broadest comedy, until the third act. Some allusions in the opening scenes are likely to be obscure or even misleading at a first hearing. When Mirabell, for example, hints that Mrs. Marwood is Fainall's mistress, an audience would have to be very quick on the uptake to take the hint:

You pursue the Argument with a Distrust that seems to be un-affected, and confesses you are conscious of a Concern for which the Lady is more indebted to you, than is your Wife.   (I. i)

It would be impossible for an audience to gather in Act I that Mirabell's uncle was an impostor, and that he was to court Lady Wishfort rather than Millamant. But such difficulties do not arise after a first hearing, and may indeed give ironical under-tones to the dialogue.

The play is fundamentally more serious than *Love for Love* and the dialogue and characterisation are continuously brilliant and more subtle. Congreve avows in his Dedication that he was aiming at greater subtlety:

Those Characters which are meant to be ridicul'd in most of our Comedies, are of Fools so gross, that in my humble Opinion, they should rather disturb than divert the well-natured and reflecting Part of an Audience; they are rather Objects of Charity than Contempt; and instead of moving our Mirth, they ought very often to excite our Compassion. This Reflection moved me to design some Characters, which should appear ridiculous not so much through a natural Folly (which is incorrigible, and therefore not proper for the Stage) as through an affected Wit; a Wit, which at the same time that it is affected, is also false.   (*Comedies*, p. 337)

The only character, however, to whom these remarks seem to apply is Witwoud, for neither Petulant nor Fainall could be so described, and Millamant, although not guiltless of affectation, is at the same time genuinely witty. But it is true that the characterisation depends less on exaggeration than it had in Congreve's earlier plays. Except in the farcical, and very funny, Sir Rowland scenes, Congreve succeeded in his aim of rivalling Terence of whom he writes in the Dedication, alluding perhaps to the defective taste of his own audience: 'The purity of his Stile, the Delicacy of his Turns, and the Justness of his Characters, were all of them Beauties, which the greater Part of his Audience were incapable of Tasting' (*Comedies*, p. 337).

The style is beautifully varied, and the voices are all distinct: the 'boudoir Billingsgate' of Lady Wishfort as she curses Foible (V. i); the endearing earthiness of Sir Wilfull, which is 'Rustick—ruder than Gothick' compared with Millamant's preciosity (IV. iv); the elaborate pretences of Marwood and Mrs. Fainall as they try to read each other's hearts (II. i); the malicious exchanges of Marwood and Millamant (III. x, xi); and the bitterness of Marwood when alone (III. vii). Best of all, perhaps, are the scenes following Millamant's first triumphant entrance (II. iv, v) in which every character—Mirabell, Witwoud, Mrs. Fainall, Mincing and Millamant herself—is superbly alive, and in which the grave meditations of Mirabell on 'Beauty the lover's gift' contrast brilliantly with Millamant's calculated affectations and Witwoud's breathless similitudes. These scenes represent the high-water mark of the Comedy of Manners, as perfect in their kind as those of Rosalind in Arden or Viola in Illyria.

Knights' remarks on Millamant seem to exhibit a misunderstanding of what Congreve was trying to do, as well as an imperfect understanding of the character. He complains that she 'expects to draw vitality from the excitement of incessant solicitation', that she shares with unattractive characters 'a disproportionate belief in the "pleasure of a chase" ', and that her way of life 'is never for a moment enlivened by the play of genuine intelligence' (pp. 146–7).

In reply to this formidable indictment it must be said, first, that Congreve is perfectly aware of his heroine's defects, and that Mirabell discourses on her acquired follies long before we see her: 'Those Affectations which in another Woman wou'd be odious, serve but to make her more agreeable.' It is Congreve's great triumph to convince us of the truth of these words.

Secondly, it is important to realise why Millamant wishes not to be 'freed from the agreeable Fatigues of Sollicitation'. She lives in a society in which constancy is regarded as a bore, and in which marriage ends in disillusionment. She wishes to avoid what Swift's Stella was to describe as the common lot of women:

> Before the thirti'th year of life
> A maid forlorn, or hated wife.[6]

Hazlitt thought Millamant was 'nothing but a fine lady',[7] and Meredith said she was 'a type of the superior ladies who do not think'.[8] Both critics were surely mistaken. Millamant's wit, like that of Rosalind and Beatrice, is a sign of intelligence; and although affectation and coquetry usually indicate a frigid temperament, Millamant's affectation is the cloak of affection, and her coquetry conceals a nature capable of a whole-hearted love. She can act the fine lady to perfection, she can pose as a woman who makes wit the be-all and end-all of her life, but fundamentally she is a sensitive girl in an insensitive society. This is made perfectly clear when just after the bargaining scene she confesses to her friend: 'Well, if *Mirabell* should not make a good Husband, I am a lost thing—for I find I love him violently.' It was made clear, too, for Congreve's original audience, by the poems he puts into his heroine's mouth just before her surrender. Suckling's lines—

> There never yet was woman made,
> Nor shall, but to be curs'd;—[9]

are part of a poem which pretends to discuss women's promiscuity, but which goes on to imply the inconstancy of men. Millamant then quotes the first stanza of another of Suckling's poems:

> I prithee spare me, gentle Boy,
> Press me no more for that slight Toy,
> That foolish Trifle of an Heart;
> I swear it will not do its part,
> Tho' thou dost thine, employ'st thy Power and Art.

---

[6] *Swift's Poems*, ed. H. Williams (1937), p. 737.
[7] *Lectures on the English Comic Writers* (ed. 1910), p. 74.
[8] *An Essay on Comedy* (ed. 1927), p. 41.
[9] *Minor Poets of the Seventeenth Century*, ed. R. C. Howarth (1931), pp. 195, 198.

Suckling goes on to explain that he calls out for the last course before the rest, and as soon as the woman capitulates he hurries off to new conquests:

> Men rise away, and scarce say grace,
> Or civilly once thank the face
> That did invite, but seek another place.

Millamant's fourth quotation is from Waller's 'The Story of Phoebus and Daphne, Applied';[10] and Mirabell, entering in the middle of a couplet, completes it, thereby showing that he understands the allusion and knows the reason for Millamant's hesitation 'upon the very Verge of Matrimony'.

Millamant's quotations—the aptness of which proves that she has 'genuine intelligence'—come at the end of nearly a century of argument on the subject of 'platonic' love. This was stimulated by the fashionable cult introduced by Henrietta Maria and by the realisation by many of the poets that absolute licence made conquests unsatisfying. So we have Suckling proclaiming that 'Fruition's dull' and that

> 'Tis expectation makes a blessing dear;

Henry King tells us that it is impossible to

> Enjoy our Love and yet preserve Desire;[11]

and Cowley tells his mistress that she would be a fool to yield:

> Much of my *Veneration* thou must want,
> When once thy *kindness* puts my *ign'rance* out;
> For a *learn'd Age* is always least devout.[12]

On the other side of the debate there were numerous poems attacking platonic love, from Donne who ridiculed those who ignored the 'right, true end of love' to Suckling who exclaimed, this time ironically:

> Oh, what a stroke 'twould be! sure I should die,
> Should I but hear my mistress once say ay.[13]

Congreve was writing more than a generation after the Cavalier poets, and he revived for his own purposes, in a more licentious society,

---

[10] *Poetical Works*, ed. Gilfillan (1857), p. 22.
[11] *Minor Poets*, ed. Saintsbury, III, p. 209.
[12] *Poems* (ed. 1903), p. 98.   [13] *Op. cit.*, pp. 83-4.

the theme that possession involves the decay of desire, and hence of love. In the world of Restoration comedy—and to some extent in the society reflected by that comedy—it was assumed that men and women were naturally promiscuous. But whereas Etherege cheerfully accepted this state of affairs, Congreve's main concern was always with the comparatively sensitive who were seeking for a more satisfactory relationship between the sexes. His heroines are fully aware of the fact that love is not supposed to outlast the honeymoon, and they all shrink from marriage until their gallants have undergone a period of probation. Cynthia, observing the behaviour of the Froths and of her own father and stepmother, asks Mellefont: 'What think you of drawing stakes, and giving over in time?' Angelica, living in the same house as Mrs. Foresight who cuckolds her husband, Mrs. Frail whose name expresses her reputation, and Miss Prue who tries very hard to be seduced, and loving the prodigal Valentine, naturally hesitates before committing herself to matrimony—he may be after her fortune. Millamant knows that her cousin is Mirabell's cast-off mistress, and that she is treated badly by her husband. This is sufficient to account for her behaviour.

The actual bargaining, where both Millamant and Mirabell pretend they are not desperately in love, is not absolutely original. Kathleen Lynch has found a parallel (pp. 83–4) in the provisos given in D'Urfé's *Astrée*:

> That no one shall exercise over the other that sovereign authority which we say is tyranny . . .
>
> That we shall love as long as we please . . .
>
> In order that we shall not be liars or slaves, words of fidelity, servitude, and of eternal affection shall never be used by us.

The bargaining between Florimel and Celadon in Dryden's *Secret Love* —also quoted by Miss Lynch (p. 146)—is closer in spirit to Congreve's scene:

> CELADON: One thing let us be sure to agree on, that is, never to be jealous.
>
> FLORIMEL: No; but e'en love one another as long as we can; and confess the truth when we can love no longer.
>
> CELADON: When I have been at play, you shall never ask me what money I have lost.
>
> FLORIMEL: When I have been abroad, you shall never inquire who treated me.

CELADON: *Item*, I will have the liberty to sleep all night, without your interrupting my repose for any evil design whatsoever.

FLORIMEL: *Item*, Then you shall bid me good-night before you sleep . . .

CELADON: Lastly, whereas the names of husband and wife hold forth nothing, but clashing and cloying, and dulness and faintness, in their signification; they shall be abolished for ever betwixt us.

FLORIMEL: And instead of those, we will be married by the more agreeable names of mistress and gallant.

CELADON: None of my privileges to be infringed by thee, Florimel, under the penalty of a month of fasting nights.

FLORIMEL: None of my privileges to be infringed by thee, Celadon, under the penalty of cuckoldom.

In spite of obvious resemblances, the enormous superiority of Congreve's scene is apparent. Dryden's lines are generalised, and they could have been spoken by almost any lovers on the verge of matrimony between 1660 and 1710; Congreve's are all perfectly in character, rich in detail, and continuously witty. No dramatist has equalled Congreve in the creation of character by diction and rhythm:

MILLAMANT: My dear Liberty, shall I leave thee? My faithful Solitude, my darling Contemplation, must I bid you then Adieu? Ay-h adieu—My Morning Thoughts, agreeable Wakings, indolent Slumbers, all ye *douceurs*, ye *Someils du Matin*, adieu—I can't do't, 'tis more than impossible—Positively *Mirabell*, I'll lye a-bed in a Morning as long as I please.

MIRABELL: Then I'll get up in a Morning as early as I please.

MILLAMANT: Ah! Idle Creature, get up when you will—And d'ye hear, I won't be call'd Names after I'm Marry'd; positively I won't be call'd Names.

MIRABELL: Names!

MILLAMANT: Ay, as Wife, Spouse, my Dear, Joy, Jewel, Love, Sweet-heart, and the rest of that nauseous Cant, in which Men and their Wives are so fulsomly familiar—I shall never bear that—Good *Mirabell* don't let us be familiar or fond, nor kiss before Folks, like my Lady *Fadler* and Sir *Francis* . . . Let us never Visit together, nor go to a Play together, but let us be very strange and well bred: Let us be as strange as if we had been marry'd a great while; and as well bred as if we were not marry'd at all. (IV. v)

This is one example of the way Congreve, writing within well-worn conventions, was able to transmute the commonplace into great dramatic dialogue. One other example may be given, where Congreve was certainly playing variation on a theme of Etherege. In *The Man of Mode*, Dorimant upbraids Mrs. Loveit for encouraging fools. She replies that fools

> really admire us, while you at best but flatter us well . . . Then they are assiduous, Sir, they are ever offering us their service, and always waiting on our will.
>
> DORIMANT: You owe that to their excessive idleness! They know not how to entertain themselves at home, and find so little welcome abroad, they are fain to fly to you who countenance 'em, as a refuge against the solitude they would be otherwise condemned to.   (V. i. 117)

So Mirabell complains that Millamant had denied him a private audience on the previous evening:

> Unkind. You had the leisure to entertain a Herd of Fools; Things who visit you from their excessive Idleness; bestowing on your Easiness that Time which is the Incumbrance of their Lives. How can you find Delight in such Society? It is impossible they shou'd admire you, they are not capable: Or if they were, it shou'd be to you as a Mortification; for sure to please a Fool is some degree of Folly.
>
> MILLAMANT: I please my self—Besides, sometimes to converse with Fools is for my Health.
>
> MIRABELL: Your Health! Is there a worse Disease than the Conversation of Fools?
>
> MILLAMANT: Yes, the Vapours; Fools are Physick for it, next to *Assa-foetida*.   (II. v)

Even those critics who admit that Congreve's plays—and especially *The Way of the World*—are incomparably the finest examples of the Comedy of Manners, and certainly superior in most ways to *The School for Scandal* or *She Stoops to Conquer*, are apt to complain of the artificiality of the genre. It is no longer possible to accept Lamb's ingenious argument, which he never intended to be taken seriously, that the plays are fantasies about an imaginary world: they reflect in a highly polished mirror the society of Congreve's day. The truly artificial comedies (as Dobrée has remarked)[14] are the sentimental plays of Congreve's successors. But, it is argued, the world with which they deal is a narrow one, the characters are 'heartless', and we do not much

---

[14] *Oxford History of English Literature*, VII (1959), p. 240.

care what happens to them. To which we may answer that this attitude reveals an insular view of the nature of comedy, that the world is not so narrow as it is sometimes painted, and that we are not bounded by the walls of a fashionable drawing-room, as we are, for example, in *Le Misanthrope*. The outside world—in the shape of Ben, Sir Wilfull, 'bouncing Margery', Trapland's widow, Pumple-Nose the Attorney— is continually breaking in; and there is a great social gulf between Lord Touchwood and Fondlewife, for example, or between Miss Prue and Millamant.

Secondly, the central characters are not heartless, although—as we have seen with regard to Mirabell and Millamant—they pretend to be less in love than they are. The fact that ladies and gentlemen are also men and women is the chief point of the play. The characters for whom our sympathies are engaged are the most sympathetic ones in the plays; and if we read them in chronological order, we notice a gradual change of attitude on the part of the dramatist. We are not asked to condemn Bellmour's promiscuity very seriously; but Congreve was criticised for his satire of female frailty in *The Double Dealer*, and Valentine's prodigal past is one reason why Angelica hesitates to marry him. All Congreve's heroines are chaste. The adultery of Fainall with Mrs. Marwood is condemned; and if the relationship of Mirabell and Mrs. Fainall is condoned, one has only to compare it with Dorimant's treatment of his former mistresses to see how much more civilised Congreve is than Etherege.

Lastly, it can be said that although Congreve inevitably deals with the relationship between the sexes in his own society, he satirised false relationships both in and outside marriage, and he tried to present, at least, by implication, an ideal of marriage based on reason and respect, although without religious sanctions. To admit the existence of adultery at a time when divorce was difficult, and to recognise that love and marriage do not always coincide, was the acceptance not of a literary convention but of one of the facts of life. And perhaps our society is not so enlightened or so inclined to accept a sacramental view of marriage, that we can afford to dismiss Congreve's reading of life as totally irrelevant to our situation.

Index

[*This index excludes the information, systematically arranged for reference purposes, given in the notes before each chapter.*]

CAPRICORN TITLES

201. *Hauser,* DIET DOES IT. $1.35.
202. *Moscati,* ANCIENT SEMITIC CIVILIZATIONS. $1.65.
203. CHIN P'ING MEI. $2.95.
204. *Brockelman,* HISTORY OF ISLAMIC PEOPLES. $2.45.
205. *Salter,* CONDITIONED REFLEX THERAPY. $1.85.
206. *Lissner,* LIVING PAST. $2.45.
207. *Davis,* CORPORATIONS. $2.45.
208. *Rodman,* CONVERSATIONS WITH ARTISTS. $1.65.
209. *Falls,* GREAT WAR. $1.95.
210. MEMOIRS OF A RENAISSANCE POPE. $1.95.
211. *Schachner,* FOUNDING FATHERS. $2.45.
212. *Viereck,* UNADJUSTED MAN. $1.85.
213. *Cournos,* TREASURY OF CLASSIC RUSSIAN LITERATURE. $2.45.
215. *Guerdan,* BYZANTIUM. $1.45.
216. *Mandeville,* FABLE OF THE BEES. $1.65.
217. *Bradford,* OF PLYMOUTH PLANTATION. $1.65.
218. *Taylor,* COURSE OF GERMAN HISTORY. $1.65.
219. *Frankfurter,* LAW & POLITICS. $1.75.
220. *Shelby Little,* GEORGE WASHINGTON. $1.95.
221. *Peterson,* ANCIENT MEXICO. $1.95.
223. *Isaacs,* IMAGES OF ASIA. $1.85.
224 *Krafft Ebing,* ABERRATIONS OF SEXUAL LIFE. $1.95.
226. *Grekov,* SOVIET CHESS. $1.65.
227. *Ernst-Loth,* REPORT ON THE AMERICAN COMMUNIST. $1.45.
228. *Adler,* THE PROBLEM CHILD. $1.85.
231. *Fine,* FIFTY CHESS LESSONS. $1.45.
233. *Barraclough,* ORIGINS OF MODERN GERMANY. $2.45.
235. *Skeat,* ETYMOLOGICAL DICTIONARY. $2.45.
236. *Hauser,* GAYLORD HAUSER COOK BOOK. $1.45.
237. *Fulop Miller,* THE JESUITS. $2.45.
238. *Shenton,* RECONSTRUCTION. $1.75.
239. *Blitzer,* COMMONWEALTH OF ENGLAND. $1.65.
240. *Wright,* GREAT AMERICAN GENTLEMAN. $1.65.
241. *Braeman,* ROAD TO INDEPENDENCE. $1.65.
242. *Bridenbaugh,* CITIES IN THE WILDERNESS. $2.65.
243. *Bridenbaugh,* CITIES IN REVOLT. $2.65.
244. *de Riencourt,* COMING CAESARS. $1.95.
246. *Weinberg,* THE MUCKRAKERS. $2.45.
247. *Hays,* FROM APE TO ANGEL. $2.65.
248. *James,* ANCIENT GODS. $2.25.
249. *Green,* LUTHER AND THE REFORMATION. $1.65.
250. *Filler,* THE ANXIOUS YEARS. $1.95.
251. *Ehrlich,* EHRLICH'S BLACKSTONE: RIGHTS OF PERSONS, RIGHTS OF THINGS. $2.95.
252. *Ehrlich,* EHRLICH'S BLACKSTONE: PRIVATE WRONGS, PUBLIC WRONGS. $2.95.
253. *Lissner,* THE CAESARS. $1.95.